Baseball and Cultural Heritage

Cultural Heritage Studies

UNIVERSITY PRESS OF FLORIDA

Florida A&M University, Tallahassee
Florida Atlantic University, Boca Raton
Florida Gulf Coast University, Ft. Myers
Florida International University, Miami
Florida State University, Tallahassee
New College of Florida, Sarasota
University of Central Florida, Orlando
University of Florida, Gainesville
University of North Florida, Jacksonville
University of South Florida, Tampa
University of West Florida, Pensacola

Baseball and Cultural Heritage

Edited by
Gregory Ramshaw and Sean Gammon

Foreword by Paul A. Shackel

UNIVERSITY PRESS OF FLORIDA
Gainesville · Tallahassee · Tampa · Boca Raton
Pensacola · Orlando · Miami · Jacksonville · Ft. Myers · Sarasota

27 26 25 24 23 22   6 5 4 3 2 1

Library of Congress Control Number: 2022943128
ISBN 978-0-8130-6940-1

The University Press of Florida is the scholarly publishing agency for the State University System
of Florida, comprising Florida A&M University, Florida Atlantic University, Florida Gulf Coast
University, Florida International University, Florida State University, New College of Florida,
University of Central Florida, University of Florida, University of North Florida, University of
South Florida, and University of West Florida.

University Press of Florida
2046 NE Waldo Road
Suite 2100
Gainesville, FL 32609
http://upress.ufl.edu

Contents

Illustrations

Foreword

Challenging Baseball's Traditional Heritage

This edited volume by Gregory Ramshaw and Sean Gammon, *Baseball and Cultural Heritage*, is a well-thought-out collection of essays that tie many aspects of baseball history and culture to the concept of heritage. The editors explain that this book explores how the "heritage of baseball is understood, interpreted, commodified, performed, and, in some cases, marginalized in order to address contemporary needs, issues, and concerns."

The process of heritage-building is about deciphering history and events and then deciding what we remember. What we remember and celebrate helps to serve and legitimize the past and the present, and it sets the foundation for future memorialization. Public history exhibits, monuments, statues, artifacts, commemorations, and celebrations can foster the myths that create a shared history that allows divergent groups to find a common bond. What we collectively decide is important impacts the way we see the past, the present, and potentially the future.

As I write this foreword in 2021, it is evident that so much has changed because of the coronavirus pandemic. We have also become more aware of racial equity and justice issues. For instance, following the murder of George Floyd in 2020, African American baseball players increasingly spoke out about the injustices they face(d) while trying to succeed in Major League Baseball. In 2020, 100 current and former Black baseball players created the Players Alliance to make the public aware of the shrinking participation of African Americans in the sport. As a result, Major League Baseball announced in 2021 that it would donate up to $150 million to help promote baseball in Black communities. It took a strong, vocal lobby to make change happen.

There have been other recent changes to make baseball heritage more inclusive. For instance, in 1969, the "Special Baseball Records Committee" declared that those who played in different leagues—like the Union Association (1884) and the Federal League (1914–1915)—would now be considered as Major Leaguers. They did not consider, or maybe they did, and rejected, including those who played in the Negro Leagues. However, in December 2020, Major League Baseball recognized seven of the Negro Leagues, including more than 3,400 players from 1920 to 1948. These players are now considered Major Leaguers. Without a doubt, this inclusion changes some of the statistics that American baseball fans so dearly love to memorize and recite. The record books will be updated and modified without an asterisk. Recognizing the Negro Leagues as being on par with the American and National Leagues acknowledges a level of competition that many baseball experts never doubted.

It is also no coincidence that in 2020 the Cleveland baseball team dropped its nickname—the Indians—which it has been known as since 1915. The team was named after one of its players, Louis Sockalexis, who played for the Cleveland team in the late 1890s. He was the first known Native American player for the club. Native American groups who have protested the use of the nickname are also hoping that Sockalexis, of the Penobscot Nation, is adequately remembered by the club in some other, respected way.

While I have highlighted only a few of the challenges to the dominant baseball heritage narrative, Ramshaw and Gammon have created an exciting and inclusive volume that broadens the scope of baseball heritage. This volume goes beyond the traditionally told American stories. For instance, in Major League Baseball, the dominant narrative had traditionally been controlled by white team owners and their created white baseball heroes. However, this volume shows that baseball is a global sport, played on four continents and in the Caribbean, consisting of players of diverse backgrounds, creating a diverse heritage. The challenges of being a Black player in the MLB are highlighted in various chapters, with the stories of Jackie Robinson, Hank Aaron, and Curt Flood. While Robinson now has a national day of recognition (April 15) and Aaron is memorialized, Flood is still somewhat ostracized because he helped challenge the game's corporate structure. In addition, the volume provides a heritage of women in baseball and challenges the notion that it has always been a man's game. Also, there are reminders of baseball in various forms of material culture, from Cracker Jack to baseball stadia. What makes this volume so compelling is that there are many baseball histories. This volume is timely as we think about a more inclusive past and help promote a more inclusive present and future.

Paul A. Shackel
Series Editor

1

Introduction: People, Place, and Promotion

Exploring the Baseball/Heritage Relationship

GREGORY RAMSHAW AND SEAN GAMMON

Some may question both the necessity and wisdom of publishing another book examining baseball's past. After all, for well over a century, baseball has been lauded, eulogized, romanticized, and idealized, escalating it to something more than just a game. It is also an academic topic that has been widely written about, particularly its history. The game's heroes, famous games, beloved stadia, and links to other social and political pasts—particularly in the United States—have been explored in many different ways by numerous scholars. And yet, as much as baseball history has been a staple of popular and academic discourse for some time, how baseball's past is used today—in other words, its heritage—remains relatively unexplored. As such, this book seeks to explore how the heritage of baseball is understood, interpreted, commodified, performed, and, in some cases, marginalized in order to address contemporary needs, issues, and concerns.

This is not to suggest that the baseball/heritage relationship is entirely absent from academic literature. Topics such as the creation and interpretation of historic and replica baseball stadia (Friedman & Silk, 2005); the narrative constructions of baseball museums and halls of fame (Springwood, 1996; Ramshaw et al., 2019; Ramshaw & Gammon, 2020); and baseball's use in nostalgia-based retro marketing (Kim, 2016), to name but a few, have been explored across various fields and disciplines. However, as clubs, leagues, fans, and sponsors—not to mention public agencies—continue to use and, at times, grapple with baseball's heritage, a collection such as this could not be more timely.

The "national pastime" is at a critical stage—both in the United States and beyond. The demise of baseball has been predicted countless times over the years, and yet each spring, like a hardy perennial, it always returns, as a reassuring constant that offers much-needed stability in a world of change and uncertainty. Indeed, during the COVID-19 pandemic, baseball was thought to be the first major U.S.-based sport to return—in part as a "tonic" to heal the nation—though it resumed well after other leagues had begun play, thus ceding the spotlight to other sporting distractions, and only continued in fits and starts due to coronavirus outbreaks within a number of different clubs. Of course, the events of the pandemic, coupled with the pessimistic perception of baseball's cultural importance, led many to opine on the future of the sport. Baseball's waning relevance in U.S. culture is of course not new—as the prophetic observations of Koppett (2016) illustrated: "The game that used to be the central sun of the spectator sports solar system is now only one of its planets—still the largest, but nevertheless only a planet" (p. 221). Today, it may not even be the biggest planet. As a result, there have been discussions exploring the feasibility of making the game more appealing to a younger, time-starved, less patient generation, while also attempting to retain some of the game's most treasured assets, specifically its rituals, traditions, and heritage. Many of the chapters in this book reflect this tension between the past and the future in the sport, particularly in the United States. Baseball's heritage can be an asset, though at times—and depending on the circumstances—it can be a millstone as well. Indeed, we are at a crossroads with regard to how we interpret and analyze baseball's heritage. Unsurprisingly, nostalgia features heavily in a sport that has changed little from its early development. As a consequence, throughout the ages, romance for an idealized past has occupied baseball fans and cultural commentators alike. Today, the nostalgia is far more self-aware than it was in the past, though the temptation to be drawn back to more innocent, uncomplicated times remains irresistible for many. Such sentimentality may in part be fueled by aims in some political circles to "Make America Great Again," though it may have more to do with an aging population that has more interest in the past than for an uncertain future—not just their own, but baseball's too. During the pandemic-shortened MLB season in 2020, many of baseball's most treasured traditions were cast aside—including drastic rule changes, game schedules, and playoff formats, not to mention spectators in the stands—while other heritages were recognized (such as the 100th anniversary of the founding of the Negro Leagues) and maintained (such as a league-wide Jackie Robinson Day) despite the pandemic and the absence of fans at ballparks. How baseball uses, celebrates, and ignores its past is very much a part of the sport's present and future in the United States.

While the sport's home may be grappling with this Janus-head approach, baseball has made great strides to reach beyond its traditional U.S. base. Baseball has a long history in many other parts of the world—including in Asia and the Caribbean—and the sport, particularly at the professional level, seeks broader global engagement, not only in terms of spectators and consumers but for labor as well. While many countries have used baseball in the U.S. as a template, including as reference points for heritage and culture, many countries have their own baseball-related heritage quite apart from (and, sometimes, in opposition to) the United States. This book recognizes and explores the fact that the baseball/heritage relationship is not only an American phenomenon; that its heritage, meanings, values, places, and performances are often quite local or regional. And yet, even then, there is a tension between the domestic and international baseball worlds. The best league is largely U.S.-based; much of the baseball labor seeks to "make it" in the U.S., and the power and allure of American baseball heritage is a global phenomenon (to illustrate, neither of the editors of this book are, in fact, American). As with all cultural markers, new generations bring new interpretations and, of course, new heritages. How such changing perceptions of the game—both at the domestic and international levels—will impact the manner in which the game is experienced and valued is largely unknown, though will undoubtedly include changes to meaning-making, cultural relevance and identity, and fandom.

People, Place, and Promotion: Exploring the Baseball/Heritage Relationship

Heritage is a complex and frequently misunderstood term, although succinctly it is best understood as "what we inherit from the past and use in present day" (Timothy, 2011, p. 3). Harrison (2013) further described the presentism of heritage, noting that heritage addresses both current considerations and inherited concerns, while Waterton and Watson (2015, p. 1) viewed heritage as "a version of the past received through objects and display, representations and engagements, spectacular locations and events, memories and commemorations, and the preparation of places for cultural purposes and consumption." There are, of course, many different heritages, each of which connects past places, people, and practices to contemporary needs, considerations, and concerns. Sport is one such topic in heritage.

Ramshaw (2020, p. 4) defined sport heritage as "the recognition and use of the sporting past as a means of addressing or illuminating a variety of contemporary social, cultural, and economic processes and practices" while the sport/heritage relationship can be viewed in a variety of contemporary sporting practices—including baseball. Ramshaw and Gammon (2005; 2017) further explored the heritage/sport relationship by delineating the *heritage of sport*—which would include intra-sport heritage such as famous players, performances, and records—and *sport as heritage*—which includes sport-based heritage, which has a broader societal recognition and impact. There are many examples of the heritage of sport in baseball—many sports have heritages which are recognized, celebrated, and commodified by the teams, leagues, and fans of particular sports. Baseball is perhaps unique in its ability to generate examples of sport as heritage. Jackie Robinson, who most certainly had heritage of sport aspects to his legacy through his on-field records and achievements, is perhaps the most pertinent representation of sport as heritage, as his breaking of the "color barrier" in Major League Baseball is an important part of both American history and heritage, as well as a well-known moment in global sport heritage. Many of the locations of baseball heritage—stadiums and venues, as well as halls of fame, statues, and memorials—tell a broader story of American culture and society, urban development, and heritage conservation. The performances of baseball heritage—whether playing or going to a game—often reflect more about the culture and heritage of a nation than they do of the sport itself. This is not only true in the American context, but internationally as well (as several chapters in this book demonstrate). As such, while the heritages of baseball are certainly important to how the sport is played, promoted, and consumed, baseball's role in revealing broader heritages is one of its most intriguing characteristics.

In approaching baseball's heritage, we are reminded of Graham et al. (2000) who explained the duality of heritage: that heritage is simultaneously a cultural and economic resource. Often the cultural and economic aims of heritage are in conflict with one another; the cultural aims look to create, solidify, or justify the cultural uses of heritage while the economic aims look to exploit the consumer demand for heritage products, experiences, and consumers. In applied terms, the duality of heritage pits the curator (who, perhaps, is most concerned with the cultural uses of heritage) against the gift shop manager (who, perhaps, wishes to sell souvenirs of the latest blockbuster exhibition). In baseball, there are times when the duality of heritage may be in conflict; when the economic uses of baseball's heritage might shape who or what is culturally remembered and celebrated. A team museum, for example, may only represent great performances and beloved players, and not more controversial seasons, teams, and incidents. On the other hand, the cultural and economic aims of baseball heritage may be in concert. The annual celebration of Jackie Robinson not only celebrates his momentous achievements but also might add to ticket and souvenir sales at the ballpark. As such, approaching baseball's heritage under the themes of *people, place, and promotion* is a recognition of the simultaneous uses of baseball's heritage—some of which are in concert while others are in conflict.

Because heritage is shaped by contemporary needs—be they economic, cultural, and/or political—what is included and discarded as part of the heritage canon will often change. The uses of heritage in baseball—though long a part of how the sport's past has been interpreted, marketed, and con-sumed—has taken on a more central role in recent years. In particular, while teams continue to use heritage in fairly typical and recognizable ways—such as in the creation of heritage-themed merchandise, promotions, and ballpark experiences—how baseball heritage is recognized and by whom, as well as how the sport is connected with larger heritage contexts has been pushed to the forefront, particularly in the United States. Indeed, during the creation of this volume, significant social movements such as Black Lives Matter and #MeToo changed how baseball's past is viewed, which in turn changed how baseball's heritage is interpreted and recognized. Historic racialized team names and logos—such as the Indians of Cleveland—have recently been discarded in light of Black Lives Matter protests, while the very history of professional baseball from a statistical perspective is no longer segregated, as statistics from players in the Negro Leagues are now harmonized with those of Major League Baseball. The #MeToo movement, which revealed the widespread impact of sexual assault, abuse, and harassment, changed base-ball's heritage as well—in particular, it spurred the removal of in-stadium heritage markers for past players who were accused of sexual assault, such as Roberto Alomar of the Toronto Blue Jays. The COVID-19 pandemic also significantly changed baseball's heritage, including the collecting of CO-VID-19 related baseball artifacts for museums and halls of fame; famous and historic baseball stadia becoming COVID-19 testing and vaccination centers (not to mention free testing and vaccination sites being part of the "ballpark experience" in 2021); MLB stadiums segregating spectators based on their COVID-19 vaccination status; and "living legends" from baseball's past—such as legendary New York Mets pitcher Tom Seaver and former

Negro Leagues player and country music star Charley Pride—being lost to COVID-19. The pandemic also accelerated broader changes in professional baseball in the United States, including a massive restructuring of the Minor League Baseball system which saw the dissolution of historic leagues such as the Pacific Coast League (founded in 1903) and the South Atlantic League (founded in 1904), suggesting that some baseball heritages—particularly in a crisis—are no longer valuable. While 2020 and 2021 may be exceptional in terms of the sheer number of changes to baseball's heritage, it will undoubtedly continue to be used, commodified, abandoned, or altered depending on the needs and values of the present. As such, understanding the uses of heritage in baseball becomes more urgent, particularly as broader interpretations of the past become part of baseball's present.

Approaching baseball's past through a heritage lens, rather than through a historical one, also requires a different approach. Heritage is broadly understood as an interdisciplinary topic area with many component parts and drawing from many fields, including management, marketing, anthropology, and, of course, history. Clearly, baseball history plays a central role in understanding baseball heritage. Historical approaches to baseball provide content and context for heritage outputs while also demonstrating where baseball heritage—with its focus often on a commodifiable contemporary product or an experience which (in many cases) may have the "feel" or "look" of history but may in fact have little relation to the historical past beyond an antiquated aesthetic—may mask, obscure, or misrepresent the factual, historical past. Taken a different way, baseball history provides baseball heritage with a fundamental research base and a factual platform on which heritage builds its narrative and creates its experiences. On the other hand, baseball heritage often provides baseball history with a public (and publicly accessible) outlet. Without heritage approaches and outputs—including heritage-based events, markers, merchandise, and experiences—the nuances of academic baseball history might be impenetrable to all but specialist audiences. Similarly, when baseball's past is presented in a heritage context (at a baseball museum or hall of fame, for example), the public has a chance to understand, and perhaps even engage in, debates about the past. Baseball history and baseball heritage are not two solitudes but are not synonymous either.

While the public engagement duties of heritage may overlap in certain ways with, say, the public history, Howard (2003) argued that heritage specialists and researchers also must consider things like visitor motivation, revenue generation, and visitor experience—aspects which may have little role in historical research—along with shared concerns about fidelity in presenting various pasts. Howard (2003) further argued that

> heritage is an applied humanity, whereas history is a pure one; history is interested in the past, heritage is interested in how the past might be conserved and interpreted for the benefit of the present. (p. 21)

While some baseball historians may still view heritage approaches as "bad history," Lowenthal (1998) argued that heritage and history—though related—have very different tasks, audiences, and outcomes and must be approached and understood distinctly. This is not to argue that baseball heritage is a "good thing" or always has noble intentions or outcomes; many of the chapters in this collection are deeply critical of baseball heritage, explicitly noting its challenges and limitations. Rather, this is to suggest that historical and heritage approaches to baseball, though overlapping in many important ways, are not identical, despite their close relationship.

Another important differentiation, though again sharing a close relationship, is that between baseball heritage and baseball nostalgia. As indicated in the discussion earlier baseball is no stranger to nostalgia (Elias, 2010; Springwood, 1996; Von Borg & Johnson, 2009). It is a deceptively simple game that celebrates the past in numerous forms. Even the primary premise of the sport—to return *home*—implies that the most important journeys always end where they first began. Yet making it "safely home" in a baseball sense differs from nostalgic remembrance, in that nostalgia's defining characteristic is the realization that the past has gone and will never be repeated. To be nostalgic is to fondly recall the way things were (or should have been) while acknowledging that they are impossible to physically return to (Gammon & Ramshaw, 2013). It is such bittersweet reflections that position nostalgia as a particularly powerful emotion that simultaneously evokes feelings of joy tempered with notions of loss.

Therefore, it will come as little surprise that discussions reflecting upon baseball's past will inevitably draw on nostalgia, as both an instigator and a reaction to a game that holds a multitude of personal and collective meanings (Aden, 1995). These meaningful recollections form an integral part of some of the contributions in this collection, which not only underscores the important emotional components of the sport but also draws attention to the inextricable relationship that nostalgia has with heritage. Smith and Campbell (2017) observed that there are notable similarities between these two concepts, identifying that, like nostalgia, heritage is somewhat of a selective process that mines those aspects of the past that hold value, in order for them to be saved and cherished in the present. In some situations, heritages such as those contained in halls of fame are arguably designed to evoke nostalgic responses—whether lived or learned (Fairley & Gammon, 2005). Similarly, retro ballparks, popularized in the 1990s (see Ramshaw & Gammon in this volume), have been described as a concoction of salient heritage-markers from older parks whose primary purpose is to offer visitors more *traditional* experiences of watching a ball game.

But to suggest that interactions with heritage are always nostalgic would be misleading, as responses to heritage are far more nuanced—providing, for example, opportunities for the affirmation of personal and collective identities, as well as the more obvious educational benefits. Ramshaw and Gammon (2005), for example, argued that nostalgic recollection—though sometimes recalling times of struggle—will invariably conjure positive associations within those pasts, whereas heritage has the capacity for a much broader canvas which may include both triumph and tragedy. Nevertheless, it is inevitable that images and objects from the past will often trigger nostalgic responses to those who come in contact with them. And while there will be more broader criticisms of the selective nature of heritage, it is the processes that lead to such choices that shed light on what is valued and cherished, as "collective memory is no longer grounded in history or social context, but also in the process of abstracting and rerouting meanings" (Goldman & Papson, 1994: 40). It is these abstractions and rerouting of meanings that are in evidence throughout this collection and which separate this text from others.

The Batting Order

The baseball/heritage relationship is multifaceted, and thus it is not a surprise that the chapters in this collection approach this relationship from a variety of standpoints. The chapter by Cory Kulczycki, Luke Potwarka, and Jonathon Edwards explores one of the quintessential forms of baseball heritage: the rituals and nostalgia of spectating experience(s). Childhood memories of attending baseball games with parents are a subgenre of baseball literature (see, for example, Stanton, 2002), though rarely are those personal heritages and nostalgic experiences viewed as an essential part of the ongoing spectator experience. As Kulczycki et al. suggest, these embodied spectating experiences—enhanced through the *sportscapes* themselves (notably, famous and beloved stadia) and the atmospherics at games, including the smells and sounds of the ballpark—have managerial implications as well. The nostalgic and heritage experiences and traditions of the ballpark can, in a sense, become ritualized and provide a familiar and enjoyable sport spectating experience. It is interesting to note that the examples that Kulczycki et al. provide are Canadian, demonstrating that baseball nostalgia and the spectating experience is not the exclusive purview of fans in the United States.

Nostalgia also plays a central role in the second chapter of the collection, though from a different perspective. In this case, Andrew McGregor challenges us to consider who we nostalgically remember and how we celebrate figures and moments from baseball's past. In this case, he compares the contemporary nostalgia for Hank Aaron and Curt Flood—both of whom are important and transformational figures in baseball's history. Aaron's nostalgic legacy is confirmed, commodified, and celebrated in the present day (including in statue form, as discussed by Chris Stride in this volume). Nostalgia for Aaron is safe, placing his sacrifices, accomplishments, and legacy as a way of overlooking or overstepping contemporary baseball issues like racism and use of PEDs. Nostalgia for Flood, on the other hand, is limited, as it raises issues about labor relations (and disputes) in baseball, not to mention significant and ongoing issues of race and racism in the game. As such, McGregor poses some central questions of critical heritage studies: who or what is remembered, by whom, and for what contemporary purposes?

How some baseball heritages are remembered—or marginalized—is also central to the next chapter in the lineup, where Leslie Heaphy explores the heritage representations of women in baseball. Heaphy argues that because there is limited nostalgia about women's baseball—save for, perhaps, representations in popular culture such as the film *A League of Their Own*—as such, there are few heritage representations of women in baseball. Heaphy finds that those heritage representations of women in baseball which do exist—such as in the National Baseball Hall of Fame and at other heritage sites and museums across the United States—are scattershot and haphazard at best, provide a limited unifying story or narrative, and give very little indication of the significant involvement of women in baseball throughout the game's history. Heaphy suggests that much of the marginalization of women's baseball heritage has to do with broader cultural constructions of baseball and masculinity, which therefore marginalizes and excludes women's involvement. Ultimately, Heaphy suggests some ways in which this heritage could be represented, including the construction of a dedicated museum about women in baseball and the creation of more public events celebrating women's baseball heritage.

Issues of marginalization in the representation of baseball heritage is focus of the next chapter, in which Benjamin J. Downs and Adam G. Pfleegor explore how (and whether) the histories and heritages of Negro Leagues teams and players are recognized at baseball stadia in the United States. Sports stadia are among the most tangible and powerful forms of sport heritage (Gammon, 2011; Ramshaw, 2020), with ballparks in particular being the repositories for much of baseball's heritage. Downs and Pfleegor argue that the recognition and celebration of Negro Leagues players and accomplishments are largely absent in many ballparks across the United States. Indeed, even as many historic ballparks were replaced with modern venues, the forms of heritage recognition—which borrowed heritage from the previous stadium and installed them in the new venue (Ramshaw et al., 2013)—were almost exclusively about white players, teams, and accomplishments. These excluded pasts—which include heritages that are unrepresented, either purposely or through historical ignorance (Stone & MacKenzie, 1994)—are often unflattering (and therefore unpalatable) to contemporary organizations and therefore hinder the "heritage work" of positively connecting the spectator/consumer to the venue. Why many of the greatest baseball players—including Satchel Paige—are not celebrated at the ballparks in which they played clearly demonstrates the selectivity of heritage discourse in sport heritage, particularly the role of heritage in constructing place identity at sports venues.

Heritage and ballparks are also the focus of Gregory Ramshaw and Sean Gammon's chapter about the emergent authenticity of Oriole Park at Camden Yards (OPCY), the venue which began the retro/heritage-themed stadium trend in the United States. Ramshaw and Gammon view OPCY in three phases or ages: the first as a nostalgia-fueled postmodern pastiche of ballparks from the past; the second as a simulacrum—or the "true copy"—for various heritage-inspired ballpark developments across the United States; and the third as existing in a form of liminality whereby it has, in essence, emerged into its own right as an authentic ballpark with its own heritage while still not yet becoming a historically recognized and protected landmark. While much of the writing about OPCY has been critical—in particular, deriding its use of "fake baseball history" as part of its atmospherics—Ramshaw and Gammon take a much more sympathetic view, arguing that while it is easy to have a cynical view about OPCY, its construction and longevity are an important part of baseball's architectural and cultural legacy. The authors claim that the sense of place it helped to create—providing spectators with some sense of baseball's past coupled with relief from the interchangeable concrete doughnuts in which many MLB teams played in from the 1960s through the 1990s—ought to be applauded. Furthermore, Ramshaw and Gammon argue that OPCY is becoming an historic ballpark in its own right, particularly given its age relative to many of its peers— despite the notion that it is a "new" stadium, as of 2020 OPCY is the 21st oldest ballpark in MLB—as well as through the many moments, teams, and players celebrated at the stadium. However, Ramshaw and Gammon caution that OPCY's future, given the portability of franchises and the desire of team ownership to derive as much revenue as they can from their stadia, is somewhat more uncertain.

Place and its construction is central to Kiernan O. Gordon's chapter about baseball museums in the United States. Baseball museums are an essential part of the game's heritage narrative. Indeed, how baseball heritage is constructed, negotiated, interpreted, and commodified can be understood through examining baseball museums, in large part because of their position and popularity as tourism destinations. Through the examination of three prominent baseball museums—the National Baseball Hall of Fame and Museum, the Louisville Slugger Museum and Factory, and the Negro Leagues Baseball Museum—Gordon argues that place plays a prominent role in the meta-narratives (and, indeed, the *raison d'être*) of these museums. In this sense, a carefully constructed sense of heritage and place *confirms*, in Gordon's analysis, the National Baseball Hall of Fame and Museum (and its home in Cooperstown) as the cradle of the game, the Louisville Slugger Museum and Factory as a brand that is essential in creating baseball's hitting heroes, and the Negro Leagues Baseball Museum as both a corrective and consumptive heritage good. In these analyses, Gordon also demonstrates the broader politization of baseball heritage, observing that baseball heritage is not value-free in its presentation at American baseball museums.

While heritage is essential in the construction of the "national pastime" in the United States, the uses of heritage in baseball are frequently found throughout the world. Japan has a significant baseball heritage, particularly in high school baseball, as Ito et al. explore. In particular, they explore the broader aspects of both tangible baseball heritage in Japan—specifically the Hanshin Koshien Stadium where the Japanese High School Baseball Championship is played—and intangible baseball heritage in Japan—specifically the star high school baseball players from yesteryear who return to play in the Masters' Koshien tournament. In their analysis, Ito et al. link two essential elements of sport heritage: authentic heritage venues, such as historic ballparks (Seifried & Mayer, 2010), and existential identities linked to the sporting past (Ramshaw, 2014). Through their exploration of the Masters' Koshien, Ito et al. not only see a way of creating and maintaining culturally resonant forms of heritage sport tourism; they also demonstrate the connections between space, place, and performance in baseball heritage.

Jungah Choi's chapter, which covers the history and heritage of baseball in South Korea, demonstrates the development of a distinctive domestic baseball heritage alongside the broader global (and, in particular, American) influence on the sport's culture. The United States undoubtedly played a significant role in the creation of baseball cultures across Asia, but, as Choi demonstrates, South Korean baseball has developed its own culture, heritage, and traditions—not the least of which is the unique cheering culture seen at games across the country. It is also part of the global baseball culture, particularly in the creation of baseball labor for MLB teams, and of its participation in international baseball tournaments such as the World Baseball Classic and the Summer Olympic Games. Choi also explores the potential of South Korean baseball heritage in the country's tourism development, noting that there is significant room to develop more tangible forms of sport heritage attractions—such as a national baseball museum and hall of fame—while also suggesting that the intangible aspects of South Korean baseball culture, such as the unique cheering style and the food culture at the ballpark, may attract international tourists. Indeed, the fact that the Korea Baseball Organization (KBO)—the professional league in South Korea—garnered international attention during the COVID-19 pandemic as it was the first baseball league in the world to a) play games and b) have spectators in the stands following the global spread of the coronavirus in 2020 may bode well for future heritage sport tourism in the country.

Felipe Bertazzo Tobar's chapter about baseball heritage in Brazil also explores the national/global relationship in constructing, developing, and maintaining a domestic baseball culture, although his argument suggests that this relationship is a struggle between past, present, and future. Brazil's baseball heritage has its beginnings not with the United States but with the migration of Japanese workers into the country in the postwar period. As Bertazzo Tobar reveals much of the culture and administration of baseball in Brazil was created for and by Japanese communities with limited input (or, at least in the initial stages, interest) by Brazilians. However, as

Brazilians became interested in the sport, there became a struggle about the culture of the sport—with the Japanese representing the heritage of baseball in Brazil. Bertazzo Tobar argues that while it is important for Brazilians to embrace the sport for it to survive in the country, it should not come at the expense of marginalizing Japanese heritage. In this, he proposes that, going forward, there can be a balance to baseball culture in Brazil which both maintains and honors its Japanese past while embracing the new and dynamic Brazilian approaches to the sport.

An exploration of baseball heritage, particularly outside of the United States, would not be complete without an analysis of baseball heritage in the Caribbean. Thomas E. Van Hyning's commentary takes a broad look at the uses and understandings of heritage across several Caribbean nations, including most notably through events—such as the Caribbean World Series—through some of the baseball halls of fame and museums in the region, as well as through the "living heritage" of the region's baseball heroes. His exploration reveals that baseball heritage in the region reflects the broader culture and politics of the Caribbean, including the creation and maintenance of national cultures and heritage; interregional rivalries (and cooperation) through sport; and the region's cultural and economic relationship with the United States. Van Hyning also posits that this region's baseball heritage, which is as rich and diverse as that of the United States, requires further consideration.

Perhaps a more surprising look at baseball heritage outside of the United States comes from Brett Lashua's chapter about Britain's baseball heritage. Baseball likely owes much of its formation to the British "ball games" of rounders and cricket. Though there have been attempts to popularize baseball in the United Kingdom, it remains largely absent—both in terms of spaces and fandom—in the British sporting landscape. As Lashua explores—both through an exploration of baseball's history and formative locations in the United Kingdom as well as his own experiences as an Anglo-American playing the sport in England—there is a rich history and heritage of baseball in the United Kingdom and as a cultural practice, although the contemporary playing of the sport is largely linked with a performance of Americanness (both for expat American players and domestic British players). Lashua notes that there is a general ignorance about Britain's baseball's history, although there have been recent attempts (such as a 2019 MLB series in London) to (re)introduce the British public to this component of American sporting culture. Indeed, as baseball has become more global—and is part of the sporting practices in countries like the Netherlands, Italy, and

Australia—Lashua provides a blueprint both for understanding baseball's hidden heritages and its contemporary cultural practices in nations where baseball is not often mentioned in popular sporting discourse.

Rounding out our lineup, we return to the United States and explore how heritage is used in the creation and promotion of ballpark spaces. Chris Stride's chapter analyzes the debates about two Atlanta baseball statues, those of Hank Aaron and Ty Cobb, and whether they would be relocated when MLB's Atlanta Braves moved to a new ballpark. Heritage plaques, statues, and monuments are some of the ways in which new sporting spaces and venues are imbued with a sense of meaning, place, and authenticity (Belanger, 2000; Ramshaw et al., 2013). While the relocation of heritage artifacts occur in part as a recognition of a team's or venue's history, it is also a form of promotion and marketing—helping fans and consumers form a connection with the new stadium. As Stride explores, Aaron's legacy—a former Brave, an African American baseball hero, and one-time holder of the career home-run record—is one which the Braves wished to relocate (in statue form) to their new ballpark, whereas Cobb—a Georgia native and great baseball player whose legacy has been diminished due to racism, and who spent his entire professional career in Detroit and Philadelphia—was not a legacy the Braves wanted to celebrate at their new venue. However, as Stride explains, while Cobb's statue was not welcome at the Braves' new stadium, it was relocated to the town of Royston, Georgia—Cobb's birthplace—which uses its association with Cobb in its community promotion and tourism. As Stride's chapter demonstrates, having a "suitable" and marketable heritage is an important part of the baseball heritage landscape.

Finally, Alana N. Seaman's examination of the food/heritage relationship at ballparks also helps shape the spectator experience. Baseball is perhaps unique in that many of the promotional aspects of the game experience—such as giveaways, mascots, and foods—are fundamental aspects of "going to the game." As Seaman demonstrates, traditional ballpark foods—such as hot dogs, cold beer, and Cracker Jack—are still part of the ballpark experience, but teams are introducing other forms of food-based heritage, in particularly local brands and delicacies, to add a new sense of place and authenticity. Similarly, at the minor-league level of professional baseball, food promotions—such as "Thirsty Thursdays," where beer and soda are sold at reduced rates—are staples of the promotional calendar, while team names and mascots—such as the Jacksonville Jumbo Shrimp and the Montgomery Biscuits—reflect local food heritages. Even the ballpark names themselves—such as Miller Park in Milwaukee—are named after and sponsored by beverage companies. As such, Seaman demonstrates that food is an integral part of the ballpark experience and an essential element of baseball heritage.

Conclusion

Few sports are as inseparable from the past as baseball. Indeed, the fact that much of the past in baseball is also linked to its present is a large part of the sport's appeal. As sports and political commentator Keith Olbermann explains in *The Tenth Inning* baseball documentary:

> What adheres me to baseball, and always has, is this sense that I am essentially watching the same game that somebody saw in 1860. The history of it . . . it is the only sport that goes forwards and backwards. Other sports have some interest in their own history and will occasionally make reference to it. But, baseball, it's there. You come in at the start of the game or the start of the season or the start of your own fandom, you feel as if you are joining the river midstream. And all that has gone before you can enjoy as much as if you were there. It's as simple as that. (Burns & Novak, 2010)

While there are innumerable academic and popular assessments of baseball's history, baseball's heritage—in particular, how baseball's past is understood, used, interpreted, commodified, or ignored in the present—remains relatively underexplored. While baseball's heritage is still largely viewed as an asset, as many of the chapters in this collection reveal, this heritage is challenging, reveals larger tensions and issues, and, in several cases, is under threat. Similarly, while heritage is still very much a part of the contemporary game, how long it will remain this way—and whether owners, leagues, and teams view heritage as more of a burden than a benefit—is a consideration that cannot be ignored. Still, as this collection reveals, baseball's heritage—like many other forms of heritage—can be a source of great enjoyment and inspiration; can be used to address numerous social, political, or economic aims and missions; can be a cause of conflict and contestation; and can reveal tensions about whose pasts are remembered and whose pasts are ignored. This collection demonstrates that baseball heritage is not strictly the purview of the United States. The "national pastime" is now shared by many nations. Indeed, the fact that much of this collection focuses on baseball heritage outside of the United States, while many non-American authors explore baseball heritage in the United States, demonstrates that an understanding of the baseball/heritage relationship is increasingly global. Finally, this collection is meant to be a starting point for further explorations of the baseball/heritage relationship. Though demonstrating a wide range of perspectives about baseball heritage, this collection is just the proverbial tip of the iceberg. We hope that readers find insight and inspiration in these pages, and that this collection begins broader explorations of baseball heritage in the United States and beyond. Play ball!

Acknowledgments

The editors would like to thank Shawna Cass for her time and effort in proofreading chapters and helping to improve the clarity and quality of the photos in this collection. The editors would also like to thank the Robert H. Brooks Sports Science Institute at Clemson University for their support.

References

Aden, R. C. (1995). Nostalgic communication as temporal escape: When it was a game's re-construction of a baseball/work community. *Western Journal of Communication, 59*(1), 20–38.

Bélanger, A. (2000). Sport venues and the spectacularization of urban spaces in North America: The case of the Molson Centre in Montreal. *International Review for the Sociology of Sport, 35*(3), 378–397.

Burns, K. (director/producer), & Novick, L. (producer) (2010). *Baseball: A film by Ken Burns, the tenth inning: Top of the tenth* [motion picture]. United States: PBS Home Video.

Elias, R. (Ed.). (2010). *Baseball and the American dream: Race, class, gender, and the national pastime.* New York: M. E. Sharpe.

Fairley, S., & Gammon, S. (2005). Something lived, something learned: Nostalgia's expanding role in sport tourism. *Sport in Society, 8*(2), 182–197.

Friedman, M. T., & Silk, M. L. (2005). Expressing Fenway: Managing and marketing heritage within the global sports marketplace. *International Journal of Sport Management and Marketing, 1*(1–2), 37–55.

Gammon, S. (2011). 'Sporting' new attractions? The commodification of the sleeping stadium. In R. Sharpley & P. Stone (Eds.), *Tourism experiences: Contemporary perspectives* (pp. 115–126). London: Routledge.

Gammon, S., & Ramshaw, G. (2013). Nostalgia and sport. In A. Fyall & B. Garrod (Eds.), *Contemporary cases in sport* (pp. 201–220). Oxford: Goodfellow Publishers.

Goldman, R., & Papson, S. (1994). Advertising in the age of hypersignification. *Theory, Culture & Society, 11*(3), 23–53.

Graham, B., Ashworth, G. J., & Tunbridge, J. E. (2000). *A geography of heritage: Power, culture & economy.* London: Arnold.

Harrison, R. (2013). *Heritage: Critical approaches*. London: Routledge.

Howard, P. (2003). *Heritage: Management, interpretation, identity*. London: Continuum.

Kim, K. K. (Ed.). (2016). *Celebrating America's pastimes: Baseball, hot dogs, apple pie and marketing?: Proceedings of the 2015 Academy of Marketing Science (AMS) annual conference*. New York: Springer.

Koppett, L. (2016). A new golden age? An evolving baseball dream. In R. Elias (Ed.), *Baseball and the American dream: Race, class, gender, and the national pastime* (pp. 214–225). London: Routledge.

Ramshaw, G. (2014). A Canterbury tale: Imaginative genealogies and existential heritage tourism at the St. Lawrence ground. *Journal of Heritage Tourism, 9*(3), 257–269.

Ramshaw, G. (2020). *Heritage and sport: An introduction*. Bristol: Channel View Publications.

Ramshaw, G., & Gammon, S. (2005). More than just nostalgia? Exploring the heritage/sport tourism nexus. *Journal of Sport & Tourism, 10*(4), 229–241.

Ramshaw, G., & Gammon, S. (2017). Towards a critical sport heritage: Implications for sport tourism. *Journal of Sport & Tourism, 21*(2), 115–131.

Ramshaw, G., & Gammon, S. (2020). Difference, dissonance, and redemption in sport heritage: Interpreting the tangled legacy of Pete Rose at two museums. *Journal of Heritage Tourism, 15*(2), 217–227.

Ramshaw, G., Gammon, S., & Huang, W. J. (2013). Acquired pasts and the commodification of borrowed heritage: The case of the Bank of America Stadium tour. *Journal of Sport & Tourism, 18*(1), 17–31.

Ramshaw, G., Gammon, S., & Tobar, F. (2019). Negotiating the cultural and economic outcomes of sport heritage attractions: The case of the National Baseball Hall of Fame. *Journal of Sport & Tourism, 23*(2–3), 79–95.

Seifried, C., & Meyer, K. (2010). Nostalgia-related aspects of professional sport facilities: A facility audit of Major League Baseball and National Football League strategies to evoke the past. *International Journal of Sport Management Recreation and Tourism, 5*(1), 51–76.

Springwood, C. F. (1996). *Cooperstown to Dyersville: A geography of baseball nostalgia*. Boulder, CO: Westview Press.

Stanton, T. (2002). *The final season: Fathers, sons, and one last season in a classic American ballpark*. New York: Macmillan.

Stone, P. G., & MacKenzie, R. (Eds.). (1994). *The excluded past: Archaeology in education*. London: Routledge.

Timothy, D. J. (2011). *Cultural heritage and tourism: An introduction*. Bristol: Channel View Publications.

Von Burg, R., & Johnson, P. E. (2009). Yearning for a past that never was: Baseball, steroids, and the anxiety of the American dream. *Critical Studies in Media Communication, 26*(4), 351–371.

Waterton, E., & Watson, S. (2015). Heritage as a focus of research: Past, present and new directions. In E. Waterton & S. Watson (Eds.), *The Palgrave handbook of contemporary heritage research* (pp. 1–17). London: Palgrave-Macmillan.

2

Unpacking the Embodied Baseball Spectator Experience

Intersections of Heritage and Nostalgia

CORY KULCZYCKI, LUKE POTWARKA, AND JONATHON EDWARDS

Sport invokes a broad range of emotions and creates positive and negative memories for sports fans and spectators (Ramshaw & Gammon, 2005). Attending a baseball game in an iconic stadium will often include traditions, stories, and reminiscences about historic and inspirational moments, where the "sportscapes" (i.e., the stadiums and their components [e.g., banners, seats]; Wakefield et al., 1996), become attractions, and "spectacles" (Ritzer & Stillman, 2001, p. 100) help enhance the intangible experience. As Ritzer and Stillman (2001) contended, "at an early point in their history, ballparks were rather enchanted, magical settings" (p. 99) and, as such, the memories and emotions that are created by attending a ball game can "hook" the spectator into becoming loyal to the team or sport. Ramshaw and Gammon (2005) indicated that "fans identify with the past of their team, even if that past does not exist in their living memory, while others see sport as a continuity of a national, regional or personal legacy and identity" (p. 232). Relatedly, Ramshaw (2020) explained the notion of "being" heritage, where there is an element of "hereditary connections" that can be associated with the fandom of a specific team that is shared among family members and over generations. Furthermore, "doing" sport heritage involves the expression and representation of participating in heritage elements, which sometimes includes collecting and displaying sports memorabilia (Ramshaw, 2020).

The individual "doing" heritage is able to share their personal sport heritage as part of their fandom within social interactions (Ramshaw, 2020). Thus, sport consumption needs to be understood as a social experience.

To expand on the intrapersonal and interpersonal aspects of "being" and "doing" heritage in this chapter, we present and apply the concept of the embodied experience. It is through this experience associated with sport spectating at games and events that people come together and build memories that form nostalgia (Fairley & Gammon, 2005). For example, pivotal moments in the game become memories for the spectator, including where they were sitting, who they were with when the moment occurred, and how the memories are shared. Thus, an individual gravitates toward a particular team or league as it relates to that sport and a personal heritage and nostalgic connections.

Therefore, this chapter will begin with an articulation about the embodied spectator experience, which positions it within the notion of the sportscape (Wakefield et al., 1996). Next, we explain heritage and nostalgia in the context of the sport fan with a specific focus on the baseball spectator. To explore the nexus of the experience, heritage, and nostalgia in a baseball context, the reader is presented with an autoethnography about a father and son game-day experience at a Toronto Blue Jays game in Toronto, Ontario. Notably, the autoethnography is written from the son's perspective. To conclude, we will unpack the meanings associated with the son's game-day account, while discussing the implications of the embodied experience for sport spectators and managers.

Embodied Spectator Experiences

Fans attend games for a variety of reasons. Researchers have suggested that the "sportscape" plays an important role in spectator experiences (Wakefield & Sloan, 1995; Wakefield et al., 1996). The sportscape includes the features of the stadium that an attending fan will interact with and includes parking, concessions, cleanliness, and fan management (Wakefield & Sloan, 1995; Wakefield et al., 1996). Hill and Green (2000) explained that fan perception of the sportscape influenced future attendance. Therefore, the setting elements, which engage the individual in an embodied experience, are in essence the sportscape.

The embodied spectator experience is a relatively new concept in the literature. Channon and Jennings (2014) defined the term *embodiment* as "the living, moving and feeling social experiences of human beings" (p. 773). Low (2003) explained, "Embodied space is the location where human experience and consciousness take on material and spatial form" (p. 9). Sport researchers have long acknowledged the importance of the body, mind, and setting in an effort to understand the lived experience of the participant (Allen-Collinson et al., 2018). For an individual to have a specific experience, they will interpret and plan their actions based on social and cultural information and past routines which are practiced and rehearsed, and the physical body will be prepared (e.g., training, wearing a jersey). The physical and mental body then responds to stimuli during the experience (Nash, 2000). Experience occurs through spectator's senses, movement, knowledge of the setting and activity, the characteristics of the setting, and the technology (i.e., equipment; Anderson, 2013; Spinney, 2006; Springgay & Truman, 2017).

Gaffney and Bale (2004) noted that the stadium is experienced through the senses. People look onto the stadium from the street and gain a sense of its scale, presence, and importance. Spectators as a collective observe or gaze upon the occurrences within the stadium. Gaffney and Bale asserted that "sound occupies space and gives fullness to experience" (2004, p. 28), where the music and chants can be orchestrated by facility management for desired experiences or impacts for spectators within the setting. Spectators also experience the stadium through touch as they interact with others in the crowd and the sportscape. Smell provides a powerful connection to memories and place, and it encapsulates nostalgia (e.g., food, typical stadium aromas).

Finally, taste is often associated with the experience of food consumption at stadiums and is "part of the larger ritual process of stadium events" (Gaffney & Bale, 2004, p. 33). Based on the identifying factors of experiences, individuals begin to comprehend the social culture, setting, and experience (Springgay & Truman, 2017), where the space is a variable (Dutkiewicz, 2015) that is part of the socially constructed setting with which and to what people interact (Sparkes et al., 2010). The act of being a fan attending a live sporting event is an example of embodied fan experience that is influenced by the sport fan's characteristics (e.g., gender, team affiliation), social and cultural interactions, and the sportscape in which the fan experience occurs.

Heritage and Nostalgia

The embodied spectator experience can be understood in relation to notions of heritage and nostalgia. The term "heritage" has been described by scholars as "awkward to define" (Ramshaw & Gammon, 2005, p. 230). Furthermore,

Heritage often seeks to remember, enliven, teach—and even create—personal and collective legacies for contemporary audiences. Its purpose is often to celebrate the achievements, courage and strength of those who have come before, consequently making it unusual to see critical examinations of the past from a heritage perspective. Such representations and interpretations are achieved using a variety of sources, including (though not limited to) history, nostalgia, memory, myth and tradition. (Ramshaw & Gammon, 2005, p. 230)

Within sport, heritage is often associated with the collective recollection of significant on-field actions of players and the play of the athletes (Ramshaw, 2014). The stadiums of sport become the locations or places of heritage. That is not to imply that heritage must be associated with large buildings and objects; heritage and meaning can be connected to large and small or tangible and intangible objects (Gammon, 2007). In addition, Ramshaw and Gammon (2005) indicated that there are four categorizations of sport heritage, which include tangible immovable, tangible movable, intangible, and goods and services.

"Tangible immovable" is in reference to those "special sites/sights of sporting significance" (Ramshaw & Gammon, 2005, p. 233). For example, Major League Baseball's oldest stadium, Fenway Park in Boston and home to the Boston Red Sox, has been branded as a heritage resource (Friedman & Silk, 2005). Conversely, "tangible movable" sport heritage "refers to objects, articles and tangible experiences that need not necessarily be spatially rooted" (Ramshaw & Gammon, 2005, p. 234), while "intangible" sport heritage includes "rituals, traditions, chants, memories, nostalgia and other forms of impalpable heritage associated with sport" (Ramshaw & Gammon, 2005, p. 234). Finally, "goods and services" of sport heritage are those "sporting goods, particularly *retro* apparel, and services with a heritage element" (Ramshaw & Gammon, 2005, p. 235). An example of retro apparel would be an original jersey from an established professional team.

Related to heritage, the term "nostalgia" has been described by Havlena and Holak (1991), Holbrook (1993), and Fairley (2003) as being an individual's or a group's desire to return to or relive a past period, which Ramshaw and Gammon (2005) suggest leads to motivating the individual or group to attend the event. Furthermore, the social interactions one has at games and the desire to return for the experience can be a motivation for repeat attendance and travel to sport games and events (Cho et al., 2017; Fairley, 2003; Kulczycki & Hyatt, 2005), as this is understood as the "nostalgia for social experience" (Fairley & Gammon, 2005, p. 182). The social interactions, along with friends, family, and atmosphere (e.g., sounds, smells), are intangibles that influence perceptions of nostalgia (Havlena & Holak, 1991). In Gibson's (1998) work, nostalgia can be understood as the physical entity that holds special meaning to an individual or community. This physical entity can have historic or symbolic importance (Fairley, 2003), which Fairley and Gammon (2005) identified as "nostalgia for place or artifact" (p. 182).

Contextualizing the Embodied Sport-Spectator Experience: A Narrative of a Father and Son's Experience of Watching Live Baseball Games

This narrative is presented as an autoethnography, which permitted the author, Luke Potwarka, to share the baseball experience and engagement on game day with his father (Alverson, 2003). Through the experiences described, we are able to gain insight into the embodied experience on game day (Larsen, 2014). We ask the reader to be mindful of the embodied experience (e.g., preparation of the mind and body for the experience; setting elements that engage the senses). Moreover, we ask the reader to be conscious of the tangible (e.g., objects) and intangible (e.g., rituals and songs) aspects of heritage described in the narrative.

The Narrative

The clock in Mrs. Climenhaga's Grade 5 classroom seemed to be stuck at 3:29 p.m. It was only one minute until we heard the buzzer that signaled the end to another school day. Today was special. In just one hour's time, I would be on the way to a Toronto Blue Jays baseball game with my dad. This was our time and our space. I had gone to hundreds of ball games with my dad in my short life. Although we had the same routine, every experience was special and unique, and conjured up the same level of excitement. It didn't matter who was playing or how well the Jays were playing. What mattered was that we were together sharing in an experience we both loved . . . watching baseball.

Beep . . . Beep . . . Beep. The buzzer had finally arrived. I quickly gathered my books and belongings and darted out the door. I raced home on foot, hoping to arrive before Dad. On this day, I beat him. I hardly made it to the kitchen before I could hear Dad's voice from the front door:

"You ready, Luke? Let's get going. Remember, it's really important to

dress in layers, because the breeze from the lake will make it really cold tonight at the stadium. You can't put on what you don't have, right?"

"Got it, Dad," I said.

I quickly threw on my sweater and grabbed a jacket. We then piled into our 1986 Oldsmobile Cutlass Supreme and away we went.

The time in the car driving to Exhibition Stadium was sacred. Dad would frequently quiz me on how to keep score at the game. "If someone hits a ground ball to the second basemen and is thrown out, how would you score it?" he asked. "4–3," I replied. Driving to the game was also a time to talk about how the Jays were doing and who to watch at the game. We would always follow the same hour-long route to the game, 401 Westbound, Gardener expressway, and then exit on Lakeshore Boulevard toward the stadium. Dad knew a secret place to park near the stadium, an abandoned gas station that only charged five dollars. Although we had parked here hundreds of times, I thought he was a genius each time. The walk to the stadium was always purposeful and quick. The smell of hot dog carts and peanut stands filled the air. Dad and I walked right past these vendors with a sense of urgency. Although we were hungry, it was not time to eat yet. Instead, our mission was to be at Gate 11 when it opened so we could stake out our spot for batting practice. Not even the finest processed meats could stop us from witnessing this pre-game tradition.

As soon as the gate opened, Dad and I rushed to find our seats. Section 118, left field line, second row from the field. We ran down the steep stadium steps, narrowly avoiding collisions with other people with the same goal. We tried our best not to slip on spilled beer and plastic cups that had already littered the aisles. When we reached the fence, it took a few inappropriate elbows and nasty looks to secure a spot in a prime location to catch a ball. For me, the most important thing about watching batting practice was catching a ball from an errant throw or batted ball. For Dad, batting practice was a chance to learn hitting techniques and futilely attempt to predict which player was going to play well. "Barfield is getting his hands back. He is going to hit two today, just watch, Luke," he would say. We would remain along the fence watching batting practice until the fateful moment when the usher cried out, "OK, folks, time to take your seats!" This moment signaled it was time for my final plea to the nearest player in earshot, "Can I have a ball?" I collected dozens of practice balls during my time with Dad. Today, they proudly adorn my mantel. Even the most casual of glances at them awakens fond memories of my times watching Blue Jays games with Dad.

Whether or not my request for a ball was granted didn't matter. The end of batting practice meant only one thing: it was time to eat! Eating at the stadium with Dad was consistent and ritualistic. Despite the multitude of available concessions and snack options, our purchase decisions were narrowly constrained and rarely deviated from. We first made our way to the concourse behind home plate. Here we lined up at the only vendor that sold French fries in the entire stadium. When we were handed our single order of fresh-cut fries, we smothered them in ketchup and malt vinegar. We then grabbed two wooden sporks, and carefully weaved in and out of groups of our fellow spectators until we reached our next concession destination adjacent to our section. Once it was our turn to order, without hesitation my dad would habitually say, "One program, two dogs, and two beers please." To avoid unnecessary interruptions to his viewership experience, Dad always ordered two beers. We would then dress our dogs. Ketchup and mustard for me; mustard and relish for Dad. We would then make our way back to our seats.

Astonishingly, we always made it back in time to stand for the national anthems (and without spilling too much of our delicious food). We would stand at attention as we stared at the Canadian Flag atop the scoreboard in right field. I remember the solemnity of these moments, and vague feelings of pride as I listened to the gentle hum of fans collectively singing "O Canada." Then, without fail, at exactly 7:05 p.m., the umpire would yell, "Play ball!" At this moment, Dad and I knew we were where we belonged. We watched the action intently. We didn't talk much. Instead, we listened. We listened to the crack of the bat, the umpire's calls, the intonations in the announcer's voice as he uniquely introduced each hitter, the collective cheers and boos, and the seagulls that circled the stadium. Dad kept score and occasionally offered insights into the nuances of the game. He would lean toward me and say, "Did you see how the pitcher backed up home plate? Every player has somewhere to go on every play. Remember that, Luke." As I watched and learned about the game with Dad, I fantasized about being a Major League Baseball player one day.

As the game went on, the cold breeze from Lake Ontario chilled me to the bone. When it became too much, I would put on my jacket and invariably think to myself, I'm glad I wore layers. You were right, Dad. Soon after, the iconic song lyrics "OK . . . Blue Jays . . . let's . . . play . . . ball," could be heard playing over the stadium speaker. This song signaled it was *time for the seventh-inning stretch. Dad and I would routinely perform a series of familiar stretching actions in tune with the song (a series of clapping and arm-pumping actions), led by the teams' entertainment staff. Although we both felt awkward each time we danced along, it served to help keep us warm on cool Toronto evenings.*

Before I knew it, it was the bottom of the eighth inning, two outs. At this instant, Dad would say, "OK, Luke, time to go." "Do we have to, Dad?" I would ask. To which he would unwaveringly reply, "Yes. We have to get ahead of the stadium traffic." Ignoring my protest, we began our journey up the stairs to the concourse. Here, we would watch the final out recorded and then make a break for the exit. Not surprisingly, we were not the only spectators trying to leave early to avoid Toronto traffic jams. Our journey back the car could be described as an Olympic sport, dodging and weaving through spectators and cars. At times, I had to run so that I could maintain my grip on Dad's hand.

Making it back to the car was cause for celebration, albeit a short-lived celebration. Immediately, Dad put the rest of the game on the radio, and we began our journey home. As we entered the expressway, I would pause for one last look at the Toronto skyline. Once we were in the clear, Dad would ask if I'd had fun. Sensing that I was growing tired, Dad would stop talking, and I would fall asleep feeling warm, safe, and loved.

Unpacking the Narrative

The narrative of Luke's baseball experiences of attending the Blue Jays' baseball games with his father at Exhibition Stadium (Figure 2.1) illustrate the blending of the embodied experience, sportscape, nostalgia, and heritage over years of sport fan attendance. The following section will explore these concepts within the context of the narrative.

Sportscape

The "sportscape" (Wakefield & Sloan, 1995; Wakefield et al., 1996) of stadium was prominent in Luke's narrative. The sportscape begins with traveling to the stadium on the expressway, obtaining a parking space, and then continuing the journey on foot. It is evident that years of game attendance have influenced how Luke and his father attended the games (e.g., the route, both driven and walked) and how Luke's senses were interacting with the sights and smells (e.g., hot dogs, peanuts) along the way to and within the stadium. Luke's narrative demonstrated the embodied experience, where

Figure 2.1. Exhibition Stadium in Toronto. Photo courtesy of Luke Potwarka.

the mental preparation occurred as the school day ended and the excitement led into preparing to attend the game with appropriate clothing and physical preparation, which can be explained through the work of Nash (2000). Throughout this experience, Luke and his dad are joined by others engaging in pre-game rituals and are becoming communal sport spectators (Figure 2.2). The social experience is continued into the stadium through the crowded gate and into stadium seating. The stadium's features (e.g., seats, stairs, field) make up an important element of the experience where even the spilled beer and trash add to the tangible elements of the memory. Finally, spectator management also influences Luke's involvement, whether it is the usher moving the crowd, or the concessions and various vendors, factors that influenced the game-day experience.

Baseball Nostalgia

Through Luke's narrative, direct connections can be drawn together between nostalgia and attending the baseball game at the stadium. These connections are demonstrated through the memories of a youth experiencing

Figure 2.2. Luke Potwarka and his father. Photo courtesy of Luke Potwarka.

the sportscape of baseball stadium (i.e., a tangible physical entity; Gibson, 1998; Kulczycki & Hyatt, 2005). Participation in sport and outdoor recreation establishes positive bonds between parent and child (Knoester & Randolph, 2019). Luke's narrative demonstrates that bonding can occur through heritage and the nostalgia associated with attending a sporting event. This bonding exemplifies the "being" heritage, where the father is imparting knowledge and a passion for baseball onto his son, building a connection to future generations (Ramshaw, 2020). Specifically, father-and-son interactions within the sporting atmosphere facilitated an opportunity for a shared baseball nostalgia (Gordon, 2013), where the stadium is the "point of attachment" for nostalgia (Cho et al., 2017, p. 1096).

This connection is evident in Luke's anticipation, interest, and the practiced routines of each excursion, which demonstrated the desire to return

(Holbrook, 1993; Fairley, 2003) with his father. For example, there was the routine of Luke being quizzed by his father on how to keep score, that the same route was always taken to get to Exhibition Stadium, the same "secret" parking place, and that the same concessions were used for the same food purchased in the same order on each visit to Exhibition Stadium. As Luke progresses through his life and perhaps has children of his own, he may choose to share his knowledge and passion with his children and desire to have similar experiences as he did with his father; in this case, he would be demonstrating the quest of nostalgia through his identity as a father and a sport fan (Cho et al., 2017), and passing on the routines that he experienced.

The social bonding between father and son highlights the important social interactions that influence the establishment of nostalgia between individuals and places (Kulczycki & Hyatt, 2005; Fairley, 2003). The time spent traveling within the car provided a safe space for social bonding, and helped establish "nostalgic recollections" (Fairley & Gammon, 2005, p. 193). Cho et al. (2017) asserted that the nostalgia and the social interaction that occurs are intertwined. The recollection of the seventh-inning stretch in which Luke participated with his father and others in the stadium is an example of nostalgia as a group identity where "positive memories are associated with group behaviour of sport spectators [which] evoke nostalgia" (Cho et al., 2017, p. 1097).

Furthermore, there are ritualistic elements that connect Luke, his father, and all sport fans through a collective, action-based experience and that connect to previous experiences of traveling (e.g., driving, parking, leaving the stadium early to beat traffic) to and from the stadium for baseball games (Fairley, 2003; Gordon, 2013; Wilhelm, 2018). These ritualistic elements reflect the "doing" heritage, where father and son are participating and creating elements of heritage associated with the game-day experience (Ramshaw, 2020).

Luke's narrative demonstrates that emotions and cognitive meanings of nostalgia are attached to the tangible spaces of the stadium (Fairley, 2003), whether it is the roads used to travel to the stadium, the "secret place to park," or the components of the stadium (e.g., Gate 11, Section 118). Therefore, the physical structure of the stadium is associated with the nostalgia associated with going to the game with his father and being a sport fan (e.g., Seifried & Meyer, 2010). Fairley and Gammon's (2005) two conceptualizations of nostalgia are also notable: "nostalgia for sport place or artifact" (p. 182), which is evident in the cityscape and the stadium's sportscape along with any baseballs collected during batting practice and the accompanying memories; and "nostalgia for social experience" (p. 182), which is evident with the recollections of parent and sport spectator interactions (e.g., parental advice, score keeping, crowding at the stadium).

Heritage, Baseball, and the Fan

The ballpark is an important part of the collective heritage of urban environments where a history of baseball occurred and is part of a collective nostalgia with place meanings (Gordon, 2013). This notion is evident in Luke's attention while traveling to and from the stadium, especially when he reflects back on the stadium's prominence in the city skyline; this is an important element of how one senses the stadium (Gaffney & Bale, 2004). Ramshaw and Gammon's (2005) conceptions of four characteristics of heritage are relevant to the lived game-day experience: tangible immovable, tangible movable, intangible, and goods and services. The "tangible immovable" heritage in Luke's narrative connects to his experience during the national anthem at the stadium. The Canadian flag present in the stadium was a key marker that connected the experience to a broader national heritage and sense of collective societal identity. It is the historical items and the heritage contained within and associated with stadiums that influence a person's stadium-based nostalgia (Ritzer & Stillman, 2001). Luke was able to collect "tangible movable" heritage through his experiences; these items include ticket stubs, game-day programs, and any baseballs collected from Section 118. These elements are part of the history of baseball and are specific to the stadium, documenting sport history (Gaffney & Bale, 2004).

Luke and his father's game-day rituals included the same route driven to the stadium, watching batting practice prior to eating from the same concessions, and participating in the seventh-inning stretch; all examples of "intangible" sport heritage (Ramshaw & Gammon, 2005). Luke needed to be present in order to experience the intangible heritage; hence he had an "embodied experience" (Channon & Jennings, 2014) in the "embodied space" (Low, 2003). Finally, purchased items or experiences provided by management (e.g., ushers) provide the "goods and services" of sport heritage. The tradition of the seventh-inning stretch is a traditional element of baseball spectatorship that has continued over time (Ramshaw & Gammon, 2005), and it is one way that Luke and his father openly participated in each game along with many fans in the stadium. Here, the collective actions of the fans helped expand the game-day experience into the history and heritage of the stadium and the collective memory of spectators (Gaffney & Bale, 2004). Other services connecting Luke to baseball heritage include those provided by the concession workers and the food served; elements that have a constant presence in baseball across venues and history and time.

Conclusion

The way in which an individual interacts with the elements of a stadium and the connections that are created is influential on the fan experience (Gammon, 2010). The premise of this chapter was to focus on baseball as it relates to the embodied fan spectator experience in the context of nostalgia and heritage. Through Luke's personal account, we exposed the nexus of the embodied experience and the "sportscape," a context within which we were able to explore the influence and relevance of nostalgia and heritage. Specifically, we explored an experience between Luke and his father in which they attended a ball game in Toronto, Ontario. Through the narrative, we exemplified that it is possible to identify the positive longing of past experiences associated with nostalgia (Ramshaw & Gammon, 2005), while also isolating how the concepts of sportscape, nostalgia, and heritage can be linked. Furthermore, heritage places (e.g., the stadium) are the markers and sites of individual and collective memories that surpass the test of time for individuals, families, and ultimately the sport fan (Ramshaw & Gammon, 2005). Finally, liminality and community are enhanced by the social interactions that occur through sport fandom in and around live-game experiences (Fairley & Gammon, 2005). Luke and his father interacted with each other and with other spectators around the baseball stadium, thereby building community and lasting memories.

The embodied experience at the stadium draws on the senses (Spinney, 2006; Gaffney & Bale, 2004); Luke navigated the crowds (e.g., touch), smelled and consumed the concession food (e.g., smell and taste), and watched (e.g., sight) the games. While the focus of the narrative is on the parent-and-child experience, the entire social experience occurred with all spectators in and around the stadium (Sparkes et al., 2010). The narrative demonstrates how the sportscape can lead into established concepts of "being" and "doing" heritage (Ramshaw, 2020) and nostalgia. This can occur through intangible stadium elements, such as Luke's father in Section 118 explaining the nuances of batting and creating those positive memories for Luke, or tangible elements, such as standing for the national anthem, looking at the Canadian flag, getting concessions, and sharing a meal.

As Ramshaw (2020) explained, "These forms of embodied heritage are important to our understanding of how sport heritage is understood and articulated . . . toward more every day, personal sport heritages" (p. 137). Therefore, we recommend that sport and facility managers acknowledge the variety of elements that influence nostalgia (Gammon, 2010) and the various points of attachment (Cho et al., 2017) that will influence the spectator experience. While nostalgia is individual and subjective, the markers of nostalgia are similar across spectators—for example, music, imagery, and smells all connect spectators to nostalgia. Managers can maintain group experiences that become ritualistic, such as the seventh-inning stretch and familiar food services such as popcorn vendors. Furthermore, management can maintain the collective actions and repetitive behaviors that are connected to nostalgia and those that spectators expect (Wilhelm, 2018). Fans experience a variety of emotions at baseball games (Wilhelm, 2018); however, nostalgia seems to bring people back to the game and stadium, as shown in Luke's narrative, as well as Kulczycki and Hyatt's (2005) and Fairley's (2003) explorations, for example. Nostalgia is connected to and influenced by points of attachment; therefore, stadium management needs to be cognizant of the tangible heritage that the spectators are embracing. For example, prominently displayed statues and banners connect historical events to memories and therefore nostalgia. In summary, on game day the fan has an embodied experience that is connected to tangible and intangible heritage and nostalgia that is associated with the baseball stadium.

References

Allen-Collinson, J., Lee, C., & Swann, C. (2018). 'Endurance work': Embodiment and the mind-body-nexus in the physical culture of high-altitude mountaineering. *Sociology, 52*(6), 1324–1341.

Alverson, M. (2003). Methodology for close up studies: Struggling with closeness and closure. *Higher Education, 46*(2), 167–193.

Anderson, J. (2013). Cathedrals of the surf zone: Regulating access to a space of spirituality. *Social & Cultural Geography, 14*(8), 954–972. doi:10.1080/14649365.2013.845903

Biaett, V., & Richards, G. (2020). Event experiences: Measurement and meaning. *Journal of Policy Research in Tourism, 12*(3), 277–292.

Channon, A., & Jennings, G. (2014). Exploring embodiment through martial arts and combat sports: A review of empirical research. *Sport in Society, 17*(6), 773–789.

Cho, H., Lee, H., Moore, D., Norman, W. C., & Ramshaw, G. (2017). A multilevel approach to scale development in sport tourism nostalgia. *Journal of Travel Research, 56*(8), 1094–1106.

Dutkiewicz, J. (2015). Pretzel logic: An embodied ethnography of a rock climb. *Space and Culture, 18*(1), 25–38.

Fairley, S. (2003). In search of relived social experience: Group-based nostalgia sport tourism. *Journal of Sport Management, 17*(3), 284–304.

Fairley, S., & Gammon, S. (2005). Something lived, something learned: Nostalgia's expanding role in sport tourism. *Sport in Society, 8*(2), 182–197.

Friedman, M. T., & Silk, M. L. (2005). Expressing Fenway: Managing and marketing heritage within the global sports marketplace. *International Journal of Sport Management and Marketing, 1*(1–2), 37–55.

Gaffney, C., & Bale, J. (2004). Sensing the stadium. In P. Vertinsky & J. Bale (Eds.), *Sites of sport: Space, place, experience* (pp. 25–38). Routledge: London.

Gammon, S. (2007). Introduction: Sport, heritage and the English. An opportunity missed? In S. Gammon, S., & Ramshaw, G. (Eds.), *Heritage, sport and tourism: Sporting pasts—Tourist futures* (pp. 1–8). Routledge: London.

Gammon, S. (2010). 'Sporting' new attractions? The commodification of the sleeping stadium. In R. Sharpley & P. R. Stone (Eds.), *Tourist experience: Contemporary perspectives* (pp. 115–126). Routledge: New York.

Gibson, H. (1998). Sport tourism: A critical analysis of research. *Sport Management Review, 1,* 45–76.

Gordon, K. O. (2013). Emotion and memory in nostalgia sport tourism: Examining the attraction to postmodern ballparks through an interdisciplinary lens. *Journal of Sport & Tourism, 18*(3), 217–239.

Havlena, W. J., & Holak, S. L. (1991). The good old days: Observations on nostalgia and its role in consumer behavior. *Advances in Consumer Research, 18,* 323–329.

Hill, B., & Green, C. (2000). Repeat attendance as a function of involvement, loyalty, and the sportscape across three football contexts. *Sport Management Review, 3*(2), 145–162.

Holbrook, M. B. (1993). Nostalgia and consumption preferences: Some emerging patterns of consumer tastes. *Journal of Consumer Research, 20,* 245–256.

Holt, N. L. (2003). Representation, legitimation, and autoethnography: An autoethnographic writing story. *International Journal of Qualitative Methods, 2*(1), 1–22. http://www.ualberta.ca/~iiqm/backissues/2_1final/html/holt.html

Knoester, C., & Randolph, T. (2019). Father-child sports participation and outdoor activities: Patterns and implications for health and father-child relationships. *Sociology of Sport Journal, 36,* 322–329.

Kulczycki, C., & Hyatt, C. (2005). Expanding the conceptualization of nostalgia sport tourism. *Journal of Sport Tourism, 10*(4), 273–293.

Larsen, J. (2014). (Auto)ethnography and cycling. *International Journal of Social Research Methodology, 17*(1), 59–71.

Low, S. M. (2003). Embodied space(s): Anthropological theories of body, space, and culture. *Space & Culture, 6*(1), 9–18.

Nash, C. (2000). Performativity in practice: some recent work in cultural geography. *Progress in Human Geography, 24*(4), 653–664.

Ramshaw, G. (2020). *Heritage and sport: An introduction.* Bristol: Channel View Publications.

Ramshaw, G. (2014). Sport, heritage, and tourism. *Journal of Heritage Tourism, 9*(3), 191–196.

Ramshaw, G., & Gammon, S. (2005). More than just nostalgia? Exploring the heritage/ sport tourism nexus. *Journal of Sport Tourism, 10*(4), 229–241.

Ritzer, G., & Stillman, T. (2001). The postmodern ballpark as a leisure setting: Enchantment and simulated de-McDonaldization. *Leisure Sciences, 23*(2), 99–113.

Seifried, C., & Meyer, K. (2010). Nostalgia-related aspects of professional sport facilities: A facility audit of Major League Baseball and National Football League strategies to evoke the past. *International Journal of Sport Management, Recreation & Tourism, 5,* 51–76.

Sparkes, A. C., Brown, D. H. K., & Partington, E. (2010). The "Jock Body" and the social construction of space: The performance and positioning of cultural identity. *Space and Culture, 13*(3), 333–347.

Spinney, J. (2006). A place of sense: A kinaesthetic ethnography of cyclists on Mont Ventoux. *Environment and Planning D: Society and Space, 24,* 709–732.

Springgay, S., & Truman, S. E. (2017). A transmaterial approach to walking methodologies: Embodiment, affect, and a sonic art performance. *Body & Society, 24*(4), 27–58.

Trothen, T. J. (2006). Hockey: A divine sport?—Canada's national sport in relation to embodiment, community and hope. *Studies in Religion/Sciences Religieuses, 35*(2), 291–305.

Wakefield, K. L., & Sloan, H. J. (1995). The effects of team loyalty and selected stadium factors on spectator attendance. *Journal of Sport Management, 9*(2), 153–172.

Wakefield, K. L., Blodgett, J. G., & Sloan, H. J. (1996). Measurement and management of the sportscape. *Journal of Sport Management, 10,* 15–31.

Wilhelm, J. L. (2018). Atmosphere in the home stadium of Hertha BSC (German Bundesliga): Melodies of moods, collective bodies, and the relevance of space. *Social & Cultural Geography,* doi:10.1080/14649365.2018.1514646

3

Killing Nostalgia

How Curt Flood and Henry Aaron Challenged Baseball Nostalgia

ANDREW MCGREGOR

During his December 2019 introductory press conference with the New York Yankees, and after signing a nine-year $324 million contract, Gerrit Cole thanked Curt Flood (Baer, 2019). The homage surprised many fans and journalists, becoming a news story of its own. Why did a 29-year-old white pitcher feel the need to thank an African American outfielder from the 1960s for his new contract? The media sought to remind fans of Flood's legacy, recalling his significant role fifty years earlier in creating free agency in professional sports, which has allowed players like Cole to earn millions (Baer, 2019). While this incident serves as an important reminder of that baseball history, it also forces Major League Baseball (MLB) players, executives, and fans to confront the racial tension within the legacy of Curt Flood.

Since his retirement in 1971, Flood's career and legacy has received less praise and attention from Major League Baseball or the National Baseball Hall of Fame than other historically significant players of his era. While scholars have repeatedly credited his accomplishments in opening up free agency in Major League Baseball, the baseball establishment has shied away from celebrating this feat (Khan, 2012; Lomax, 2003; Snyder, 2007). The question of "why" once again emerges. This chapter explores the legacy of Curt Flood parallel to that of Henry "Hank" Aaron to consider this question.

During the early 1970s, Henry Aaron began to approach George Herman "Babe" Ruth's all-time career home-run record. As Aaron inched closer, the home-run race captured the attention of fans and the media. Aaron became a cultural phenomenon discussed not only in the sports pages but in the comics as well. The Peanuts—the famous comic strip featuring characters such as Charlie Brown and Snoopy—commented on his pursuit of Ruth and the responses of fans who struggled to conceptualize an African American home-run champion.

Contemporaries Aaron and Flood both threatened what David Leonard (2017) has described as "white nostalgia" by forcing fans to re-write the history of the game in ways that not only included African American accomplishments but displaced traditional views of players as the property of teams and fans. As Leonard (2017) explained "Contemporary sports often waxes for the moment when sports were more about the games and less about the money, when athletes were role models, and when passion, hard work, and determination were central to sporting culture" (p. 7). Jeffrey Lane (2007) further described white nostalgia as "a rampant paranoia that white society has relinquished too much," which contributes to an anxiety that "produces a mournful longing for a romanticized, racially homogeneous past" (p. 115). Indeed, because nostalgia is often triggered by a threat, scholars view it as a reactionary emotion where people recall previous positive experiences or memories to cope with change (Sedikides et al., 2004; Gordon, 2013; Cho et al. 2019). Cho et al. (2019) have suggested that those "who are unsatisfied with their present situation escape reality by experiencing nostalgia" (p. 322). Similarly, Sedikides et al. (2004) contended that "nostalgia soothes the self from existential pangs by solidifying and augmenting identity, regenerating and sustaining a sense of meaning, and buttressing and invigorating desired connectedness with the social world" (p. 206). Because, as Gordon (2013) explained, nostalgia is an "important component of individual and collective sport-related memory" (p. 219), it plays a powerful role in sport heritage. White nostalgia, in particular, presents idyllic imaginations of the past that obscure moments of discomfort and confrontation, selectively remembering heroes who fit neatly into narratives of continuity and who do not bely the hegemonic position of the status quo.

The impact of Aaron and Flood, however, made these players difficult for baseball fans to ignore when trying to cope with a changing America. Each received hate mail and disdain from the sport's primarily white fans. Yet, unlike Aaron, Flood's actions attacked baseball's bottom-line in ways beyond acknowledging African American athletic equality through breaking records. Just as the quest for economic equality splintered the Civil Rights Movement, Flood's efforts to nullify the Reserve Clause left many fans and executives bitter and angry, blaming Flood and other "entitled" athletes for disrupting the game they love. As time went on, Aaron's accomplishments have become accepted, and he is celebrated as an African American home-run king, which promotes a view of interracial equality. Flood, on the other hand, remains seldom lauded as his legacy forces fans and owners to confront complicated issues of exploitation, capitalism, and race, which remain unresolved points of contention in larger society.

Curt Flood Challenges the Reserve Clause

The story begins in October 1969, when the St. Louis Cardinals traded Curt Flood to the Philadelphia Phillies. The trade signaled the end of a strained relationship between Flood and Cardinals owner August Busch Jr. Prior to the season, Flood asked for a $100,000 contract and joined a group of teammates in holding out of Spring Training for a higher salary. This came on the heels of a league-wide boycott in which 450 players refused to sign contracts until MLB owners resolved a pension dispute with the Major League Baseball Players Association (MLBPA) (Lomax, 2003). The actions angered Busch, who responded cruelly toward his players.

The Cardinals, who won the 1968 National League Pennant, underperformed during the first half of the 1969 season. This lackluster performance, as well as Busch's disdain for older, entitled players, like Flood, resulted in Busch replacing veterans with younger players in the lineup. The move soured their relationship and foreshadowed Flood's eventual trade.

As Lomax (2003) has argued, Busch viewed the rising labor unrest in Major League Baseball, particularly by Flood and his team, as being connected to the disruptive and militant turn toward "Black Power" among the Civil Rights Movement. The controversial phase of activism took on a number of different meanings for white Americans, but most viewed it as antagonistic to American values and unnecessarily disruptive. They saw the racial uprisings in Detroit, Newark, and Watts during 1967 and 1968 as indicative of an out-of-control, destructive, and occasionally violent movement that revealed deep-seated views about the pathology of African Americans that confirmed their second-class nature. African Americans activists within the Civil Rights Movement similarly did not subscribe to a cohesive or universal understanding. For some, it simply meant a demand for respect and equality, a pivot toward racial pride, and a refusal to settle for a second-class designation. Economic rights frequently became a component of this view, which unsettled even the most progressive whites.

August Busch followed the lead of the white sporting establishment not only to protect the status quo but also to put "disruptive" Black athletes "in their place." Just as Avery Brundage condemned the 1968 Olympic demonstrations by Tommie Smith and John Carlos, Busch berated his players in front of the media. Brent Musburger captured the prevailing view of many white Americans, writing in 1968, "The way things are going, someone better save all of us before it's too late" (1968, n.p.). Busch's trade of Flood served as his attempt to "save all of us," by maintaining the status quo of the white sporting establishment.

Flood, however, refused to accept the trade. On December 24, 1969, he sent a letter to MLB Commissioner Bowie Kuhn requesting the right to consider offers from other teams. Kuhn denied his request, setting off a legal fight to nullify Major League Baseball's Reserve Clause. In simple terms, the Reserve Clause within every MLB contract kept each player under team control in perpetuity. Each contract reserved the rights to the player for the following year, preventing him from negotiating or signing with other teams. Teams held control over players, including the right to trade them, while players had no autonomy. Flood took issue with this, pointedly writing to Kuhn, "I do not feel that I am a piece of property to be bought and sold irrespective of my wishes" (Rhoden, 2019, n.p.).

At the time of the trade, Flood had played twelve seasons in Major League Baseball. Although 37 years old, Flood won seven Gold Glove Awards (including 1969) and two World Series with St. Louis. Only a year prior, he graced the cover of *Sports Illustrated*. The magazine celebrated his career, describing him as "the most solid and consistent player for St. Louis" (Leggett, 1968, p. 20) Indeed, during the 1966 and 1967 seasons, he compiled a 226-game errorless streak, then a National League record. As a veteran player, he knew he still had what it took to compete and hoped to end his career in St. Louis. In addition to his outstanding play on the field, Flood also sought to improve the playing conditions of baseball players, white and Black. He played an important role in desegregating the Cardinals' Spring Training facilities and openly spoke out against double-headers and expanded schedules (Lomax, 2003). Like Busch, Flood considered himself an activist and his fight against the Reserve Clause became perhaps his most important fight.

As a consequence of Kuhn's refusal to grant his request, Flood sat out the entire 1970 season. Backed by MLBPA Executive Director Marvin Miller, he filed a series of lawsuits to challenge the legality of the Reserve Clause. Although the case eventually reached the Supreme Court in 1972, Flood lost in a 5–3 decision. His struggle, however, illustrated a need for change within MLB's labor structure. Miller used the Flood case to negotiate minimum salary increases for players and impartial arbitration of disputes between players and owners, as well as what became known as the "Flood Rule," which gave ten-year MLB veterans with five years of experience on their current team the power to veto trades (Roberts & Olson, 1989). Flood's legal struggle brought awareness to other players, who continued his fight. Catfish Hunter, Andy Messersmith, and Dave McNally additionally pushed the envelope, using this new framework to further weaken the Reserve Clause. Within four years, Major League Baseball adopted a new "Basic Agreement" that again revised the sport's salary structure, pension, and negotiation rules. No longer did the Reserve Clause rule baseball. Players now had access to arbitration and a structure for free agency after six years of service. Curt Flood paved the way for these changes, though he never benefited from them himself.

Safely Supplanting Ruth: Henry Aaron and Nostalgic Continuity

Amid this climate, Henry Aaron approached Babe Ruth's career home-run record. At the dawn of the 1973 season, he trailed Ruth by 41. *Sports Illustrated*'s William Leggett (1973) rooted for Aaron to break the record but wondered if the pressure might surmount the efforts of the aging slugger. He wrote:

> Is this to be the year in which Aaron, at the age of 39, takes a moon walk above one of the most hallowed individual records in American sport, the 714 home runs hit by George Herman Ruth? Or will it be remembered as the season in which Aaron, the most dignified of athletes, was besieged with hate mail and trapped by the cobwebs and goblins that lurk in baseball's attic? (Leggett, 1973, p. 29)

Indeed, as Leggett (1973) observed, Aaron faced more than a simple record. The home-run record represented the enormity of Ruth's legacy and his meaning to the game. Becoming the "home-run king" meant more than baseball history. The title came cloaked in the nostalgia of what Hobsbawm and Ranger (2012) described as an "invented tradition," tying strength, skill, and masculinity to whiteness.

Leggett (1973) took special care to describe the initiation of Ruth as the home-run king, recounting the history of the title. Although he retired in 1935 with 714 home runs, Ruth became the career leader in 1921. At the time, according to Leggett (1973), no one really knew who held the career record. Researchers disagreed on the total number, but most suggested that the tally fell between 117 and 136. Either way, Ruth easily surpassed the number and spent the remainder of his career extending his own record. The fact that Ruth took a largely overlooked record and turned it into a piece of trivia memorized by generations of fans reflected his immortal influence on the game. He represented the modernization of the sport as it moved into the live-ball era, contributing a larger-than-life personality that saw the New York Yankees overtake the Boston Red Sox as the sport's dominant franchise following a puzzling trade.

African American players did not figure into Leggett's (1973) brief history of the career home-run record. They also did not factor into his recollection of other significant Major League Baseball landmarks that Henry Aaron had or would soon pass in 1973. Indeed, he trailed only Ty Cobb in career at-bats, only Stan Musial in extra-base hits, and lurked 13 hits behind Honus Wagner for the most by a right-handed hitter (Leggett, 1973). While Ruth's 714 home runs remained the target, Aaron had slowly etched his name into the record books on a number of fronts.

Integrating into the record books presented a challenge for African American athletes. Deep-seated white nostalgia created resentment and hatred as the heroes of generations of white fans were eclipsed by Black athletes. Aaron received over 2,000 letters per week during the 1973 season. While the majority of these fan letters offered encouraging words and reflected admiration, a significant number also wished him ill and demeaned him with racial epithets.

Charles Schulz took note of Aaron's plight in his popular Peanuts comic strip. Over the course of several days in August, his pursuit of Ruth inspired the comic's storyline. Beginning on August 8 and continuing until August 22, the comic portrayed Snoopy in the role of Aaron. In a number of the comics, Snoopy responds to the mounting pressure to break the record. For example, in reaction to Linus counting to 714 and informing Charlie Brown that one of their players could tie Babe Ruth's record, Snoopy lying atop of his doghouse, which is covered in tally marks, says, "Yes, I, for one, am aware of it!" (Schulz, August 8, 1973). The next day, the comic explains that Snoopy is chasing Ruth alongside Aaron (Schulz, August 9, 1973). Schulz (1973) addresses the pressure of fan mail in the comic strips on August 10 and 15. The first letter he receives reads, "Dear Stupid, who do you think you are trying to break Babe Ruth's record? Why don't you go back to where you came from? Drop dead! Get lost! Sincerely, A True Baseball Fan" (Schulz, August 10, 1973). Snoopy tells Charlie Brown that the letter is from an admirer. Later, Snoopy receives another threatening letter. This one includes the lines "We hate your kind!" and "We'll run you out of the country!"

(Schulz, August 15, 1973). A concerned Charlie Brown asks if the hate mail has been causing Snoopy to lose sleep. While lounging atop his doghouse with a stack of envelopes next to it, Snoopy replies, "Only when it falls on me" (Schulz, August 15, 1973).

In these comics, Schulz uses Snoopy to highlight the racist treatment of Henry Aaron. On other days, the comic takes on a more subversive and clever twist that conveys the treatment of Snoopy as a dog in juxtaposition with Aaron as a Black man. On August 11, Lucy praises Henry Aaron, wishing that he will break Ruth's record. She reveals that she is actively rooting against Snoopy because, as she tells him, "You're not even human!" (Schulz, August 11, 1973). Snoopy elects to view that "as a point in my favor," but the implication is clear (Schulz, August 11, 1973). Anyone viewed as "not even human" should not break Babe Ruth's record.

The Peanuts Henry Aaron–inspired storyline comes to its conclusion in late August. Snoopy emerges in his last at-bat in the ninth inning of the season with 713 home runs, one behind Babe Ruth. Downplaying the pressure to equal the record, Snoopy focuses on the pitch, thinking, "I just want to be a credit to my breed!" (Schulz, August 18, 1973). Never mind that Schulz accurately predicts that Aaron would end the 1973 season trailing Ruth by one, the comic once again uses Snoopy's canine status to comment on the racial divisions in America. The comic playfully mirrors the cliché of an athlete being "a credit to their race," which frequently appears as a racial microaggression that uplifts certain African American athletes in comparison to others. The exceptional nature of this phrasing allows one to appear above expectation and as an acceptable or model minority without offering full acceptance to others who have not accomplished the same feats. Here again, Schulz offers sharp commentary on race in America.

Two days later, the comic reveals that Snoopy failed to tie Babe Ruth's record because Charlie Brown got picked off second base while rooting for him to hit a home run (Schulz, August 20, 1973). Finally, on August 22, the saga comes to an end. An angry Snoopy refuses to talk to Charlie Brown, who he blames for stealing his chance to break the record. Trying to re-establish order, Charlie Brown apologizes to Snoopy before scolding his behavior. "I also don't think you should get so mad at me . . . after all, I'm still your master . . . you're still my dog . . ." he tells him (Schulz, August 22, 1973). "Just remember, one little phone call and I could have you sent right back where you came from!" (Schulz, August 22, 1973). The strip ends with a still-silent Snoopy handing Charlie Brown the phone.

In this last frame, Charlie Brown and Snoopy's relationship comes full circle. Although Charlie Brown roots for Snoopy to break the record and worries about the weight of the hate mail, off the field he fails to view Snoopy as an equal. Instead, after the season ends, he seeks to cull any disrespect or ill will toward him by reminding Snoopy of his place. In this simple frame, Schulz is once again reminding Americans about the complicated nature of race in society. While sports can sometimes offer equality, it is frequently conditional. When one threatens a record or a memory held sacred, the person is often attacked. Similarly, equality often ends when one walks off the field. While some in society may respect an athlete's accomplishments, few apologize for their role in supporting an oppressive system or understand the entitlement of asking for forgiveness.

With a barrage of letters continuing to arrive, Henry Aaron entered the off-season fixed at 713 home runs. As opening day approached, no longer did fans wonder *if* he would break Ruth's record but *when*. In his first at-bat, on his first swing, just six minutes into the 1974 season, Aaron hit number 714. He described the accomplishment as "just another home run" but "a load off my back" (Anderson, 1974, p. 1). Four days later, during the Atlanta Braves' home opener, he slugged 715 to surpass Babe Ruth.

Vin Scully, calling the game for the visiting Los Angeles Dodgers, described it as "a marvelous moment for baseball . . . a marvelous moment for Atlanta and the state of Georgia . . . a marvelous moment for the country and the world" ("Vin Scully," 2014). He recognized the significance of the moment in baseball history as well as for race relations. "A Black man is getting a standing ovation in the Deep South for breaking a record of all-time baseball idol" ("Vin Scully," 2014). For Scully, like many Americans, the sight reflected tremendous progress. Not only had baseball successfully desegregated, but it now had an African American hero capable of standing on equal footing with the most legendary of white players. The ovation for Aaron signaled respect and acceptance from a majority of fans, who claimed the South's only baseball team as their own.

While Aaron's assault on nostalgia earned him disdain and hatred during his pursuit of Ruth, it all seemed to dissipate in the moment and he quickly ascended to iconic status. He joined Jackie Robinson as an instrumental figure in changing the game of baseball by showcasing the talent and fortitude of Black athletes. Aaron represented the staying power of African American baseball players. He played for two more seasons after breaking the record, amassing 755 career home runs. Upon his retirement, he continued to receive widespread praise. He was inducted into the National Baseball Hall of Fame in 1982 after receiving 97.8 percent of the vote, only nine shy of a unanimous selection (Muder, n.d.). During his induction speech, Aaron recalled his connection with Babe Ruth, likely referring to those who were upset and did not want him to eclipse Ruth's record. "I never want them to forget Babe Ruth," he said, "I just want them to remember Henry Aaron" ("Hank Aaron," n.d.).

Although a generation younger than Robinson, Aaron represented not only sustained African American success but also the transition to a world without the Negro Leagues. Aaron ushered baseball history across the divide of segregation through his play and by his integration into the record book. At the time of his retirement, no other Major League Baseball player had played in the Negro Leagues. He played an integral role in killing white nostalgia and forging a new, integrated baseball history. The new nostalgia created by Aaron, however, appealed to white fans because it offered positive continuity and an acceptable progressive narrative that celebrated the democratic nature of the sport as a leader in racial integration.

Unreconciled White Angst and Curt Flood's Legacy

Like Henry Aaron, Curt Flood is also frequently compared to Jackie Robinson. But Flood's legacy differs in profound ways. The question of why remains important. It requires a deeper reading of Flood's impact and a parsing of the white nostalgia he confronted. As Khan (2012) observed, "Flood may be the most remembered forgotten athlete in the history of professional American sport" (p. 169). Indeed, it is not necessarily a case of forgetting Flood. Gerrit Cole knew about and remembered Curt Flood, as did the media who retold his story. Instead, the question of memory and legacy are tied to the type of narrative, both official and unofficial, that Major League Baseball and its fans employ.

In his analysis, Khan (2012) explored the media and scholarly depiction of Flood. He expressed concern about how Flood's public memory and legacy fed into nostalgia for the activist-athlete and informed the political tension between celebrations of racial progress and concurrent struggles for further equality. Rather than summarize or replicate Khan's work, it is instead fruitful to meditate on the contexts that surround the narratives of Curt Flood.

White nostalgia is a key factor in this analysis, as, like Aaron, Flood upset many baseball fans. Perhaps more important, Flood upset the baseball establishment and did so off the field. On the surface, the labor changes in Major League Baseball that resulted from Curt Flood's activism bear no direct connection to baseball nostalgia. Yet the move toward free agency and players no longer spending their entire careers tethered to one team disrupted a world in which fans and star players became intimately connected through years of service. Without the Reserve Clause, players no longer had to spend their entire careers with one team. Instead, after a number of years, they had the opportunity to sign contracts with new teams. This left many fans feeling rejected as their favorite players failed to return their loyalty in search of bigger contracts. Within a generation, the idea of a hometown player who spent his entire career with the same team disappeared. In this way, Flood's quest for economic self-determination threatened the nostalgic days for older—and, in particular, white—fans. These fans felt that baseball had lost a part of its uniqueness when the special relationship between a team, fanbase, and its players was severed by players' free agency. They resented players who sought big paydays, labeling them entitled, greedy, and selfish (Smith, 2018). Players already made astronomical sums compared to blue-collar workers. Why did they need more, fans wondered?

Because of his connection to the Civil Rights Movement, use of the phrase "a well-paid slave," and skin color, Flood received the brunt of this criticism. As Busch led the charge in connecting Flood to militant and radical protesters, during his legal fight and a year spent playing with the Washington Senators, Flood received death threats and hate mail (Brown, 1992). White players, such as Catfish Hunter, David McNally, and Andy Messersmith, who ultimately succeeded at achieving free agency, received relatively less negative criticism (Kahn, 2012). The racial connotations of Flood's rebelliousness and his insistence that he is not a piece of property reflected the uneasy tension that Schulz observed years later when Snoopy refused to "know his place" as Charlie Brown's dog. As de Jong (2016) documented in her book *You Can't Eat Freedom*, the war on poverty and the later phase of the Civil Rights Movement after 1965 focused on economic issues with the understanding that legal and social protections did not do enough to ensure racial equality. Within this context, Flood and Aaron demanded humane treatment in terms of respect and pay. While some suggest that Flood contributed to the commodification of athletes, particularly African Americans, he did so while demanding agency within that context (Nichol, 2019). Indeed, as Smith (2018) argued, Reggie Jackson built on Flood's assertiveness in his self-expression and swagger. Typified as arrogant and selfish, Smith (2018) suggested that Jackson personified the new "me decade" of the

1970s. To be sure, Flood openly told reporters that he stood up against the Reserve Clause primarily for himself (Khan, 2012).

In this way, Flood's assault on nostalgia appeared more systemic and could not be downplayed with condescending statements like "He's a credit to his race." Rather than garnering comparisons to heroic white athletes (like Ruth), Flood's fight frequently attracted associations with radical (and controversial) Civil Rights activism as well as the new "me decade" that followed. In short, Flood's achievements, although largely race-neutral, afforded little room for whitewashing. To many white baseball fans, he appeared to be a greedy and entitled Black athlete in an era of militant activism during the upswing of the conservative Silent Majority, and, as Jackson's example suggests, other Black athletes followed suit (Blumenthal, 2018; Lassitter, 2006; Smith, 2018).

Few white fans saw the validity in comparing Flood to the heroic Jackie Robinson. Given the fact that the white working class increasingly lost its collective bargaining power, they felt little sympathy for athletes paid to play a child's game (Cowie, 2010; Smith, 2018). Instead, the emergence of million-dollar salaries, the disruption of competitive balance, and the end of players' loyalties to their cities and teams further stripped fans of one of the few remaining comforts in their lives. To many white fans, African American athletes cooperating with their white teammates no longer reflected democratic values and superior character that offered a testament to racial unity; instead, these athletes looked more like a threat to the racial and economic status quo of America. As a result, the national pastime no longer looked like itself. As Scott Flood recounted of his father's impact, "He represented an affront to the pureness of baseball and what 'America's pastime' as an institution stood for and continues to try to uphold" (Rhoden, July 19, 2019. n.p.). This created angst among fans, particularly in small markets where their teams could no longer compete in the new economic system and their favorite players left for bigger paydays. The blame for that anxiety fell predominantly at the feet of Curt Flood. His association with a disappearing hegemonic status quo meant his legacy posed a threat to white nostalgia, ultimately rendering him incompatible with tidy narratives that celebrate racial progress and continuity within the game.

Conclusion

Henry Aaron and Curt Flood forced Americans to rewrite baseball history by challenging long-held traditions and white nostalgia within the game.

They represented a transitional period in Major League Baseball, bridging the progressive integrationist period of Jackie Robinson with the rising economically focused competition seen in Reggie Jackson during the 1970s and Gerrit Cole in the present day. They also reflected a tension as America came to realize that the Civil Rights Movement did not simply end in 1965. As Charles Schulz's Peanuts comic strip illustrated, racism lived on in American society, and especially among fans of its national pastime. Aaron, however, overcame much of this tension through reliable narratives that celebrated his accomplishments as signs of progress and democracy. Economic equality remained a more difficult pill for some Americans to swallow, however, and Flood, though not forgotten, became largely excluded from heroic baseball lore.

Today, Aaron no longer threatens white nostalgia and instead has since emerged as a popular figure that reinforces a similar form of nostalgic purity. Although no longer centered on race, this new nostalgia emerged during an era when baseball became tainted by performance-enhancing drugs (PED). "Pure" athletes from yesteryear, who played the game "the right way," contrast sharply from "juiced" younger stars. The threat of PEDs calls into question the continuity and integrity of the game's history and has led some fans to consider Aaron the "true" home-run king even after Barry Bonds surpassed his record in 2007. The reluctance of the National Baseball Hall of Fame to enshrine athletes suspected of PED use reinforces this view, providing a nostalgic foundation that seeks to define who is and is not a baseball hero worthy of recognition. In short, PEDs as well as the desire to move past baseball's long history of racial exclusion are important factors in the celebration of Aaron's career. His ability to fit into progressive narratives that provide continuity and comfort soothes contemporary baseball fans, enabling his legacy's integration into an updated version of baseball nostalgia.

The omission of Flood continues, however. Baseball has not found a way to comfortably include his legacy in its heartfelt narratives of progress and continuity. Instead, he serves as a reminder of baseball's contentious labor history, which has threatened the sport for the last fifty years. Following his challenge to the Reserve Clause, Major League Baseball experienced a number of labor disputes, culminating in the 1994 Strike and cancelled World Series. Although not directly related to these confrontations, it is impossible to fully consider Flood's legacy without them. Within baseball's larger labor history, the introduction of free agency inspired by Flood extends beyond its initial nostalgic threat of hometown player discontinuity and limitations on small-market competitiveness to an attack on the entire sport itself. Indeed, the cancellation of the 1994 World Series caused many fans to renounce their support of baseball. Although reductionist, narratives like this position Curt Flood as central to the decline of Major League Baseball over the past few generations. Within these accounts there is little room to celebrate him as a heroic figure or place him within a part of a nostalgic past. As Sedikides et al. (2004) argued, "nostalgia is an effective resource for coping with existential threat" (p. 208). Little about Flood's legacy eases the ongoing existential threat to baseball nor does it contribute to a positive historical narrative of continuity.

Given these concerns, it is no surprise that the National Baseball Hall of Fame has not enshrined Curt Flood. Yet Marvin Miller's election into the Hall of Fame in 2020 changes all of that and forces us to once again consider the role of race and white nostalgia. While some fans believe that Flood as a player is a borderline Hall of Famer, his overall contributions to the game remain profound. His exclusion is confounding and suggests that it serves as a warning to players, particularly outspoken players of color, to fit in and get along. White nostalgia has no room for agitators and disruptors, unless they are white executives. (The NFL's treatment of Colin Kaepernick, for example, also affirms this.) Moreover, teams do not give away bobbleheads and jerseys honoring labor activists. Doing so would tacitly approve of the behavior of players like Flood, who contributed to ongoing existential threats to the sport, and those who potentially inspire other players to act.

Still, Curt Flood's children and William Rhoden continue to campaign for Flood's election to the National Baseball Hall of Fame. Although the Hall of Fame posthumously honored him with an award in 2015, only enshrinement will cement his legacy and ensure that the museum reflects the sport's complicated history rather than the white nostalgia of its fans. Until that happens, Gerrit Cole's homage helps remind people of Curt Flood's important legacy and his place in baseball history, no matter how uncomfortable it makes us feel.

References

Anderson, D. (April 5, 1974). Aaron ties Babe Ruth with 714th homer. *New York Times.* n.p.

Baer, B. (December 18, 2019). Gerrit Cole thanks Curt Flood and Marvin Miller during introductory press conference. *Hardball Talk, NBC Sports.* https://mlb.nbcsports.com/2019/12/18/gerrit-cole-thanks-curt-flood-and-marvin-miller-during-introductory-press-conference/ (accessed December 5, 2020).

Barra, A. (July 12, 2011). How Curt Flood changed baseball and killed his career in the process. *The Atlantic.* https://www.theatlantic.com/entertainment/archive/2011/07/how-curt-flood-changed-baseball-and-killed-his-career-in-the-process/241783/ (accessed December 5, 2020).

Blumenthal, S. (2018). *Children of the silent majority: Young voters and the rise of the Republican Party, 1968–1980.* Lawrence: University of Kansas Press.

Brown, P. (1992). Interview with Curt Flood. Oral History Collection. *Society of American Baseball Research.* https://oralhistory.sabr.org/interviews/flood-curt-1992/ (accessed December 5, 2020).

Cho, H., Pyun, D. Y., & Wang, C. K. J. (2019). Leisure nostalgia: Scale development and validation. *Journal of Leisure Research, 50*(4), 330–349.

Cowie, J. (2010). *Staying alive: The 1970s and the last days of the white working class.* New York: The New Press.

de Jong, G. (2016). *You can't eat freedom: Southerners and social justice after the civil rights movement.* Chapel Hill: University of North Carolina Press.

Firmite, R. (April 15, 1974). End of the glorious ordeal. *Sports Illustrated.* n.p.

Goold, D. (December 24, 2019). Fifty years ago on Christmas Eve, Curt Flood mailed a letter that changed baseball history. *St. Louis Post-Dispatch.* https://bit.ly/3uxWLWA (accessed February 7, 2022).

Gordon, K. O. (2013). Emotion and memory in nostalgia sport tourism: Examining the attraction to postmodern ballparks through an interdisciplinary lens. *Journal of Sport & Tourism, 18*(3), 217–239.

Hank Aaron. (n.d.) National Baseball Hall of Fame. https://baseballhall.org/hall-of-famers/aaron-hank (accessed December 5, 2020).

Hobsbawm E., & Ranger T. (Eds.). (2012). *The invention of tradition.* Cambridge: Cambridge University Press.

Khan, A. I. (2012). *Curt Flood in the media: Baseball, race, and the demise of the activist-athlete.* Minneapolis: University of Minnesota Press.

Lane, J. (2007). *Under the boards: The cultural revolution in basketball.* Lincoln: University of Nebraska Press.

Lassitter, M. (2006). *The silent majority: Suburban politics in the sunbelt South.* Princeton, NJ: Princeton University Press.

Leggett, W. (August 19, 1968). Not just a flood, but a deluge. *Sports Illustrated.* n.p.

Leggett, W. (May 28, 1973). A tortured road to 715. *Sports Illustrated.* n.p.

Leggett, W. (April 8, 1974). Poised for the golden moment. *Sports Illustrated.* n.p.

Leonard, D. J. (2017). *Playing while white: Privilege and power on and off the field.* Seattle: University of Washington Press.

Lomax, M. (2003). 'Curt Flood stood up for us': The quest to break down racial barriers and structural inequality in Major League Baseball. *Culture, Sport, Society 6*(2–3), 44–70.

Muder, C. (n.d.). Aaron, Robinson elected to hall of fame. National Baseball Hall of Fame. https://baseballhall.org/discover-more/stories/inside-pitch/hank-aaron-frank-robinson-elected-1982 (accessed December 5, 2020).

Musburger, B. (October 19, 1968). Bizarre protest by Smith, Carlos tarnishes medals. *Chicago Daily News.* n.p.

National Baseball Hall of Fame (June 23, 2015). Hall to Honor Curt Flood's legacy, World War II players during awards presentation at HOF weekend." https://baseballhall.org/discover-more/news/hall-to-honor-curt-flood-world-war-2-players-at-2015-awards-presentation (accessed December 5, 2020).

Nichol, M. (2019). *Globalization, sports law and labour mobility: The case of professional baseball in the United States and Japan.* Cheeltenham, UK: Edward Elgar Publishing Limited.

Rader, B. G. (2008). *Baseball: A history of America's game* (3rd ed.). Urbana: University of Illinois Press.

Rhoden, W. C. (April 15, 2019). Like Jackie Robinson, baseball should honor Curt Flood's sacrifice. *The Undefeated.* https://theundefeated.com/features/like-jackie-robinson-baseball-should-honor-curt-flood-sacrifice/ (accessed December 5, 2020).

Rhoden, W. C. (July 19, 2019). 'I want my father in the baseball hall of fame': Curt Flood's heroic legacy. *The Undefeated.* https://theundefeated.com/features/curt-flood-and-the-legacy-of-his-children/ (accessed December 5, 2020).

Rhoden, W. C. (December 24, 2019). The push for Curt Flood's enshrinement into the Baseball Hall of Fame intensifies." *The Undefeated.* https://theundefeated.com/features/cause-for-curt-flood-enshrinement-into-baseball-hall-of-fame-continues-fifty-years-since-letter/ (accessed December 5, 2020).

Roberts, R., & Olson, J. (1989). *Winning is the only thing: Sports in America since 1945.* Baltimore: Johns Hopkins University Press.

Schulz, C. (August 8, 1973). "Peanuts." https://www.gocomics.com/peanuts/1973/08/08 (accessed December 5, 2020).

Schulz, C. (August 9, 1973). "Peanuts." https://www.gocomics.com/peanuts/1973/08/09 (accessed December 5, 2020).

Schulz, C. (August 10, 1973). "Peanuts." https://www.gocomics.com/peanuts/1973/08/10 (accessed December 5, 2020).

Schulz, C. (August 11, 1973). "Peanuts." https://www.gocomics.com/peanuts/1973/08/11 (accessed December 5, 2020).

Schulz, C. (August 13, 1973). "Peanuts." https://www.gocomics.com/peanuts/1973/08/13 (accessed December 5, 2020).

Schulz, C. (August 14, 1973). "Peanuts." https://www.gocomics.com/peanuts/1973/08/14 (accessed December 5, 2020).

Schulz, C. (August 15, 1973). "Peanuts." https://www.gocomics.com/peanuts/1973/08/15 (accessed December 5, 2020).

Schulz, C. (August 16, 1973). "Peanuts." https://www.gocomics.com/peanuts/1973/08/16 (accessed December 5, 2020).

Schulz, C. (August 17, 1973). "Peanuts." https://www.gocomics.com/peanuts/1973/08/17 (accessed December 5, 2020).

Schulz, C. (August 18, 1973). "Peanuts." https://www.gocomics.com/peanuts/1973/08/18 (accessed December 5, 2020).

Schulz, C. (August 20, 1973). "Peanuts." *https://www.gocomics.com/peanuts/1973/08/20* (accessed December 5, 2020).

Schulz, C. (August 21, 1973). "Peanuts." https://www.gocomics.com/peanuts/1973/08/21 (accessed December 5, 2020).

Schulz, C. (August 22, 1973). "Peanuts." https://www.gocomics.com/peanuts/1973/08/22 (accessed December 5, 2020).

Sedikides, C., Wildschut, T., & Baden, D. (2004). Nostalgia: Conceptual issues and existential functions. in J. Greenberg, S. L. Koole, & T. A. Pyszczynski (Eds). *The handbook of experimental existential psychology* (pp. 200–214). New York: Guilford Press.

Smith, J. (2018). "The magnitude of me": Reggie Jackson, baseball, and the seventies. *Journal of Sport History, 45*(2), 145–164.

Snyder, B. (2007). *A well-paid slave: Curt Flood's fight for free agency in professional sports.* New York: Penguin.

Vin Scully calls Hank Aaron's historic 715th home run. (November 13, 2014). *MLB,* YouTube. https://www.youtube.com/watch?v=QjqYThEVoSQ (accessed December 5, 2020).

4

Women's Baseball

A Story Not Told

Leslie Heaphy

Baseball's cultural heritage can be seen every day in different venues across the United States. There are numerous museums, mural, statues, memorabilia, and stadiums to celebrate the players and the history of the game. Within that history, there are a variety of different stories to be told. One of those tales involves the celebration of women's baseball. The story of women in the game is not as well documented as that of Major League Baseball or even Minor League Baseball. Few statues or exhibits can be visited and even fewer stadiums remember the women of the All-American Girls Professional Baseball League (AAGPBL) or other women's teams or individual players. Even fewer opportunities exist to learn about women's roles off the field. The real questions are: Why has this story not been told? What has been lost because the cultural artifacts are not celebrated any longer? What story is being supported or not being represented because of the lack of cultural artifacts that tell the story of women in the game? The following essay will explore these questions by examining both the cultural representations of women in baseball and the lack thereof to demonstrate the increased need to preserve and promote women's baseball history.

Greater attention must be paid to the roles women have played in the game of baseball since the sport's beginnings. Their stories contribute not just to the history of baseball but to the narrative of American history as well. The record of women's achievements has not been preserved and celebrated with monuments, stadiums, museum exhibits and other typical forms of cultural remembrance. Women's baseball heritage has to be broadened and expanded to tell the full and complex story of women's contributions to

America's "national pastime." The need for this expansion will be shown by examining what collections and related materials can be found at places such as the National Baseball Hall of Fame, the Negro Leagues Baseball Museum, and the Children's Museum in Indianapolis, as well as collections and other artifacts preserved in museums and on websites. The lack of representation of women in the baseball heritage story creates a narrative that implies that women are not important to baseball.

The story of women in baseball is a complicated one. Until recently, the general narrative talked about women's exclusion from the game until the 20th century, when women began to break the barriers and find a slow opening, starting with the bloomer girls in the 1910s. The real start, in this typical narrative, began with the AAGPBL in 1943. Philip Wrigley created a professional league that gave women the chance to be a part of America's national pastime through 1954. That prevailing narrative was challenged by Debra Shattuck's 2018 book *Bloomer Girls*. Shattuck convincingly argues that women were a part of the game from the start but were actually pushed out by the end of the 19th century and then had to fight to return, rather than be admitted as newcomers. Shattuck provides ample evidence to support this new narrative, which raises the question of why most people believe women are newcomers to the game. One reason this larger story is not as well known is the lack of attention paid to the history and heritage of women's involvement. Another is the basic problem inherent to sports in general. How does one preserve the moment of a great achievement at a sporting event? It is not like a speech where the recording or the written document is made available. The achievements of female ball players have few tangible artifacts (Ramshaw, 2015).

Baseball heroes are all men because baseball is considered a masculine sport. They define the sport and the ideals society considers important, and they often embody a higher ideal. Roberto Clemente fits this ideal perfectly, as his skill made him significant but his humanitarian work made him a hero. We hold up players such as Clemente to give us something to aspire to, to show us what we could be. Statues and monuments are erected to help us know who our heroes are meant to be (Gammon, 2014). But what about the heroine? How do we define and remember her? With our statues and plaques, it seems that society is trying to fit women into the same mold— providing someone for women to aspire to be like. But if this is the case, why are there so few statues of women more generally and even fewer of women in baseball? The lack of such commemorative items suggests that the role of women is not as important, that baseball history does not really include them.

Different audiences hear and understand stories based on a variety of evidence. Stories in newspapers and official documents can tell the story of baseball, but so can monuments, stadiums, exhibits, and memorabilia. This is where the story begins to diverge when analyzing women's roles in the game. Shattuck looked to newspapers and archives to challenge the existing narrative, but for many the cultural artifacts are what dictate the story. Who has been commemorated with a bobblehead? What stadiums have been named for players? Who has their own statue or museum exhibit? Since baseball is America's national pastime, what national identity has been created with women who have been left out of the history of the game? What will happen to the narrative with the addition of women's accomplishments?

Within a discussion of understanding the past, the idea of nostalgia certainly comes into play. Nostalgia has been defined in a variety of ways throughout history, beginning with the idea of homesickness but evolving into a more complex yearning for an ideal past when the present is lacking (Cho et al., 2014). Others have acknowledged that nostalgia can incorporate both positive and negative feelings (Baker & Kennedy, 1994). Researchers have also identified the difference between nostalgia and reminiscence. The idea of reminiscing simply means remembering without any further consideration or thought, a chance to look back on something fondly. When looking at how women's baseball has been remembered, reminiscing seems to be the more common process—if their participation is considered at all. Nostalgia does not work with the narrative most are familiar with, since women are generally missing from the baseball stories that are remembered. An exception to that idea is the 1993 movie *A League of Their Own*, which was directed by Penny Marshall. Marshall's film not only tells audiences a story they did not know but also makes viewers yearn for that better time when women had a league and when opportunities in baseball seemed possible for women. In an interview, Marshall also wanted to inspire a desire to build on the contributions of those pioneers (Hollywood's Master Storytellers, n.d.).

The movie *A League of Their Own* is the connection point for so many who, before having watched the movie, knew nothing about the participation of women in baseball. The movie is a classic, feel-good baseball story, but the film goes far beyond that when considering the history told. Thousands became interested in learning more about the history of women in baseball and more about the actual women. The movie creates nostalgia and romanticism, a longing for a better time. To move the story beyond nostalgia, we need to see the story as one that has continued and is bigger than just the movie.

To help accomplish a goal larger than nostalgia, there is the idea of heritage. This concept has been defined in a variety of ways, but one key area of heritage centers around the ideas of history and education. Another important definition focuses on the idea that heritage is made up of events and people that we value, but that we also want to be sure are remembered in the future (Gammon & Ramshaw, 2007). So, if women's baseball is not part of the legacy of the sport, does that mean it has not been valued? Heritage is what is chosen to be passed on by contemporary society. That also means heritage includes that which is decided not to be passed on or that which should be forgotten (Tonkin, 2011). That idea fits the women's baseball story. Efforts have been made to try to preserve places and exhibit artifacts so that future generations know about the history, but many achievements have been omitted and forgotten. Women's baseball history is what really needs to be explored to understand the story being told and the one that has been left out. Museums are a great place to begin this journey, and none is more important to baseball than the National Baseball Hall of Fame in Cooperstown, New York.

National Baseball Hall of Fame

The largest celebration of baseball happens at the National Baseball Hall of Fame in Cooperstown, New York, which not only promotes the best players or heroes of baseball's past but also highlights the history of the game. When the Hall of Fame was founded in 1939, the inaugural class of players represented the image of the game up to that point. Naturally, there were no women included then—not until 2006, when Effa Manley was elected to the Hall of Fame as part of the group of 17 Negro Leaguers chosen. When one visits the Hall of Fame today, Manley's bust can be found among all the other Hall of Famers. After seeing her bust, visitors can wander through the various galleries to learn about the history of the game. Since 1999, there has been a women's exhibit that encompasses a small section of the second floor. Visitors are introduced to the story of women's involvement since the 19th century when the Vassar Resolutes and other college teams formed. There are various photos, uniforms, news articles, and the like to help paint a picture of women's roles. The exhibit is updated with more recent stories, as well, such as Mo'ne Davis pitching in the Little League World Series and Justine Siegal throwing batting practice.

One can also see women's baseball being recognized via the outdoor sculptures at the Hall of Fame. There are three sculptures in Cooper Park near the library entrance. Two are male figures and the third is a female player meant to represent all women ball players. The sculpture, created by Stanley Bleifeld in 2006, is entitled "Woman at the Bat." She is set off to the side, away from the male pitcher and catcher who are shown as if they are a part of a real ball game. These sculptures are all easily missed if you do not know they are there.

On closer examination, one asks: what story about women's baseball is being told and remembered at the Hall of Fame? The first answer is that the story of women's baseball is not comprehensive but simply highlights, creating something to see as an exception (Ramshaw, 2015). As often happens in exhibits, the focus is on firsts and important or significant events. Most of the emphasis is on field experience and not on other baseball personnel. Amanda Clement, the first umpire, is mentioned along with such topics as members of the All-American League, bloomer girl teams, the Colorado Silver Bullets, and the USA National team. Visitors do not walk away from the exhibit knowing that women have been playing baseball since its origins and have been working in baseball nearly as long. Through these omissions, there is no effort to change the dominant narrative of baseball as a man's game (Ramshaw, 2015). The first female owner of an MLB team was Helene Britton with the St. Louis Cardinals in 1911. There have been a host of women owners ever since, but that is not really a part of the story. Most people do not travel to the Hall of Fame to learn about the history of women's baseball. They travel there to see their favorite Hall of Famer and to see memorabilia from Major League Baseball. The Hall of Fame is a place for heroes, heritage, and a constructed history of the game. Sometimes when organizations are commercial ventures, such as museums, their agendas can get in the way of telling a story or deciding what story gets told. The past becomes commodified. Since museums and other heritage sites rely on donations and sponsors as well as political support, their decisions have to consider what will attract or retain their funding. Women's baseball, or women's sports in general, often falls into a category where the question being asked is: will this bring in visitors and fans, or would money be better spent elsewhere (Ramshaw, 2010)?

Websites

So, where does one find women's baseball heritage? The places are few and far between. There is no list one can look up or a comprehensive directory of collections. The closest one comes to finding the collected materials is on the website for the AAGPBL. On their website, there is a section called Resources that lists 27 museums, exhibits, and libraries in the United States and Canada that have any collection related to the All-American Girls Professional Baseball League (www.aagpbl.org/resources/museums). The resources listed here focus on one aspect of women's baseball, the AAGPBL, and are not at all comprehensive.

The AAGPBL's website provides the full history of the league. Each collection helps to tell the complete story of the league through photos, newspaper articles, and league records. Visiting the online presence of these sites shows how they each have chosen to display women's baseball history. At the Grand Rapids Public Library, for example, if one searches for the "Chicks 19," most of the results are photographs. At Midway Village Museum (www.midwayvillagemuseum.com), one can search for the "Rockford Peaches" within the digital collection and find 100 items listed. Almost all results are photos of games and fans at various Peaches events between 1943 and 1954. These photos have been on display at the museum at various times, so there is a place to visit—a heritage site. Each of these sites provides a piece of the larger history, telling the story of both the famous and the less well-known players in the league as well as those who came and watched them play. These collections offer more than just memorabilia; they can also tell us about how the country viewed baseball at any given time and who was able to participate or be prohibited from playing (Gammon & Ramshaw, 2007).

The Society for American Baseball Research (SABR) Bio Project (sabr.org/bioproject) has over 5,000 biographies of all people related to the game. There are currently 26 biographies of players who played in the AAGPBL. A category entitled "Spouses" includes eight biographies of women, such as Eleanor Gehrig and Ethel Posey. In the "Executives" category, there are also only eight biographies of female owners. What is most interesting about the bio project is that members choose who they wish to write about; the meager representation of women is revealing. In part, it represents members' preferences but also what they are most familiar with or projects for which they know they can find research. As a result, the bio project website is not a primary resource for learning about women in baseball.

Physical Artifacts

What are the physical artifacts that commemorate women's place in baseball? Where can one go to experience and see stadia, monuments, and the like that tell the story of women in the game? Who are the sporting heroines? Again, much of what one can visit focuses primarily on women and teams in the All-American League, since this was the only professional league. Even that story was not familiar to most people before Penny Marshall's movie *A League of Their Own* came out in 1993. With the movie's popularity, suddenly fans became aware that there had been a league and the women who were depicted in the film started to get attention. Contrast that with the Colorado Silver Bullets, the women's professional team that played from 1994 to 1997 with the support of Coors. The year 2019 marked the 25th anniversary of their formation, and still few people know anything about their story. The Hall of Fame has a couple of commemorative items from the club in their exhibit and has some files in their collection but that is all that exists. Without places to visit or collections to see, the stories of most women in baseball have been forgotten or lost to history. There is little or no nostalgia for women's baseball because there is not a "better time" remembered. There is also no heritage because the history is not being told.

If one travels to Rockford, Illinois, the story of the Rockford Peaches is still alive. The Peaches were one of the two teams who existed for the entire length of the AAGPBL (1943–54). Beyer Stadium has been restored and teams play there today. A women's tournament is held there every Labor Day weekend, hosted by the Rockford Starfires. Baseball for All has held its National Girls Tournament there twice. At one corner of the field is the original gate and ticket booth with the Rockford Peaches' name above it. Murals depicting the Peaches' history have been painted in the rebuilt dugouts. A small series of monuments tells the sporting history of Beyer Stadium. Here, the Peaches are recognized with plaques for local players such as Helen Waddell, Lou Erickson, and Dottie Ferguson. One monument also lists all the teams that played in the league. Alongside these memorials are a series of plaques about football, Olympic athletes from Rockford, and the original Fall City's baseball team from the 19th century. The restoration of the field has made this a bit of a destination.

The story told by the ticket booth and murals highlights the local players on the Peaches but rests mainly on a bit of nostalgia. There is no complicated history told here, as the Peaches are simply part of the local Rockford sport history story. The ticket booth reminds people of a better time when they came to see the Peaches playing the South Bend Blue Sox or the Grand Rapids Chicks. But there is no information about who won the individual games or how many times the Peaches won the League Championship. There is no context provided for the time period when roles for women in baseball were more limited than today.

By placing commemorative items in museums or preserving a site and encouraging tourists to visit, the values represented become institutionalized (Ramshaw, 2011). Saving Hamtramck Stadium because it was a site for Negro League baseball implies that remembering a time when America was segregated, and African American players had to play in a separate league, is important to America's history. Preserving Beyer Stadium's ticket booth indicates that the Peaches played an important role in local Rockford history. Effa Manley's plaque in the Hall of Fame cements her place in the history of the game. The plaque also tells people that at least one woman held an important role.

Other Ways to Remember

There are few places that tell the story of women's baseball. Few stadiums that women played baseball in regularly have been preserved. There are a handful of plaques at places like Horlick Stadium (Racine Belles 1943–50) and at South Bend Four Winds Field, where there is a Wall of Fame which includes a plaque for local AAGPBL player Lou Arnold. Again, the details are limited and not much is learned. These plaques are simply an acknowledgment that women's baseball existed. Where can one find the stories of the Vassar Resolutes, the St. Louis Black Bronchos, or the Dolly Vardens? The history of baseball in America is incomplete without the inclusion of these accounts and so many others. Finding an isolated photo in a book or a single plaque is not enough to create a sense of heritage.

The Negro Leagues Baseball Museum (www.nlbm.com/) dedicated three busts in November 2016, celebrating the contributions of Toni Stone, Connie Morgan, and Mamie Johnson. Sculptor Kwan Wu created the piece "Beauty of the Game" to highlight the contributions of the three women who starred in the Negro Leagues during the 1950s. Their story is an important part of American history as well as baseball history. Learning their individual achievements provides an education that cannot be found in a traditional baseball book. But the problem with most of these types of exhibits is that they tend to forget about the audience and the need for variety to attract visitors. They are static and unchanging.

Toni Stone played baseball in the Minneapolis/St. Paul area before moving on to play in San Francisco and then for the Kansas City Monarchs of the Negro Leagues. She was the first woman to play for one of the major Negro League teams, and she paved the way for two others to follow her onto the diamond. Many years later, in 1997 the city of St. Paul renamed a field in her honor. Along with the sign at the field when one visits, there is also a second sign that includes information about her background. To add to that story, if one visits the new St. Paul City of Baseball Museum, not only is Toni Stone included in the displays but so is a picture of Ila Borders, who pitched over 40 years after Stone played in the area ("Saints to Open City of Baseball Museum on Opening Day, May 16"). Borders pitched for the St. Paul Saints in 1997 (Johnson, 2017). Her larger story was published in *Making My Pitch* (Ardell & Borders, 2017). Here, the story of local baseball more comprehensively includes the story of the women who played a role.

The story of Toni Stone has been added to with a recent off-Broadway play based on the only book written about her by Martha Ackmann (*Curveball*, rept. 2017). The play, written by Lydia Diamond, is about Stone's triumphs as well as her struggles. The audience is left with a deep appreciation for what she was able to accomplish at a time in American history when an African American woman had limited opportunities in life. There is also a series of bronze sculptures that include Toni Stone, Mamie Johnson, and Hank Aaron at the Children's Museum in Indianapolis. The sculptures are part of the Sports Legend Avenue highlighting old-time sports heroes in the local community. There is also a mural that fans can visit near Target Field next to the light rail station. The mural, entitled "A History of Minnesota Baseball," was dedicated as part of a three-part series created between 2009 and 2010. Artists Craig and Jennifer David included Toni Stone as part of the local story, even if she has not been recognized on the national level (David, n.d.).

One of the other African American women who played in the Negro Leagues has also had her story celebrated with a field in Washington, DC, named in her honor in 2013. More significant than the field is an entire Little League group called the Mamie Johnson Little League, beginning in 2015. That designation honors both her time pitching for the Indianapolis Clowns but also connects her story to Mo'ne Davis, the first woman to pitch her team to a win in a Little League World Series. These efforts celebrate the importance of women who were among the first to make significant achievements in baseball, the heroines of the game.

Memorabilia and Tournaments

Memorabilia can help provide a way to remember the past. There are bob-bleheads, pennants, artwork, pins, T-shirts, and even replica uniforms of the figures in women's baseball. Seeing a bobblehead of Ila Borders makes people wonder who she was and why she is being honored in such a way. As a result, some fans may research her background and learn her history. Others will simply accept the gift without ever knowing her baseball story. A pennant with the name of the Muskegon Lassies in their team colors lets fans know that such a team existed, but it does not provide the team's full backstory. Again, a little background information is given, but not enough to change the larger story of American baseball. Artwork depicting a female ball player or umpire can be found, but such works simply celebrate a single player or a moment in time. T-shirts of AAGPBL teams can be found, as can replica uniforms, but almost no other women's baseball teams or players are found with this merchandise. It is as if the AAGPBL is the only venue for women's involvement in the game of baseball.

Another effort to remember and celebrate key individuals who have made a contribution for women in baseball has been the recent trend to name tournaments in their honor. Today, there are series to honor Shirley Burkovich, Maria Pepe, Jane Forbes Clark, Suzyn Waldman, and Tamara Holmes. The fascinating part of these games is that they honor key women at a variety of levels of the game, expanding our education beyond the AAGPBL. Waldman was an announcer for the New York Yankees. Clark is the Chairman of the Board of Directors for the Hall of Fame. Pepe tried to break the barrier in Little League when she pitched three games in Hobo-ken, New Jersey, in 1972.

Women's Baseball Heritage

In trying to understand the stories of women's baseball through various cultural artifacts and heritage sites, one needs to compare their stories to those of men's baseball. What is immediately apparent is how different they are, resulting in huge disparities in the artifacts and memorabilia available. Women's baseball in America has only had one professional league, which lasted for 12 seasons. There has been only one other professional team in the 1990s, the Colorado Silver Bullets. The number of individual women who have played professionally is under 10, and no female umpire has ever made it to the Majors. There have been a number of female owners but no GM of a Major League ball club. As a result, one could argue that there is less women's history to be remembered so there are fewer places and artifacts to be preserved. While that is partially true, it is not the whole story.

The whole story would require telling a different narrative. The history of women in baseball challenges the notion that the sport has always been a man's game, that baseball is for men and softball is for women. It also challenged the idea that the game is essential to understanding America's identity. After all, the Mills Commission was created to declare baseball an American game and not an English one. The game is part of America's heritage (Frost, 2002). Reinforcing that idea are a number of softball fields named for women who played in the AAGPBL. Anna Petrovic-Meyer had a softball field named in her honor in Kenosha, Wisconsin. Alva Jo Fischer had a softball complex dedicated to her in San Antonio, Texas, in 1975. Mary Nesbitt Wisham also had a softball field dedicated in her name in Inter-lachen, Florida.

America's identity is partly tied up in the masculinity associated with baseball, and so the story of women in the game has been permanently rel-egated to the sidelines. At the Memorial Stadium in Terre Haute, Indiana, a granite monument was dedicated to Max Carey in 2001. Carey was born in the city of Terre Haute, and the monument does discuss his time as manager in the AAGPBL. So, the only mention of the women's teams is through one of the men who managed in the league. Without Penny Marshall's movie, many people would have no idea that women have played baseball for de-cades. Women's baseball needs more celebrations and remembrances like *A League of Their Own* in order for women baseball players to take their place in the annals of American baseball history. To move from nostalgia, reminiscing, and heritage studies to history, more attention needs to be paid to the full history and education to bring the story of women's baseball into its proper place—one that does more than just celebrate a few select heroines and teams (Lowenthal, 1998). Each generation both intentionally and unintentionally selects what is remembered and what is forgotten. To change the story about women's baseball, more intentional thought must be given to what artifacts are preserved and what stories are passed on to future generations.

What Can Be Done?

What can we do to recognize this heritage and keep the sport alive for future generations of women and girls? First, building a dedicated museum that tells the history of all women's participation in baseball would go a long way. Exhibits and research facilities would tell the stories and bring this heritage to a much larger audience. Penny Marshall's movie introduced many to the history over 25 years ago, but something must move that interest forward. A museum connects people to the past in many ways. People would be able to learn that women have been in the game since the beginning. Women are not newcomers—just their stories are. Individual communities and ball clubs can do their part by hosting events to highlight the women of the past and present in their own organizations. Some teams have taken this a step further by inviting women ball players to come and throw out the first pitch. A short biography of the player could be included in the program.

Hosting public events to recognize women in baseball gives people another venue to connect. These events should be expanded beyond just Women's History Month and should occur throughout the year. Local companies can support a girls' team in their local Little League or start a division for girls. Inviting former players from the AAGPBL, the Colorado Silver Bullets, USA National team, and others can show today's women players that they are not alone. Seeing others who have taken part before helps break down some of the barriers for today's players. The same holds true for umpires and front office personnel. Showcase those who have been involved to celebrate their legacy, and keep the heritage alive. Make it about more than nostalgia.

Conclusion

By exploring the story of women's baseball and how players' contributions are remembered, we see clearly how little has been preserved and how much more needs to be done. Expanding on current exhibits, murals, memorabilia, websites, and tournaments will give women's achievements and contributions a broader place in the game's history and will affect how that history is passed down as more than just reminiscing or nostalgia. In doing so, the narrative of women in baseball will become a larger part of baseball's heritage.

References

Ardell, J., & Borders, I. (2017). *Making my pitch: A woman's baseball odyssey.* Lincoln: University of Nebraska Press.

Baker, S. M., & Kennedy, P. F. (2014). Death by nostalgia: A diagnosis of context specific cases. *Advances in Consumer Research, 21,* 169–174. https://www.acrwebsite.org/volumes/7580

Cho, H., Ramshaw, G., & Norman, W. C. (2014). A conceptual model for nostalgia in the context of sport tourism: Re-classifying the sporting past. *Journal of Sport & Tourism, 19*(2), 145–167. https://www.tandfonline.com/doi/full/10.1080/14775085.2015.1033444

David, C. (n.d.). Sustainability reborn. Art Davidi. http://artdavidii.com/TargetFieldMuralsFrontViews.htm (accessed March 4, 2022).

Frost, W. (2002). Heritage, nationalism, identity: The 1861–62 England cricket tour of Australia. *International Journal of the History of Sport, 19*(4), 55–69. https://research.monash.edu/en/publications/heritage-nationalism-identity-the-1861-62-england-cricket-tour-of

Gammon, S. J. (2014). Heroes as heritage: The commoditization of sporting achievement. *Journal of Heritage Tourism, 9*(3), 246–256. https://www.researchgate.net/publication/271927520_Heroes_as_heritage_The_commoditization_of_sporting_achievement

Gammon, S., & Ramshaw, G. (Eds.). (2007). *Heritage, sport and tourism: Sporting pasts tourist futures.* London: Routledge.

Johnson, S. (23 May 2017). *Twenty years ago, Ila Borders broke gender barriers playing for the St. Paul Saints.* City Pages. www.citypages.com (accessed December 5, 2020).

Hollywood's Master Storytellers (n.d.). *Hollywood's Master Storytellers Presents "A League of Their Own with Penny Marshall and Lori Petty"* [Video]. YouTube. https://www.youtube.com/watch?v=ZMpETGQ6Tjs (accessed March 4, 2022).

Lowenthal, D. (1998). *The heritage crusade and the spoils of history.* Cambridge: Cambridge University Press.

Ramshaw, G. (2010). Living heritage and the sports museum: Athletes, legacy and the Olympic Hall of Fame and Museum, Canada Olympic Park. *Journal of Sport & Tourism, 15*(1), 45–70. https://www.researchgate.net/publication/233375797_Living_Heritage_and_the_Sports_Museum_Athletes_Legacy_and_the_Olympic_Hall_of_Fame_and_Museum_Canada_Olympic_Park

Ramshaw, G. (2011). The construction of sport heritage attractions. *Journal of Tourism Consumption and Practice, 3*(1), 1–25. https://pearl.plymouth.ac.uk/handle/10026.1/11568

Ramshaw, G. (Ed.). (2015). *Sport heritage.* London: Routledge.

Saints to open City of Baseball Museum on opening day, May 16. St Paul Saints. https://www.saintsbaseball.com/team/news/saints-open-city-baseball-museum-opening-day%09may-16 (accessed December 5, 2020).

Shattuck, D. A. (2017). *Bloomer girls: Women baseball pioneers.* Urbana: University of Illinois Press.

Tonkin, S. (2011). *What is heritage?* https://environment.gov.au/system/files/pages/ f4d5ba7d%09e4eb-4ced-9c0e%09104471634fbb/files/essay-whatisheritage-tonkin. pdf (accessed December 5, 2020).

Walk among the greatest all time on the Old National Bank Sports Legends Avenue of Champions (13 September 2017). https://www.childrensmuseum.org/content/walk %09among-greatest-all-time-old-national-bank-sports-legends-avenue-champions (accessed December 5, 2020).

5

Physical Reminders of Empowerment

Heritage, Baseball Stadia, and African American Communities

BENJAMIN J. DOWNS AND ADAM G. PFLEEGOR

At the age of 59, future Hall of Fame pitcher Leroy "Satchel" Paige started his final Major League Baseball game in front of a crowd of 9,289 fans at Kansas City Municipal Stadium. His three-inning effort as the starting pitcher for the last-place Kansas City Athletics on September 25, 1965, against fellow American League bottom-dwellers the Boston Red Sox capped a two-week publicity campaign by mercurial Athletics owner Charles O. Finley to boost late-season attendance, as fans were growing intolerant with the Athletics' team performance ("Another Finley Gimmick," 1965). After signing Paige to a professional contract on September 10 of that year, a decision on which he did not consult Athletics manager Haywood Sullivan, Finley announced that Paige would start for the Athletics on September 25 (McGuff, 1965). In advance of the September 25 contest, Finley and Paige emphasized the legendary pitcher's advanced age in promoting both the game and Salute to Satchel Paige Night rather than his numerous wins as a Negro League pitcher—28 as a Major League Baseball pitcher, and seven all-star appearances and two championships between the leagues.[*] Over-the-top stunts were not uncommon for Finley, and in this case he petitioned the American League to permit Paige to sit outside of the Athletics below-field level bullpen because Paige believed he was "close enough to being below the ground level as it is" ("A's Install Rockin' Chair," 1965, p. 14). Furthermore, Finley arranged for a novelty rocking chair and nurse to assist Paige in an effort to

---

[*] Negro League statistics for Satchel Paige are an approximation, as official stats were often not kept for Negro League contests. These figures are meant to serve as an indication of Paige's dominance in Negro League performances.

make the contest a spectacle for ticket sales rather than a celebration of one of the greatest pitching talents in baseball history. Paige's immensely successful career was trivialized in order to increase revenue for Finley.

Although Paige pitched three scoreless innings for the Athletics and yielded just one hit, a first-inning double to former (and future) batting champion and Hall of Famer Carl Yastrzemski, he did not appear again as a player in the Major Leagues. After the game, Finley stated he would keep Paige on the Athletics roster for the remainder of the season, even though he would not play, in order to satisfy the minimum five-year service time requirement for a $125 monthly pension payment, an offer Paige would discuss with his manager Abe Saperstein (Broeg, 1965). In the days following the game against the Red Sox, Paige went on the record with his personal and professional frustrations with his career in both segregated and integrated baseball, stating, "All they ask me is how old I am. But nobody asks me why I stayed out of the major leagues for 15 years. That's a long time, isn't it" ("Satch Can't Forget," 1965, p. 12). Despite his frustration, Paige appreciated the opportunity to play one last game in the Major Leagues because it allowed fans to "see that I must have had a lot more going for me and deserved to be in the big leagues when I was in my prime" ("Satch Can't Forget," 1965, p. 12).

The recognition of Satchel Paige's career before and during a Major League Baseball contest was symbolic. Although he won a World Series championship in 1948 as a member of the Cleveland Indians and made two all-star teams as a member of the St. Louis Browns, Paige only played parts of five seasons in the Major Leagues. He spent the majority of his career as a barnstorming attraction for various teams, including stops in Chattanooga, Birmingham, Baltimore, Cleveland, Pittsburgh, Kansas City, New York, Memphis, and Philadelphia, in the loosely associated and organized Negro Leagues. Despite his propensity to change teams, Satchel Paige's most notable organizational affiliation was with the Kansas City Monarchs, a team that also played in what would become Kansas City Municipal Stadium (Grundy & Rader, 2015). Beyond recognizing Paige's return to the Major Leagues, "Salute to Satchel Paige Night" paid homage to the history of professional baseball in Kansas City and at Municipal Stadium by including a one-inning exhibition game between former players of the Monarchs and the American Association Minor League team Kansas City Blues (van Valkenburg, 1965).

In addition to serving as the home facility for both the Athletics and Monarchs, Municipal Stadium's other major tenant, the Blues, was affiliated with the New York Yankees from 1936 to 1954. Future Yankee greats such as Mickey Mantle and Phil Rizzuto called Municipal Stadium home during the early stages of their careers. Given its association with highly recognizable Negro League and Major League organizations and players, Municipal Stadium holds a unique place in baseball history. Few stadia hosted both Negro League and Major League competition, although several ballparks across the country, such as Sulphur Dell (in Nashville, Tennessee), hosted a combination of White and Negro Minor League teams.* Other stadia supported White Minor League and Negro League teams, as was the case of Rickwood Field hosting the Birmingham Barons (Southern Association) and Birmingham Black Barons (Negro National League), as well as the Newark Bears (International League) and Newark Eagles (Negro National League) playing in Ruppert Stadium.

Despite the segregated status of the game on the field, organized Negro League teams competed in Major League stadia such as Comiskey Park (Chicago), Forbes Field (Pittsburgh), Griffith Stadium (Washington, DC), League Park (Cleveland), and Yankee Stadium (New York City). While these stadia have been examined as part of Major League history (e.g., Seifried & Pastore, 2009), their significance in the context of the Negro Leagues and the broader African American community is less understood.

Beyond showcasing African American baseball talent, the organized Negro Leagues served as a highly visible African American economic enterprise (Peterson, 1992). The organized Negro Leagues also became a site for debate within the broader Civil Rights Movement and the role and degree of White involvement in African American social, political, financial, and economic causes (Peterson, 1992; Ribowsky, 1995). Moreover, and paramount to the discussion, the relationship between African American and White baseball entrepreneurs highlighted the structural inequality faced by the African American community. One physical manifestation of the different realities experienced by African Americans and White Americans was the Major League Baseball stadium. Those facilities have previously been identified as important sociocultural symbols (e.g., Mason et al., 2005; Pfleegor et al., 2013; Ramshaw, 2020; Rosentraub & Ijla, 2008; Trumpbour, 2007). Furthermore, Major League stadia are particularly important structures

---

* Sulphur Dell in Nashville, TN, was home to the Nashville Vols (Southern League) from 1901–1961/1963, the Nashville Stars (Negro Major League) in 1942, and the Nashville Black Vols/Cubs from 1945–1951. The stadium also hosted exhibition Negro American League (majors) attractions.

within their communities, and many residents of Major League communities feel that those facilities improve a city's national reputation (Schwester, 2007).

Importantly, Major League Baseball stadia were not the only locations of dual-use, segregated baseball, and an examination of Minor League facilities would likely be a valuable endeavor. However, the disparity in access to Major League facilities and the rental agreements offered by Major League teams may imply that the cultural heritage of facilities is more complex than previously investigated. For example, Ribowsky (1995) found the New York Yankees charged Negro League teams $3,500 rent per game for the use of Yankee Stadium during the late 1930s, but famed sports promotors like Eddie Gottlieb and Abe Saperstein intervened on behalf of Negro League teams to negotiate a reduced rate as low as $1,000 for the teams' use of the facility.

For Ramshaw (2020), "built sporting structures such as sport stadia are some of the most identifiable forms of sport heritage" (p. 13). Although the physical spaces bring about positive memories of family and triumph for many, invoking heritage can also reinforce divides in communities. This duel form of cultural heritage, or dissonant heritage, illuminates that different groups can have vastly different interpretations of the past (e.g., Graham et al., 2005; Tunbridge & Ashworth, 1996). This leads to the question of who owns the past. For heritage purposes, the majority, wealthy, and culturally elite generally establish what version of history is celebrated in the present. This is known as Authorized Heritage Discourse (AHD) (Smith, 2006). In looking at the "other side" of heritage, Seifried and Meyer (2010) stated, "old buildings like Fenway Park (Boston, MA), Wrigley Field (Chicago, IL), and Lambeau (Field) (Green Bay, WI) are filled with ghosts of old players and memories which can also importantly fill people with moments of sadness and melancholy" (p. 53). Although they focused on the feelings of fan nations, the same concept can be applied to communities of different races, ethnicities, and religions. The harsh reality for African Americans and other minority groups is that stadia across the country celebrate heroes and organizational triumphs, but, all too often, non-White heroes and their impressive athletic accomplishments are left out of the celebration in lieu of White heroes and White-centric stories. In other words, heritage represents the majority way of thinking and the dominant values of the group in power (Smith & Waterton, 2012).

In the years immediately after World War I, many college football facilities were designated as memorial stadiums to honor service members, thereby constructing a patriotic symbol that simultaneously capitalized on the growing popularity of American football and the groundswell of national pride that emerged following the victory of the United States and its allies in the Great War (Schmidt, 2007). In recent years, the politics of memory has become more prevalent in heritage academic discourse. Throughout the United States, this politicization of memory has come to the forefront of local and national governments as politicians and constituents grapple with how to handle confederate statues, war monuments, and building names that display those that held openly racist or ethnocentric viewpoints. This identity and celebration thereof through memorialization is "closely connected to place promotion power relations" (Zhang et al., 2018). Within the politics of memory, what is forgotten is equally important to understand as what is memorialized. For Renan (1998), national history is constructed through this combination of remembrance and forgetting. Throughout history, ruling classes and the majority often deem African American heroes as forgettable. This lack of historical respect has dire and immediate consequences on modern race relations.

In recent years, Major League teams and facilities have made attempts to honor the complicated history of segregated professional baseball in the United States. The Kansas City Royals wear throwback uniforms inspired by the Kansas City Monarchs as part of the Salute to the Negro Leagues Day. After the game, the Royals auction off the uniforms and other game memorabilia and donate the proceeds to the Negro Leagues Baseball Museum (Salute to the Negro Leagues, n.d.). The Washington Nationals placed a statue honoring famed Homestead/Washington Grays catcher Josh Gibson outside of Nationals Park as part of an exhibit commemorating Washington, DC, baseball legends that also includes statues of Walter Johnson and Frank Howard. Additionally, PNC Park, the home stadium of the Pittsburgh Pirates, honored seven Negro League players, including Gibson, with statues as part of the facility's Legacy Square of Pittsburgh baseball history in 2006. Following an ownership change in 2015, the organization dismantled the exhibit citing lack of fan interest, then asked Gibson's great-grandson if he would retrieve all seven statues from the stadium (Harris, 2016).

In framing our discussion of African American communities and Major League Baseball stadia, Tunbridge and Ashworth's (1996) presentation of dissonant heritage and Smith's (2006) discussion of Authorized Heritage Discourse (AHD) are critical to understanding the complexities of heritage, especially within marginalized communities. Dissonant heritage describes two parallel interpretations of something of cultural value. As a cultural product, heritage is prone to dissonance. For Graham et al. (2005), "the creation of any heritage actively or potentially disinherits or excludes those who do not subscribe to, or are embraced within" the heritage (p. 34). The authors also expanded the definition to specifically include underrepresented communities: "despite the development of multicultural societies, the content of heritage is also likely to reflect dominant ethnicities" (p. 35). This understanding of dissonant heritage is easily combined with Smith's (2006) concept of AHD. For Smith, AHD is a naturalization process in which culturally elite (i.e., Western, White-centric, upper-class) values are dominant and select what is to be preserved, remembered, and celebrated. In Major League Baseball stadiums, the AHD is that of the White team owners and White baseball heroes. The dissonant heritage of African American communities in baseball and the Negro Leagues seems to be largely forgotten.

In this chapter, we will discuss the connection of sporting physical spaces to heritage, or what Ramshaw and Gammon (2017) identified as tangible immovable sport heritage, and why these physical spaces are important for modern communities. Next, we will examine how middle-class White team owners and facility owners utilized Negro League talent for profits in the early- to mid-1900s. Finally, we establish a call for contemporary Major League Baseball stadiums to more overtly recognize and memorialize the heritage established by Negro League players in ballparks.

Baseball Stadiums and Heritage

Sport and heritage go together, as both constructions possess a combination of tangible and intangible assets and qualities for a variety of stakeholders such as community members, fans, and organizations. Several scholars have offered definitions of heritage, primarily focusing on legacies and meaning-making. For Ramshaw and Gammon (2005), heritage seeks to "remember, enliven, teach—and even create—personal and collective legacies for contemporary audiences. Its purpose is often to celebrate the achievements, courage and strength of those who have come before" (p. 230). The authors added, heritage is an "active process of meaning-making which is tied to present needs, circumstances, and ideologies" (Ramshaw & Gammon, 2017, p. 120). Importantly, heritage is intrinsically tied to contemporary events and can change with time, circumstances, and happenings. For the purposes of this chapter, it is also important to note that heritage takes on very different meanings for various individuals and groups of people.

As part of their definition, McKercher et al. (2005) included places, "built environments," and structures as a primary component to heritage (p. 541). Sport stadia and venues have been identified as both tourist attractions and heritage-based attractions (e.g., Bairner, 2015; Gammon, 2011; Gordon, 2013; Ramshaw & Gammon, 2010; Wright, 2012). Famous and historic stadia across the globe highlight their importance in history and the historical events they have housed in order to evoke heritage as a financial or organizational advantage. For example, Madison Square Garden (in New York City) has been dubbed the world's most famous arena due to the historic events and accomplishments that have taken place there over the years (Seifried & de Wilde, 2014). Throughout the newly renovated facility, Madison Square Garden displays photos of past sporting championships, famous plays, shots, and goals, as well as historic non-sporting moments such as hosting Pope Francis, or the record-setting concert runs from Elton John and Billy Joel.

Specifically, within sport, several scholars have discussed the importance of stadia and physical sporting spaces (e.g., Pfleegor et al., 2013; Rosentraub & Ijla, 2008; Seifried, 2010; Seifried & Meyer, 2008). For Seifried and Meyer (2008), "sport facilities . . . appear as culturally relevant places to study because they are celebrated as sacred spaces which regularly host large gatherings" (p. 54). In a taxonomy of heritage in sport, Ramshaw and Gammon (2017) identified these spaces as primary elements of tangible immovable sport heritage, which "is a category of sport heritage that encompasses sport heritage buildings or places; that is to say, a famous golf course or historic stadium that remains *in situ* and cannot be moved" (p. 119). The connection here to sport, and, further, sport and baseball stadia, is abundant. Contemporary baseball is a sociocultural phenomenon that regularly celebrates its past achievements, heroes, and contests. This is done by highlighting legendary players, coaches, and other figures, attempting to relive memorable moments and historically significant games, and paying homage to the built environments that played host. While baseball stadiums are impressive architectural and engineering feats, their fame is more often attributed to legendary players and unforgettable sporting moments. This is evident in the nicknames surrounding many stadia, such as "The House That Ruth Built" (Yankee Stadium in New York City). Notably absent from these cultural celebrations, however, are important African American players from the Negro Leagues and their sporting achievements and history.

The question becomes, why should we care about physical structures in a discussion of heroes and heritage for African American communities? The answer may lie within the meaning attributed to these large-scale structures by the communities who consider them to be home. While discussing the potential moral obligation to preserve heritage through stadia, Pfleegor et al. (2013) focused on the idea of sport facilities as synecdochical images. Most simplistically, synecdoche is when "an element of a larger set (such as a building in a city) comes to represent the set" (Maennig & du Plessis, 2009, p. 67); in other words, when a part is fully representative of the whole. For example, we can see synecdochical images when a painting represents an artist's life work (e.g., the Mona Lisa representing the work of Leonardo da Vinci). It is also common for physical structures to be synecdochical images, especially buildings within a city skyline, to come to represent the city as a whole, including community members and constituents residing in the city, area, or country. Consider the Eiffel Tower in Paris, the Opera House in Sydney, the Empire State Building or One World Trade Center in New York City, the Gateway Arch in St. Louis, the Burj Khalifa in Dubai, and the Taj Mahal in Agra—all are iconic structures that most individuals immediately identify as a representation of their location (i.e., community, city, and country). As a representation of the geographical location, the structure also represents the community members, constituents, and history of the locale. Essentially, the structures become synonymous with the location, its people, and the culture. Ergo, the Eiffel Tower equals Paris, France, the Burj Khalifa equals Dubai, and so on. However, these physical manifestations of historical celebration are often determined by the cultural elite (i.e., historically, White, upper-class male leaders or entrepreneurs) through AHD in order to tell the version of history that best suits their desired narrative.

The same can be said concerning synecdoche about sport and baseball stadia. As imposingly large structures that regularly house some of the largest gatherings of community members, sport stadia act as synecdochical representations of their communities. Consider Wembley Stadium in London, the Old Course in St. Andrews, Lambeau Field in Green Bay, or Fenway Park in Boston. These stadia are recognized and can be acknowledged by both sport and non-sport fans as important community anchors. Perhaps more than any other sport due to the reliance on history, heritage, statistics, as well as legendary figures and heroes, baseball stadia are recognizable community anchors across the United States. Yankee Stadium (both old and new) in New York City, Fenway Park in Boston, Wrigley Field and Comiskey Park in Chicago, and Camden Yards in Baltimore are prominent examples of synecdochical baseball stadia. But what transitioned these baseball facilities from mere physical conglomerations of concrete, steel, and wood, to homes of significant cultural heritage that are representative of their local communities? The answer falls within the sporting heroes that graced the spaces and the important sporting moments shared by community members within the physical boundaries of the space. Yankee Stadium, with its recognizable white-pillared facade, witnessed the Yankees organization win 27 World Series titles with the likes of Babe Ruth, Mickey Mantle, Roger Maris, and Lou Gehrig. In more recent history, in 2003 New Yorkers cheered as Aaron Boone hit an improbable walk-off homerun in the 11th inning of game seven of the American League Championship Series (ALCS) off Boston Red Sox knuckleball pitcher Tim Wakefield. This magical moment for Yankees fans, and correspondingly heart-breaking moment for Red Sox fans, earned Boone the nickname Aaron "f-in" Boone.

While Black players have also been involved with building history and memories at Yankee Stadium (e.g., Elston Howard, Reggie Jackson) and other baseball stadia (e.g., Satchel Paige in Comiskey Park), the narratives surrounding the history are predominantly White-centric, with nearly complete omission of past Negro League contests and heroes. This White-centric narrative has been established by years of limited access into facilities for Black patrons, the forced gentrification of predominantly Black neighborhoods, and organizations being led by wealthy, White businessmen. As baseball continues to celebrate its heritage with dedicated spaces and special events (e.g., plaques, halls of fame, Old-Timers' Day, jersey retirements, etc.) in built environments, the narratives of heroes have been firmly focused on the accomplishments, acts, and feats of White players. Despite the fact that all-time Negro League greats—such as Satchel Paige, Oscar Charleston, Buck Leonard, John Henry "Pop" Lloyd, and Josh Gibson—played in Major League stadiums across the country, there are few honors bestowed to them in the physical environments. For example, Comiskey Park, former home of the Chicago White Sox, located in the predominantly African American community of Chicago's South Side, hosted 27 East-West Negro League All-Star Games between 1933 and 1960. Considered one of the top baseball talents of all time, Oscar Charleston brought to the field his signature combination of defensive speed and batting power, but he was not honored in Comiskey Park, nor in its successor, Guaranteed Rate Field. Charleston, a member of the Baseball Hall of Fame, had a career batting average of .339 and received the most votes for selection into the first East-West game in 1933.[*] Negro League players such as the talented Oscar Charleston were regularly used to facilitate financial gain for team and facility owners, as these players were invited for exhibition games in Major League Baseball stadiums across the country. However, the players saw few returns on their efforts.

African American Players and "Tangible Immovable" Sport Heritage

For most of the history of modern sport, the viability of professional sport teams and leagues rested with their ability to generate revenue through the sale of game tickets. As early as the 1860s, entrepreneurial baseball businessmen such as William H. Cammeyer were able to better control and monetize fan interest by building walls around the open fields where baseball was played (Grundy & Rader, 2015). This initial step of formalizing the location and construction of a baseball stadium established the foundation from which future baseball facilities and leagues would expand and evolve (Seifried, 2010). Though rudimentary by contemporary standards, the first facilities of club and professional baseball presented facility owners with the opportunity to charge higher admission fees and present more games to customers interested in consuming baseball (Grundy & Rader, 2015). The desire to play and watch baseball was certainly not limited to White audiences.

One of the earliest demonstrations of African American interest in the game of baseball was in Philadelphia, where Civil Rights activist Octavius Catto formed the Philadelphia Pythians in 1866, an amateur baseball club that also served as a mutual aid society within the city with the largest African American population in the United States (Lomax, 2003). African American interest in baseball was such that the Pythians were able to play up to 20 games per season against regional African American competition and turn a small profit (Lomax, 2003). Despite fan support for the club, the Pythians were limited in their ability to establish their own stadium in Philadelphia, as racial hostility, particularly between Philadelphia's White Irish and African American communities, often forced the club to play its games in South Jersey or across the city at the home grounds of the Athletics Baseball Club of Philadelphia (Lomax, 2003; Rothenberg, n.d.). The

---

[*] Charleston's Negro League stats are provided as an indicator of his playing dominance, as exact statistics for Negro League contests were rarely kept.

governance structure of modern baseball further limited opportunities for the Pythians and other African American baseball clubs to operate in the sport's mainstream.

The combination of local interest in the Pythians, growing desire in the African American community to see the team play the best available competition, and the Civil Rights–focused leadership of the Pythians contributed to the team's decision to petition for access into the White-controlled National Association of Base Ball Players (NABBP) and the Pennsylvania Association of Amateur Base Ball Players. The Pythians were denied admission into both organizations on racial grounds (Lomax, 2003; Rothenberg, n.d.; Whirty, 2015). White control of league memberships and facility ownership exacerbated the social and economic divides that existed between African American and White baseball clubs and later professional teams within the social and economic realities of the United States (Lomax, 2014). The system of formal, legal segregation established following the 1896 U.S. Supreme Court's *Plessy v. Ferguson* decision underscored the de facto separation of African American and White communities existing in free states that created a burgeoning African American urban economy. Though growing, that economy was limited in terms of its overall buying power compared to the larger White population (Lomax, 2014; Ribowsky, 1995). Therefore, while African American baseball entrepreneurs were able to form professional teams and had access to players excluded from Major League Baseball by the organization's color barrier, these entrepreneurs lacked the necessary resources to build the large, permanent, steel, and concrete facilities of the Major Leagues (Lomax, 2014; Seifried & Pastore, 2009).

During the early 1900s, the availability of relatively inexpensive steel and concrete, coupled with improved construction methods, created the conditions for individuals to erect baseball stadiums to a size, scale, and level of permanence not previously possible (Seifried & Pastore, 2009). Despite control of the stadium and its events calendar, the mostly middle-class makeup of stadium and Major League owners contributed to the desire to increase the profitability of their facilities by holding as many events as possible (Seifried & de Wilde, 2014; Veeck & Linn, 1962). Major League owners such as Charles Ebbets (Brooklyn Dodgers) and Charles Comiskey (Chicago White Sox) rented their stadia to Negro League teams in the early 1900s (Lomax, 2014; Ribowsky, 1995). The financial incentive of operating as many profitable events in stadiums as possible became more overt during the Great Depression.

Limited disposable income and opportunities for leisure spending brought on by the Great Depression spurred stadium owners to pursue new, profitable events (Seifried & Pastore, 2009). During the 1930s, Major League owners entered business agreements with Negro League owners and promoters to open dates in Major League facilities for regular season and all-star competition (Ribowsky, 1995). The involvement of White middle-man promoters in African American professional sport was not uncommon. Jess McMahon, the patriarch of the McMahon professional wrestling family, operated African American baseball and basketball teams before taking a promoter position at Tex Rickard's Madison Square Garden (Kuska, 2004). Similarly, Harlem Globetrotters founder Abe Saperstein and Philadelphia Sphas operator Eddie Gottlieb negotiated rental agreements on behalf of Negro League teams (Ribowsky, 1995). Facilities like Griffith Stadium, Yankee Stadium, and Comiskey Park hosted successful and profitable Negro League events. In 1942, Yankee Stadium made $100,000 ($1,577,963.19 in 2019) by hosting Negro League games, with Negro League teams clearing $16,000 ($252,474.11 in 2019) (Ribowsky, 1995). Beyond regular-season games, the Negro League East-West All-Star Game events were famously held at Comiskey Park beginning in 1933. Those events outdrew the Major League All-Star Game in 1938, 1942, 1943, and 1946, respectively (Ribowsky, 1995).

The importance of profitability and financial health of their business to White stadium operators cannot be overstated. Plainly, White owners were not concerned with the financial health of their African American counterparts. The profit split between the New York Yankees and their Negro League renters in 1942 illustrates this point. Economic disparities between the White and African American communities created a sometimes troubling reliance by Negro League teams on the Major Leagues. Attempting to operate outside of the White sport apparatus during the Great Depression had dire economic implications for Negro League teams, as games played in parks operated by African American owners could generate total profits as low as $12 (less than $200 in contemporary dollars) for a single game. In addition to relying on White professional baseball for the survival of their business, the use of Major League stadiums gave scouts ample opportunity to identify inexpensive talent to whom they could offer contracts, as the impending desegregation of Major League Baseball seemed certain following World War II (Ribowksy, 1995).

Ultimately, the system under which the Negro Leagues operated to maintain financial viability through the 1940s ceded control over the fate of the league and its players to White-owned Major League Baseball. The exploitation and later decimation of the Negro Leagues during the mid-20th century, and the role iconic Major League stadia played in providing the setting for the demise of the Negro Leagues, is noticeably absent from the broad narrative of the desegregation of Major League Baseball. It is also missing from the pride in the heritage of Major League teams and on the legacies of their iconic facilities.

Summary and Conclusion

On February 9, 1971, Satchel Paige became the first player selected for recognition by the Baseball Hall of Fame specifically for his accomplishments in the Negro Leagues. The announcement of Paige's recognition came days after Bowie Kuhn, the commissioner of Major League Baseball, announced that professional baseball players who played at least 10 years in the Negro Leagues would be eligible for recognition by the Baseball Hall of Fame (Rathet, 1971). Interestingly, any Negro League players selected for recognition by the Hall of Fame would not be official inductees because induction into the museum required that a player's career last a minimum of 10 seasons in the Major Leagues ("Paige becomes first," 1971). Kuhn supported this restriction because "through no fault of their own these stars of the Negro leagues didn't have major league exposure" (Rathet, 1971, p. 28). Therefore, players who were denied the opportunity to participate in Major League Baseball because of their race were being offered a separate and unequal place in a museum honoring the history of the game.

Although Satchel Paige had previously voiced his frustrations regarding the racial restrictions of Major League Baseball during his athletic prime, he accepted the recognition by the Hall of Fame, stating, "I'm proud wherever they put me in the Hall of Fame" ("Paige becomes first," 1971, p. 13). Despite Paige's apparent contentment with being honored in any fashion by the Hall of Fame, the public backlash against the segregation of Paige within the Hall led Kuhn and Hall of Fame president Paul Kirk to announce in July 1971 that Paige and all future inductees from the Negro Leagues would be honored as full members of the Hall of Fame ("Baseball's front door," 1971). Following the announcement that Paige and his fellow Negro League stars would be full members of the Hall of Fame, Paige admitted that his previous comments about being proud of his special recognition were not honest, stating, "I was just going along with the program and I didn't have no kick or no say when they put me in that separate wing" (Verigan, 1971, p. 35).

Paige's observation about his lack of input in the Hall of Fame's decisions was an astute commentary on nearly a century of experiences in African American professional baseball. While there was elite talent capable of playing and excelling at the Major League level, access and recognition to the Major Leagues and its stadia was controlled and dictated by the White ownership and leadership of Major League Baseball. Indeed, the power imbalances present at the highest levels of professional baseball during the first three quarters of the 20th century were rooted in the discriminatory practices of the National Association of Base Ball Players and the Pennsylvania Association of Amateur Base Ball Players (Lomax, 2003; Rothenberg, n.d.; Whirty, 2015). Economic disparities within the United States afforded the middle-class owners of professional baseball clubs the opportunity to leverage their access to resources in order to secure favorable terms for modern facility construction in the early 20th century (Lomax, 2014). Control of modern facilities allowed White owners to influence and exploit the financial health and public perception of rival professional leagues for their benefit. That control still existed more than two decades after the desegregation of Major League Baseball by Jackie Robinson and Larry Doby in 1947.

As objects of tangible immovable sport heritage, baseball stadiums in communities across the United States play a significant role in maintaining the history of heroes, organizations, fans, and community members. Throughout the existence of the Negro Leagues, African American baseball heroes performed outstanding athletic feats in Major League Baseball stadiums owned by middle-class White entrepreneurs. In an attempt to maintain heritage, and financially capitalize on the stadiums' histories, contemporary team owners and managers evoke historic moments and players throughout their modern facilities with photos, plaques, halls of fame, and other physical monuments. This is an attempt to more strongly connect the fans to organizations' and stadiums' pasts. However, the physical representations of heroes and greatness across modern ballparks overwhelmingly represent historic White baseball players, excluding current and past African American members of local communities.[*] This culturally selected representation is a defining feature of both dissonant heritage and Authorized Heritage Discourse, as well as the politics of memory. African American

---

[*] Several parks across Major League Baseball have statues and monuments to African American players (e.g., Jackie Robinson in Dodger Stadium). However, the majority of Negro League players, especially from early years, are largely forgotten.

communities have parallel interpretations of the structures as representing physical and cultural barriers, whereas White communities can celebrate achievements of their White heroes within "hallowed halls." The stadiums and teams are predominantly owned and operated by White upper-class tycoons, which has authorized baseball's heritage to be celebrated as that of White players in the past. In order to best represent the history of baseball's constructed spaces, appropriate, permanent homages must be established to celebrate the achievements of Negro League greats in baseball heritage.

References

Another Finley gimmick-A's sign Satchel Paige (1965, September 11). *Chillicothe Constitution Tribune*, p. 5.

A's install rockin' chair (1965, September 16). *The Anderson Herald*, p. 14.

Bairner, A. (2015). The Stockholm and Helsinki Olympic stadia as living memorials. In R. Holt & D. Ruta (Eds.), *Routledge handbook of sport and legacy* (pp. 120–130). London: Routledge.

Baseball's front door opens to Satchel Paige (1971, July 8). *New York Times*, p. 45.

Broeg, B. (1965, September 28). Paige could pitch forever and coach, too. *St. Louis Post-Dispatch*, p. 5C.

Gammon, S. (2011). "Sporting" new attractions? The commodification of the sleeping stadium. In R. Sharpley & P. Stone (Eds.), *Tourism experience, Contemporary perspectives* (pp. 115–126). London: Routledge.

Gordon, K. O. (2013). Emotion and memory in nostalgia sport tourism: Examining the attraction to postmodern ballparks through an interdisciplinary lens. *Journal of Sport & Tourism, 18*, 217–239.

Graham, B., Ashworth, G. J., & Tunbridge, J. E. (2000). A geography of heritage: Power, culture and economy. London: Routledge.

Graham, B., Ashworth, G. J., & Tunbridge, J. E. (2005). The uses and abuses of heritage. In G. Corsane (Ed.), *Heritage, museums, and galleries: An introductory reader* (pp. 26–37). London: Routledge.

Grundy, P., & Rader, B. G. (2015). *American sports: From the age of folk games to the age of televised sports* (7th ed.). London: Routledge.

Harris, J. (2016, November 1). Is there no place in Pittsburgh for Negro League all-stars? *The Undefeated*. https://theundefeated.com/features/is-there-no-place-in-pittsburgh-for-negro-league-all-stars/

Kuska, B. (2004). *Hot potato: How Washington and New York gave birth to black basketball and changed America's game forever*. Charlottesville: University of Virginia Press.

Lomax, M. E. (2003). *Black baseball entrepreneurs, 1860–1901: Operating by any means necessary*. Syracuse, NY: Syracuse University Press.

Lomax, M. E. (2014). *Black baseball entrepreneurs, 1902–1931: The Negro National and Eastern colored leagues*. Syracuse, NY: Syracuse University Press.

Maennig, W. & du Plessis, S. (2009). Sport stadia, sporting events and urban development: International experience and the ambitions of Durban. *Urban Forum, 20,* 61–67.

Mason, D. S., Duquette, G. H., & Scherer, J. (2005). Heritage, sport tourism and Canadian junior hockey: Nostalgia for social experience or sport place? *Journal of Sport Tourism, 10,* 253–271.

McGuff J. (1965, September 11). Athletics can't believe it. *The Kansas City Star,* p. 33.

McKercher, B., Ho., P. S. Y., & du Cros, H. (2005). Relationship between tourism and cultural heritage management: Evidence from Hong Kong. *Tourism Management, 26,* 539–548.

Paige becomes first 'special' inductee (1971, February 10). *Jefferson City Post Tribune,* p. 13.

Peterson, R. (1992). *Only the ball was white: A history of legendary black players and all-black professional teams.* New York: Oxford University Press.

Pfleegor, A. G., Seifried, C. S., & Soebbing, B. P. (2013). The moral obligation to preserve heritage through sport and recreation facilities. *Sport Management Review, 16,* 378–387.

Ramshaw, G. (2020). *Heritage and sport: An introduction.* Bristol: Channel View Publications.

Ramshaw, G., & Gammon, S. (2005). More than just nostalgia? Exploring the heritage/sport tourism nexus. *Journal of Sport Tourism, 10,* 229–241.

Ramshaw, G., & Gammon, S. (2010). On home ground? Twickenham stadia tours and the construction of sport heritage. *Journal of Heritage Tourism, 5,* 87–102.

Ramshaw, G., & Gammon, S. (2017). Towards a critical sport heritage: Implications for sport tourism. *Journal of Sport & Tourism, 2,* 115–131.

Rathet, M. (1971, February 4). Negro diamond stars may get recognition in Hall of Fame. *The Cumberland News,* p. 28.

Renan, E. (1998). What is a nation? In C. Christie (Ed.), *Race and nation* (pp. 39–48). London: Tauris.

Ribowsky, M. (1995). *A complete history of the Negro Leagues, 1884–1955.* Secaucus, NJ: Carol Publishing.

Rosentraub, M. S., & Ijla, A. (2008). Sport facilities as social capital. In M. Nicholson & R. Hove (Eds.), *Sport and Social Capital* (pp. 339–358). Burlington, MA: Elsevier.

Rothenberg, M. (n.d.). Fighting for equality on the baseball grounds. *National Baseball Hall of Fame.* https://baseballhall.org/discover/octavius-catto-philadelphia-black-baseball

Salute to the Negro Leagues (n.d.). *Kansas City Royals.* https://www.mlb.com/royals/tickets/specials/salute-negro-leagues

Satch can't forget those lost years (1965, September 29). *The Kansas City Times,* p. 12.

Schmidt, R. (2007). *Shaping college football: The transformation of an American sport, 1919–1930.* Syracuse, NY: Syracuse University Press.

Schwester, M. (2007). An examination of the public good externalities of professional athletic venues: Justifications for public financing? *Public Budgeting & Finance, 27*(3), 89–109.

Seifried, C. S. (2010). The evolution of professional baseball and football structures in the United States, 1850 to the present: Toward an ideal type. *Sport History Review, 41,* 50–80.

Seifried, C. S., & de Wilde, A. (2014). Building the Garden and making arena sports big time: "Tex" Rickard and his legacy in sport marketing. *Journal of Macromarketing, 34,* 452–470.

Seifried, C. S., & Meyer, K. (2010). Nostalgia-related aspects of professional sport facilities: A facility audit of Major League Baseball and National Football League strategies to evoke the past. *International Journal of Sport Management, Recreation, & Tourism, 5,* 51–76.

Seifried, C. S., & Pastore, D. (2009). Analyzing the first permanent professional baseball and football structures in the United States: How expansion and renovation changed them into jewel boxes. *Sport History Review, 40,* 167–196.

Smith, L. (2006). *Uses of heritage.* London: Routledge.

Smith, L., & Waterton, E. (2012). Constrained by commonsense: The authorized heritage discourse in contemporary debates. In R. Skeates, C. McDavid, & J. Carman (Eds.), *The Oxford handbook of public archeology* (pp. 153–171). New York: Oxford University Press.

Trumpbour, R. C. (2007). *The new cathedrals: Politics and media in the history of stadium construction.* Syracuse, NY: Syracuse University Press.

Tunbridge, J. E., & Ashworth, G. J. (1996). *The management of the past as a resource in conflict.* Chichester: Wiley.

van Valkenburg, J. (1965, September 27). *Moberly Monitor Index & Evening Democrat,* p. 8.

Veeck, B., & Linn, E. (1962). *Veeck as in wreck: The autobiography of Bill Veeck.* Chicago: University of Chicago Press.

Verigan, W. (1971, July 8). Legendary Satchel Paige given full "Hall" honors. *The Cumberland News,* p. 35.

Whirty, R. (2015, February 19). Philadelphia Pythians made baseball history in 1800s. *The Philadelphia Inquirer.* https://www.inquirer.com/philly/sports/phillies/Philadelphias_Pythians_made_baseball_history_in_1800s.html

Wright, R. W. (2012). Stadia, identity and belonging: Stirring the sleeping giants of sports tourism. In R. Shipway & A. Fyall (Eds.), *International sports events* (pp. 195–207). London: Routledge.

Zhang, C. X., Xiao, H., Morgan, N. & Ly, T. P. (2018). Politics of memories: Identity construction in museums. *Annals of Tourism Research, 73,* 116–130.

6

The Historicization of a Heritage Icon

The Three Ages of Oriole Park at Camden Yards

GREGORY RAMSHAW AND SEAN GAMMON

Oriole Park at Camden Yards (OPCY), home of Major League Baseball's (MLB) Baltimore Orioles, opened in 1992 and quickly became the template for new baseball stadiums across the United States. Unlike other multiuse stadiums constructed in the 1960s through the 1980s, OPCY was built only for baseball and, most notably, the heritage features of other historic baseball parks were employed in its design. This heritage—or "retro" design—included an asymmetrical field, a brick stadium facade, wrought iron railings in the seating areas and, most prominently, it also included the existing Baltimore & Ohio Railway warehouse. The warehouse was constructed in 1899, left largely derelict by the 1970s, but was renovated and now houses retail businesses and commercial offices—as part of its design (Figure 6.1). This ballpark also became an anchor for the redevelopment of Baltimore's Inner Harbor, creating a kind of tourist bubble which since has been replicated in many other post-industrial American cities. The OPCY has been much discussed—and, to a degree, derided—in academic literature, particularly as a postmodern pastiche of baseball nostalgia as well as a simulacrum for other retro/nostalgia-inspired baseball stadium projects in the United States. OPCY-inspired stadium projects became so prevalent that subsequent stadium projects were said to have become "Camdenized." In recent years, stadium design—most prominently, Marlins Park in Miami—actively rejected the OPCY "retro" model and, as such, fewer new baseball stadia appear to reference OPCY aesthetic themes (Ramshaw, 2020).

While the OPCY model reflects a relatively recent shift in baseball stadium design, OPCY is now approaching its 30th year in operation. In fact, it is now among the oldest MLB stadia in use, given that many clubs

Figure 6.1. The Baltimore and Ohio (B&O) Railway warehouse at Oriole Park at Camden Yards. Photo by Gregory Ramshaw.

have moved into new venues in the past quarter century. While the design of OPCY borrowed heritage from other baseball stadia from around the United States (Ramshaw et al., 2013), Baltimore has a long history of baseball and, in many ways, OPCY simply reinterprets existing local heritage at a new venue—as many new stadia do, particularly when housing historic teams (Belanger, 2000). Given its decades of service, OPCY has also created its own historic moments and heritage, many of which are displayed throughout the ballpark. As such, a reassessment of OPCY is in order. In many respects, OPCY is entering a third phase in its history—not as a postmodern pastiche or a simulacrum for other retro ballparks, but as a historic baseball stadium in its own right. This chapter therefore explores the three ages of OPCY and wonders whether OPCY will soon attract attention and reinterpretation because of its age and history as much as its heritage design.

The First Age of OPCY: The Postmodern Retro Ballpark

OPCY opened on April 6, 1992, and its design was remarkably new, yet completely familiar—or, as it was described at the time, "brand new, but still old-fashioned . . . at less than a day old, it was already a classic" (Baltimore Orioles, 2020, n.p.). The ballpark's design was a meant to be an homage to baseball's past—and, in particular, a reference to numerous beloved, historic ballparks—while also being contemporary and comfortable, particularly in terms of the spectator experience. The Orioles organization described OPCY as

> state-of-the-art, yet unique, traditional and intimate in design. It blends with the urban context of downtown Baltimore while taking its image from baseball parks built in the early 20th century. Steel, rather than concrete trusses, an arched brick facade, a sun roof over the gentle slope of the upper deck, an asymmetrical playing field, and natural grass turf are just some of the features that tie it to those magnificent big league ballparks built in the early 1900s. Ebbets Field (Brooklyn), Shibe Park (Philadelphia), Fenway Park (Boston), Crosley Field (Cincinnati), Forbes Field (Pittsburgh), Wrigley Field (Chicago), and The Polo Grounds (New York) were among the ballparks that served as powerful influences in the design of Oriole Park. (Baltimore Orioles, 2020, n.p.)

OPCY also served as the anchor of Baltimore's Inner Harbor redevelopment, specifically helping to transform the city's derelict city center into a desirable leisure space for both local residents and tourists alike—what Judd and Fainstein (1999) termed a "tourist bubble," where tourism amenities (accommodations, shopping, entertainment, etc.) are within a safe, condensed space, often within a community's urban core. As Chapin (2004) noted OPCY quickly became one of the city must-see attractions—even on non-event days. During the early years of OPCY, in particular from 1992 through 1999, games were regularly sold out—a significant feat, given that MLB teams such as the Orioles host at least 81 home games each season (plus any post-season matches). Furthermore, attendance remained strong following the 1994 MLB labor dispute, which saw the 1994 World Series being cancelled and attendance drop 20 percent league-wide in 1995 (Burns & Novack, 2010). Besides baseball fans—many of which were tourists visiting the city—flocking to experience OPCY itself, attendance was also helped by the consecutive games streak of Cal Ripken Jr. Specifically, on September 6, 1995, Ripken Jr. played in his 2,131st consecutive game, breaking Lou

Gehrig's seemingly unbreakable record (Ripken Jr.'s streak finally ended on September 20, 1998, at 2,632 consecutive games). The Orioles were also regularly a competitive team, which likely also helped to sustain interest in OPCY's early years.

Although OPCY was undoubtedly popular during much of its first decade, it was also derided for being little more than a pastiche of uncritical and decontextualized baseball nostalgia. As Friedman et al. (2004) argued, OPCY "randomly cannibalizes the past, as storied signifiers are torn from their spatial and temporal moorings and are unselfconsciously juxtaposed in a pastiche of postmodern baseball historicism" (p. 128). Furthermore, OPCY perhaps used nostalgia-based design as a palliative intervention—in other words, the nostalgia experience provided at OPCY was used to paste over the challenges of baseball's past and present and provide spectators with an uncomplicated view of baseball's glorious past. Ritzer and Stillman (2001) further contended that postmodern ballparks like OPCY are little more than a temporal imitation rendering an imprecise—but highly seductive—past as a backdrop for increased consumption. Most importantly, as Goldburger (2019) noted in his reflection on OPCY's authenticity vis-à-vis historic ballparks,

> [OPCY] was not truly a return to the past at all: if it had been, it would have been far smaller, and would probably have had a third as many restrooms, scant eating options, cramped corridors, and minimal accommodations for luxury seating. The Camden Yards ballpark may have looked like an old-fashioned ballpark, but that was merely its external garb; underneath, it was very much the product of modern baseball. (p. 217)

Ultimately, OPCY employed the aesthetics of baseball's past as a way of creating the new Major League Baseball stadium. According to its critics, a highly romanticized and sanitized view of baseball's past was used at OPCY, not as a representation of baseball history but merely as a commodity. As such, while OPCY was undoubtedly popular in its first age—perhaps driven by its design, although there were certainly other factors at play, such as the consecutive games streak and the overall performance of the team—its references to the past were perhaps unearned. It was the epitome of Hewison's (1989) critique of many heritage products—that it had been "antiqued" to give a sense of *gravitas* it simply did not possess.

The Second Age of OPCY: Simulacrum and Camdenization

The perceived popularity and success of OPCY led to the ballpark becoming a simulacrum of sorts, with it being recognized as the "true copy" for other stadia and urban redevelopment initiatives (Goldberger, 2019). Within a decade, numerous other American cities sought to replicate the Baltimore model, including employing the same architect and retro style of OPCY and enticing similar retail services, tourism amenities, and attractions to their tourist bubbles (Mason et al., 2008). Even truly historic stadia—such as Boston's Fenway Park, which opened in 1912—began to replicate some of the features of OPCY, including replicating the Eutaw Street public promenade (Figure 6.2) as well as incorporating more nostalgia and retro-themed atmospherics in the stadium (Friedman & Silk, 2005; Friedman, 2007). The so-called Camdenization of ballparks, where retro designs became the norm, as well as the accompanying tourism development around the stadium, meant that OPCY and Baltimore's Inner Harbor were no longer unique destinations (Lamster, 2009; Petchesky, 2012). By 2012 and the opening of Marlin's Park in Miami (now LoanDepot Park)—which was flashy, colorful, a bit garish, and viewed as a rebuke of the OPCY aesthetic—the retro ballpark movement and the era of "Camdenization" appeared to be over (Byrnes, 2012; Wiedman, 2012). As Petchesky (2012) noted on the 20th anniversary of its opening, OPCY had become just another ballpark and was no longer an essential destination—for baseball fans and non-fans alike—like Chicago's Wrigley Field or Boston's Fenway Park.

Indeed, from 2002 onward, OPCY certainly appeared to become just another ballpark, at least in terms of attendance. In 2002, the team failed to draw over three million fans per season to OPCY for the first time, and since 2006 the team has rarely averaged over 30,000 fans per game (the lone exception being in 2014, when the team had one of the best records in baseball). At the end of the 2019 season, when the Orioles won only 54 of 162 games, the team averaged just over 16,000 spectators per game in the 46,000-seat ballpark (ESPN, 2019) In fact, 2019 marked the lowest attended season in OPCY's history and included the lowest attended game ever at OPCY, when a paid attendance of 6,585 was announced for a game versus Oakland on April 8 (Meoli, 2019). Given that OPCY became just one of many retro-themed stadia in the United States, not to mention the poor on-field performance of the baseball team, it is not surprising that OPCY has not attracted spectators as it once did. In recent years, Baltimore has also had challenges with crime and negative perceptions of the city (MacGillis,

Figure 6.2. Eutaw Street promenade at Oriole Park at Camden Yards. Photo by Gregory Ramshaw.

2019), which in turn have impacted the city's destination image and economy (Yeager, 2018). Furthermore, since OPCY was built, Baltimore reacquired an NFL franchise in 1996 who play at M&T Bank Stadium (adjacent to OPCY) and who have had recent success (winning the Super Bowl twice, including most recently in 2013). As such, OPCY appears to be just another retro stadium, rather than the "original retro," in a country filled with similar heritage-themed downtown baseball parks, housing a team with little success and few star players (and certainly none becoming as widely known as Cal Ripken Jr.), in a city that has well-publicized social and economic problems and whose residents have a winning team in a different sport to support.

The Third Age of OPCY: An Emerging Historic Ballpark?

As of 2020, OPCY is the 21st oldest ballpark in MLB, with the tenants of two older stadia (Oakland and Tampa) currently looking to replace their current homes, though two of MLB's stadia (in Chicago and Boston) are over a century old. It is therefore safe to say that OPCY exists in a state of liminality—older than many of its peers, but still new enough not to be considered a beloved historic stadium. Couple this with the fact that the Orioles do not have a national or international fanbase in the same way as the New York Yankees, Chicago Cubs, Boston Red Sox, and Los Angeles Dodgers do (all of whom play in much-loved and, in some cases, historic stadia), and it is not surprising that Baltimore is not on the same level—particularly in terms of tourism, investment, and media attention—of these much more famous cities. Add to this that the Orioles are currently in a period of poor on-field performance; it seems unlikely that, in the short term, OPCY will be a significant lure in attracting spectators.

However, given its longevity, perhaps OPCY is becoming that which it initially sought to imitate: namely, a historic ballpark. It has clearly had a significant influence on urban architecture in the United States (Goldberger, 2019), although it will likely require several decades for its historic value to be truly assessed. More importantly, OPCY has generated its own history quite apart from the historic stadia it sought to emulate. The aforementioned consecutive games streak of Cal Ripken Jr. was one of OPCY's most famous moments, with several historic markers of Ripken's achievement sprinkled throughout the stadium. The pedestrian promenade on Eutaw Street also marks with permanent historic plaques the home-run balls that landed on the street—including, most famously, the only ball to hit the B&O warehouse (Figure 6.3). OPCY was also not a blank slate; like other stadia, it inherited the history and heritage of its predecessor (Belanger, 2000). Baltimore had an important historical connection to baseball before OPCY, and this relationship is reflected throughout the stadium in billboards, plaques, and statues. As such, OPCY could be viewed as a repository for Baltimore's baseball history and heritage, as well as the place where these pasts are performed in the present and future. OPCY history intersected with broader historic moments in the city—most notably, the 2015 protests in response to the death of Freddie Gray, a 25-year-old man who sustained injuries while in custody of the Baltimore Police Department. Reflecting Ramshaw and Gammon's (2005) discussion of "sport as heritage" (where sporting people and events transcend the sports themselves), due to the 2015 protests the Orioles played their April 29 game at OPCY behind closed doors—the first time this occurred in MLB history (Cowherd, 2019) (though empty ballparks would later become a familiar sight during the coronavirus pandemic). Of course, the Orioles could become competitive again in the future, generating future heritage memories and moments at OPCY.

Figure 6.3. Commemorative plaque at Oriole Park at Camden Yards. Photo by Gregory Ramshaw.

It may be some time before OPCY is perceived as historic, but it is important to note that this point may not be as distant as one might think. Official heritage agencies at both the international and national levels have recognized that the preservation of built sport heritage, such as stadia and other sporting venues, is an important part of contemporary heritage conservation. As Ramshaw (2020) noted, international heritage agencies such as the International Council on Monuments and Sites (ICOMOS) recently recognized the heritage of sport as important to conserve, while national agencies such as the National Trust for Historic Preservation (NTHP) and the National Register of Historic Places (NRHP) have been active in the preservation of numerous built sport heritage sites, including Boston's Fenway Park (current home of the Boston Red Sox), the Astrodome in Houston (former home of the Houston Astros), and Hinchliffe Stadium in New Jersey (former Negro Leagues baseball stadium). To qualify for historic designation through organizations such as NTHP, a built structure must be at least 50 years old—a mark OPCY will hit in 2042, and it is certainly possible that the stadium will survive until this date and beyond. It is also important to note that many other historic stadia were not always treasured and went through several stages of public perception before becoming irreplaceable icons. Wrigley Field in Chicago, for example, went through several phases— including being perceived as an ultra-modern stadium through much of its life, to being considered a decrepit liability in the 1970s and 1980s, to now being the historic and beloved home of the Chicago Cubs (Shea, 2014). In the 1990s, the Red Sox strongly considered replacing Fenway Park (Friedman & Silk, 2005), arguing that the historic park was not generating enough revenue. Whether OPCY will soon be considered on the same level as these historic ballparks has yet to be seen. However, should it continue to host ball games summer after summer for decades to come, it may emerge into historic status—both in terms of protective status and public perception.

Discussion

It is tempting to over-intellectualize the construction and development of OPCY; viewing it as little more than a postmodern pastiche that clumsily conflates the best of the past, softened with the comforts of the present. Some may even suggest that OPCY is inextricably moving along Baudrillard's (1988) successive phases of the image to the extreme simulacrum of hyperreality, and so offers the consumer what Gammon (2002) analogously offers as "edited highlights of a game that probably never took place" (p. 63). In short, OPCY simply exemplifies the cravings of postmodern society to experience the genuine or authentic—however overstated they may be (Eco, 1987).

Yet such cynicism should be tempered with an acknowledgment that retro ballparks provide a taste of what watching a ball game was like in the halcyon days of the sport. Moreover, they provided a welcome change from the placeless concrete bowls that had dominated many urbanscapes during the previous two decades. In this sense, OPCY (along with other retro ballparks) is not just a manifestation of a broad societal movement but a reminder of a period where people mattered more than commerce (however misplaced the sentiment). To consider the importance of OPCY today is ultimately dependent upon its perceived value. As Caple (2009) succinctly observed when discussing heritage: "societies retain objects because they have value for the members of that society" (p. 25). The question, then, is quite straightforward: what value(s) does OPCY have for both the baseball community and society in general? Clearly, to identify and potentially operationalize values is no easy task, a point summarized by Fredheim and Khalaf (2016) when exploring the manner in which value is utilized in heritage designation. For values can be subjective constructs based upon opinion, as well as being multidimensional, tangible, intangible—and, unsurprisingly, highly contested. Clearly, OPCY is some distance from achieving heritage status, but this should not curtail discussions relating to its current and future value. If we are to explore the notion that OPCY has entered its third age, then we must at least attempt to consider where its potential values lie—however diverse. As discussed in the previous section, the development of the ballpark can be viewed broadly in economic, cultural, and experiential terms, which in turn may act as starting points to assess its current value.

From a cultural perspective, it could be argued that OPCY is nothing more than a romanticized facsimile of older parks and, as such, holds little value. There is, after all, very little that is authentic about a venue that solely relies on salient markers from other ballparks. Yet over the last three decades, it has created its own history that exemplifies an emergent authenticity, which equates to more intrinsic value and verisimilitude (Cohen, 1998). Not only have great games and important players graced the natural turf, but the structure itself has also begun to age naturally. Moreover, the park is an integral component of the Inner Harbor development (Friedman et al., 2004) and could be viewed as one of Baltimore's hallmark venues. While its architectural style is easy to dismiss as commodified faux heritage, spawned by a mixture of nostalgia and sound investment, it belies the notion that it represents an example of a 1920s revivalist style that provided (and continues to provide) solace for countless fans. It also gives visitors, both young and old, a sense of how watching a game was experienced in the past, irrespective of how manufactured an experience that may be. OPCY is a tangible representation of a time when baseball reached out and gripped onto a past that was thought to be lost. OPCY may be a copy—but it is the original copy that contains cultural values that celebrate the history of the game, as well as personal and collective meanings to those who visit.

Providing experiences has always been an important component of stadium design—though the focus of such provision has evolved from the strictly utilitarian structures of the past through to the commodified, consumerist priorities provided in many modern stadia (Lisle, 2017). The experiences offered by retro ballparks ostensibly moved the emphasis away from secondary consumption, directing attention to the experience of place.

However, such laudable sentiments ignore the fact OPCY was designed as a money-making venture, as its 61 luxury suites attest to—not to mention the numerous opportunities for commerce within and surrounding the stadium. Nevertheless, the carefully patinated exterior, complete with retro-styled advertising and distressed signage, accelerates notions of place and place attachment—an important attribute of numerous important sports structures (Gaffney & Bale, 2004; Higham & Hinch, 2009; Gammon, 2015). It must be remembered that many fans of the Orioles have only known the current park as their home ground, so there exists a deep attachment that transcends the nostalgic features that draw in visitors and tourists. This is of course no different from other ballparks, but it reminds us that the relationship that Baltimore's fans have with the park is different from those who come to experience the traditional environment that it offers. Therefore, the experiential values of OPCY are entwined with meaning, memory, and belonging—qualities that significantly add to the lives of many who visit. Yet to assess the cumulative values of such experiences is problematic, primarily due to their intangible nature and the interpretivist approaches that grade them.

In contrast, the economic values that the park offers would appear to be more straightforward. However, judgments are at best discordant, with local politicians unsurprisingly viewing the Inner Harbor development as a positive example of successful urban renewal (Baltimore Mayor Bernard "Jack" Young), while others view it as either partially successful (Chapin, 2004) or as a largely ineffective use of public funds (Friedman et al., 2004). The chief concerns over the development are that it has created a tourist bubble that contains economic investment, with all its benefits, to only one area of the city. Meanwhile, other parts of Baltimore still suffer from poor education, high crime rates, and uneven health care. This disparity highlights the limited reach of the Inner Harbor development with some believing that OPCY is complicit to such inequality, as it "represents a disingenuous abdication of the city's responsibility to its citizens" (Friedman et al., 2004, p. 134).

In an anthropomorphic sense, OPCY is slowly becoming that which it desired to be—a historic ballpark. And while it might be tempting to view this process as a steady march toward broad heritage recognition and adoration, it is not a foregone conclusion that OPCY will become a "venerated old ballpark" like Fenway Park or Wrigley Field. As was discussed in this chapter, many beloved historic ballparks—including both Fenway and Wrigley—were at various points in their histories seen as outmoded, inadequate, and replaceable, and it has only been in recent years that they have been viewed as irreplaceable and priceless baseball heirlooms. Heritage and the meanings we put into places are not fixed; they change and are inexorably dynamic. Of course, both of these historic ballparks required significant renovations which blended historical importance and aesthetics with contemporary sport consumption and spectator expectations. Indeed, the use of heritage aesthetics in OPCY's design was in large part a commercial decision; it used something old to create a new spectator experience. OPCY will likely be renovated in the coming years, and current plans appear to mirror those of other heritage-style ballparks: upgrade the spectator amenities while maintaining the historic charm (Reichard, 2020). Of course, renovations of OPCY—particularly significant ones—place the ballpark in a "ship of Theseus" conundrum (Scaltsas, 1980): how much of the original stadium should need remain to still be considered the same historic ballpark? Perhaps a larger threat, however, would come should OPCY not generate enough revenue, or be viewed as outmoded; it could also be replaced by a newer ballpark. While this appears to be unlikely, two MLB ballparks built *after* OPCY (in Arlington, Texas, and in Atlanta, Georgia) have been replaced, and most MLB ballparks do not reach 50 years of use (and eligibility for historic protection). In fact, as of 2020, only five MLB ballparks are 50 years or older. In addition, the portability of sports franchises in the United States should not be overlooked. Should another city—perhaps with a lucrative stadium deal—lure the Orioles away, the future of OPCY would be in doubt. Again, though this is unlikely, it cannot be ruled out as the Orioles have gone through a number of tense lease negotiations over the years (Reichard, 2020). And as Baltimore sports fans know all too well—given the surprise move of the Colts NFL franchise from Baltimore to Indianapolis in 1984—sports franchises in the United States are not wedded to their cities of origin. Ultimately, the three ages of OPCY demonstrate the malleable nature of heritage and, perhaps more importantly, that heritage commodification and heritage restoration/preservation are sometimes not in concert with one another. What may have been a saleable and desirable form of heritage in the 1990s may no longer be the lure it once was. And yet, while the design of OPCY was certainly more of an economic than a cultural decision, the commercial uses of baseball heritage and nostalgia in the 1990s now have conservation and preservation implications into the 2020s and beyond.

Conclusion

As OPCY enters its fourth decade of use, it is important to assess its legacy. Indeed, its architectural legacy cannot be denied—it was the template for many ballparks (both MLB and smaller, Minor League Baseball stadiums) and urban redevelopment initiatives across the United States—though how this architectural movement will ultimately be judged remains to be seen. The critique of its decontextualized use of baseball's past remains, although through its own age and historic moments it is no longer a new ballpark. As such, it appears to exist in a liminal state between being an agenda-setting sports venue and becoming a beloved baseball cathedral.

While it would be tempting to conclude that an assessment of the cultural and personal values of OPCY will determine its future, the reality is that its fate will be based on more prosaic considerations. Ultimately, baseball parks are visitor attractions, and if the Orioles continue to struggle, it's likely that attendance figures will too. The balance sheet will undoubtedly have the final say, but this can only be truly evaluated when the pandemic subsides and fans are once again allowed back in. However beloved OPCY may be, it needs to draw in visitor numbers that make it a viable attraction. Baltimore cannot afford, symbolically or financially, to fund a white elephant that once lay at the hub of the Camden Yards redevelopment. Consequently, the extent to which OPCY's third age will be a fruitful one is down to visitor numbers, which in turn is dependent on how the ballpark is perceived and valued. Time will tell whether the baseball community will view OPCY as an anachronistic experiment that has had its day, or as an important example of 1920s architectural revivalism that offers an insight into how the game once was—or perhaps should have been.

References

Baltimore Orioles (2020). Oriole Park at Camden Yards History. https://www.mlb.com/orioles/ballpark/information/history (accessed November 18, 2020).

Baudrillard, J. (1988). Simulacra and simulations. In M. Poster (Ed.), *Baudrillard: Selected writings,* Stanford: Stanford University Press.

Bélanger, A. (2000). Sport venues and the spectacularization of urban spaces in North America: The case of the Molson Centre in Montreal. *International Review for the Sociology of Sport,* 35(3), 378–397.

Burns, K. (director/producer), & Novick, L. (producer) (2010). *Baseball: A film by Ken Burns, the tenth inning: Top of the tenth* [motion picture]. United States: PBS Home Video.

Byrnes, M. (2012, March 30). Is the retro ballpark movement officially over? *CityLab*. https://www.citylab.com/design/2012/03/retro-ballpark-movement-officially-over/1597/ (accessed January 30, 2019).

Caple, C. (2009). The aims of conservatism. In A. Richmond & A. Braker (Eds.), *Conservation: Principles, dilemmas and uncomfortable truths* (pp. 25–31). London: Butterworth-Heinemann.

Chapin, T. S. (2004). Sports facilities as urban redevelopment catalysts: Baltimore's Camden Yards and Cleveland's Gateway. *Journal of the American Planning Association, 70*(2), 193–209.

Cohen, E. (1988). Authenticity and commoditization in tourism. *Annals of Tourism Research, 15*(3), 371–386.

Cowherd, K. (2019). *When the crowd didn't roar: How baseball's strangest game ever gave a broken city hope*. Lincoln: University of Nebraska Press.

Eco, U. (1987). *Travels in Hyper-reality*. London: Picador.

ESPN (2019). MLB Attendance Report—2019. http://www.espn.com/mlb/attendance/_/year/2019 (accessed December 1, 2019).

Fredheim, L. H., & Khalaf, M. (2016). The significance of values: Heritage value typologies re-examined. *International Journal of Heritage Studies, 22*(6), 466–481.

Friedman, M. (2007). The spectacle of the past: Leveraging history in Fenway Park and Camden Yards. In S. Gammon & G. Ramshaw (Eds.), *Heritage, sport and tourism: Sporting pasts–tourist futures* (pp. 103–122). London: Routledge.

Friedman, M. T., Andrews, D. L., & Silk, M. L. (2004). Sport and the façade of redevelopment in the postindustrial city. *Sociology of Sport Journal, 21*(2), 119–139.

Freidman, M., & Silk, M. (2005). The Camdenization of Fenway Park. *International Journal of Sport Management and Marketing, 1*(1–2), 37–55.

Gaffney, C., & Bale, J. (2004). Sensing the stadium. In P. Vertinksky & J. Bale (Eds.), *Sites of sport: Space, place, experience* (pp. 25–38). London: Routledge.

Gammon, S. (2002). Fantasy, nostalgia and the pursuit of what never was. In S. Gammon & J. Kurtzman (Eds.), *Sport tourism: Principles and practice* (pp. 61–71). Eastbourne: LSA Publications.

Gammon, S. (2015). Sport tourism finding its place? In S. Elkington & S. Gammon (Eds.), *Landscapes of leisure: Space, place and identities* (pp. 110–123). London: Palgrave Macmillan.

Goldberger, P. (2019). *Ballpark: Baseball in the American city*. New York: Knopf.

Hewison, R. (1989). Heritage: An interpretation. In David L. Uzzel (Ed.), *Heritage interpretation volume 1: The natural and built heritage* (pp. 15–23). London: Methuen.

Higham, J., & Hinch, T. (2009). *Sport and tourism: Globalization, mobility and identity*. Oxford Butterworth-Heinemann.

Judd, D. R., & Fainstein, S. S. (Eds.). (1999). *The tourist city*. New Haven, CT: Yale University Press.

Lamster, M. (2009, July 1). Play Ball. *Metropolis*. https://www.metropolismag.com/uncategorized/play-ball/ (accessed November 18, 2020).

Lisle, B. D. (2017). *Modern coliseum: Stadiums and American culture*. Philadelphia: University of Pennsylvania Press.

MacGillis, A. (2019, March 12). The Tragedy of Baltimore. *The New York Times Magazine*. https://www.nytimes.com/2019/03/12/magazine/baltimore-tragedy-crime.html (accessed November 18, 2020).

Mason, D., Ramshaw, G. & Hinch, T. (2008). Sports facilities and transnational corporations: Anchors of urban tourism development. In C. M. Hall & T. Coles (Eds.), *Tourism and international business: Global issues, contemporary interactions* (pp. 220–237). New York: Routledge.

Meoli, J. (2019, April 8). Orioles draw lowest attendance for open-admission game in Camden Yards history Monday. *The Baltimore Sun*. https://www.baltimoresun.com/sports/orioles/bs-sp-orioles-athletics-lowest-attendance-20190408-story.html (accessed November 18, 2020).

Petchesky, B. (2012, April 3). Marlins Park, Camden Yards, And The End of the Retro Ballpark. *Deadspin*. https://deadspin.com/marlins-park-camden-yards-and-the-end-of-the-retro-ba-5898747 (accessed November 18, 2020).

Ramshaw, G. (2020). *Heritage and sport: An introduction*. Bristol: Channel View Publications.

Ramshaw, G., & Gammon, S. (2005). More than just nostalgia? Exploring the heritage/sport tourism nexus. *Journal of Sport Tourism, 10*(4), 229–241.

Ramshaw, G., Gammon, S., & Huang, W. J. (2013). Acquired pasts and the commodification of borrowed heritage: The case of the Bank of America Stadium tour. *Journal of Sport & Tourism, 18*(1), 17–31.

Reichard, K. (2020, June 15). Orioles, stadium authority negotiating new Oriole Park lease. https://ballparkdigest.com/2020/06/15/orioles-stadium-authority-negotiating-new-oriole-park-lease/ (accessed November 18, 2020)

Ritzer, G., & Stillman, T. (2001). The postmodern ballpark as a leisure setting: Enchantment and simulated de-McDonaldization. *Leisure Sciences, 23*(2), 99–113.

Scaltsas, T. (1980). The ship of Theseus. *Analysis, 40*(3), 152–157.

Shea, S. (2014). *Wrigley Field: The long life and contentious times of the friendly confines*. Chicago: University of Chicago Press.

Wiedeman, R. (2012, April 6). The end of the retro ballpark. *The New Yorker*. https://www.newyorker.com/sports/sporting-scene/the-end-of-the-retro-ballpark (accessed January 30, 2019).

Yeager, A. (2018, December 27). Year in Review 2018: City's image struggles as tourism industry pushes for more visitors. https://www.bizjournals.com/baltimore/news/2018/12/27/year-in-review-2018-citys-image-struggles-as.html (accessed November 18, 2020).

7

American Baseball Museums and the Politics of Meta-Narrative

Kiernan O. Gordon

Museums arguably represent the most recognizable form of sport heritage (Ramshaw, 2020). The United States has the largest number of sport museums in the world, with more than 400, half of which have opened since the 1960s (Phillips, 2012). As of 2020, 34 baseball-specific museums exist in the United States (Reference USA, n.d.). Like other sites of cultural heritage, museums have become an essential element in the planning and design of contemporary urban spaces. This is particularly true for baseball museums in the United States, which, in recent years, have become increasingly integrated with larger redevelopment projects and/or sports venues for those cities and communities that aspire to increase tourism. The baseball museum has thus become a tool for the positioning of urban space as a sport tourism destination. Turning a critical eye toward baseball museums assists in seeing the degree to which sport heritage has become a strategy for urban placemaking, where politicians and local residents work to establish "place anchors," sites that generate emotion and memory for attendees to facilitate touristic consumption.

American Baseball Museums as Place

Implicit in these museums, and significant across all of heritage sport tourism scholarship, has been "place," a broad term that describes a physical venue or space to honor the sporting past as well as the broader architectural, geographical, sociological, and historical context(s) within which such venues and spaces are located. Place-oriented scholarship within heritage sport tourism has typically focused on the value of, for example, stadium tours (Gammon, 2004), halls of fame (Redmond, 1973; Snyder, 1991), and the aesthetic of American ballparks (Gordon, 2013) to the sport tourism experience. Place has been a sometimes central and often implicit focus of scholarship examining baseball heritage as well.

Examples of place-oriented scholarship in baseball heritage include Springwood's (1996) examination of the dynamic through which the town of Cooperstown, New York, where the Baseball Hall of Fame and Museum is located, both shapes and is shaped by the presentation of baseball heritage. Adelman (1990) argued that the increasingly modern conditions that emerged during the mid-19th century within New York City were significant in shaping the practice and administration of baseball as we know the sport today. Riess (1999) asserted that the relationship between baseball entrepreneurs, railroad magnates, and members of the urban political machine enabled the intentional design and placement of ballparks near a city's transportation hubs during the Progressive Era, which played a significant role in the consumption of baseball at that time. Place also plays a significant role in the placement and design of contemporary American baseball museums.

American Baseball Museums as Heritage

The symbols, artifacts, and narratives that are inherent to museums are perhaps more enmeshed with baseball than any other American sport. As a sport that has been linked to American nationalism, baseball museums and their materials take on symbolic meaning; their artifacts are imbued with nationally historical significance as well as sport-specific relevance. Thus, baseball museums serve as important sites of sport heritage in the United States where artifacts and symbols are aggregated and displayed for public consumption.

Museums have evolved into a "spectacular repository" in which "creative practitioners" design a compelling space that generates "meaningful experiences" for guests through physical and social engagement (Acarin & Adams, 2015, p. 69). They are not, however, homogeneous. Museums are often sites of tension where competing ideologies and values may be present among museum employees and community stakeholders, which often manifest themselves in the display of exhibitions (Davies et al., 2013). Key to yielding meaningful experiences for attendees is the role of narrative, a concept that has evolved among scholars from an emphasis on textual analyses of various forms of media, such as literature and film, to immersive, interactive environments where "narrativity" takes on a scalar-like quality of experience such that it is described according to its capacity to inspire some level of human response (Grimaldi, 2015). That is, an environment possesses more or less narrativity to the degree that it is successful in yielding desired human responses.

Similar to other forms of heritage, American baseball museums take their "cue from the grand narratives of nation and class" by constructing and regulating a range of values and understandings (Smith, 2006, p. 11) for the contemporary visitor. Scholars (Conn, 2010; Harrison, 2013; Kirshenblatt-Gimblett, 1998; Smith, 2006; Wertsch, 2002) have noted that museums influence the present through their presentation of the past, where what is perceived is considered an authentic, legitimate, and objective representation of historical "truth" (Hollinshead, 1997) in contrast to an "actively used, remade, and negotiated" (Smith, 2006, p. 34) past to suit the needs of the present. Heritage is not a passive practice of the preservation of objects from the past. Instead, it is an active process of assemblage that "hold[s] up as a mirror to the present, associated with a particular set of values that we wish to take with us into the future" (Harrison, 2013, p. 4). Those values are evident in the "heritage-making" that is on display in museums, which is intended to "address contemporary political needs and aspirations" and is not executed "simply by 'experts' and professional bodies, but by nations, groups, and individuals" (Wetherell et al., 2018, p. 9).

The Phenomenology of American Baseball Museums

The recognition that the meanings inherent to American baseball museums, like other heritage forms, are actively (re)made through cultural practice that represents and reinforces political motivations that are linked with their existence connotes a phenomenological epistemology. Consequently, a full understanding of baseball museums requires a phenomenological approach to better understand the ways in which they establish and attempt to define baseball heritage. Phenomenology is a philosophical perspective that is often linked to German philosophers Edmund Husserl and Martin Heidegger. Fundamental to phenomenology is that one must experience the world in order to develop an interpretation of it. That is, the world is devoid of meaning until we experience it and ascribe meaning to it. To view something phenomenologically, then, is to first recognize that it emerges from the status quo. Several scholars have employed phenomenology in their analyses within such place-based fields as architecture, urban studies, and geography (see, for example, Norberg-Schulz, 1980; Relph, 1976, 1981; Tuan, 1977). A theme across this stream of literature is that places are centers of meaning that are constructed out of lived experience (Relph, 1976).

A phenomenological perspective toward museums, for example, is to recognize that, while many of us encounter them on a daily basis, they are without meaning until we assign some meaning(s) to them. They have not always occupied a place in existence. Instead, they came into being. Others have argued for a phenomenological approach to the study of museums. Smith (2006), for example, did this when she asserted that what makes a place "heritage" "are the present-day cultural processes and activities that are undertaken at and around them, and of which they become a part" (p. 3). Such places are devoid of meaning. Instead, we project our own meanings of heritage onto them. In this way, museums serve an important function in society. They mediate a past that many of us have never encountered that we then interpret through our contemporary lived experience, serving as a bridge between collective recollection and individual retention (Carr, 2014).

Baseball museums are designed and made by humans. This itself is not newsworthy. A phenomenological perspective, though, requires us to conceptualize what humans designed them to accomplish. So, our task is to arrive at an understanding of why they came into being and how they have been situated to construct the meaning that we assign to them relative to baseball heritage. Consequently, we need a framework that is broad enough to assist us in accounting for any similarities that might be present among all baseball museums in the United States.

Let us begin with a very general presupposition: the purpose of American baseball museums is to inform those who visit them. To accomplish this, the artifacts, images, and symbols that fill these museums serve to tell a larger story, or they may function to tell a smaller story that fits within the museum's broader narrative. For example, the Baseball Hall of Fame and Museum in Cooperstown, New York, houses artifacts that honor notable baseball achievements, as well as enshrines those players who are deemed to be great performers in the game's history and other prominent contributors to the sport. Thus, everything within the Baseball Hall of Fame and Museum either contributes to the larger story of baseball or to the stories of individual performers, contributors, and teams that fit within this larger baseball story. There is an intentionality to the space and the contents within it.

I would like to turn our attention toward this larger story. While there may be variation across the different narratives that are present within baseball museums, our concern is with their overarching narrative, their *raison d'être*. This could be referred to as a baseball museum's "meta-narrative"; that is, the mere existence of a baseball museum is intended to tell or contribute to a story that is in accordance with baseball's historical narrative, its heritage.

Consequently, the existence of baseball museums is inherently political. They reside at the intersection of culture and politics (Conn, 2010) where their meaning is in a constant state of negotiation. Since they are human-made, their existence is intentional; they are intended to accomplish something larger than simply exposing their attendees to the artifacts, images, and symbols that exist within them to present an objective truth. They are not political in the sense that they are inherently linked with the American governmental system, political process, or political parties. Instead, American baseball museums are political in that the meta-narratives that are linked with their presence exist to accomplish specific objectives. Their administrative gatekeepers make decisions that represent, reinforce, and contest public conceptions of their subject matter while simultaneously working to satisfy consumer demands (Davies et al., 2013). These meta-narratives, then, serve as tools to accomplish specific outcomes, such as to situate the museum's subject matter as integral to baseball heritage and, of course, to increase tourism. This leads us to two questions. Do these museums use meta-narrative as a tool in similar ways? If so, how might we describe these museums' use of "meta-narrative as tool"?

The Framing of Museums' Meta-Narrative

Sociology gives us a useful way of describing the political meta-narrative inherent to American baseball museums. Sociology has been previously applied to scholarship within heritage sport tourism in compelling ways, particularly with regards to the symbolic and cultural capital at the root of this tourism form (see Gordon, 2013; Harris, 2006; Kulczycki & Hyatt, 2005; Redmond, 1973; Slowikowski, 1991; Snyder, 1991). It has been considered one of sport tourism's parent disciplines (Gordon, 2013).

Continuing this line of sociological inquiry, I would like to proffer a

sociological framework in an attempt to understand the universality inherent to American baseball museums' political meta-narrative. The sociological concept of "frame analysis" (Goffman, 1974) is particularly helpful
in theorizing how the respective meta-narratives of American baseball museums are crafted to define their subject matter in accordance with baseball
heritage.

"Frame analysis," a term coined by sociologist Erving Goffman, is a lens
through which to view the various ways that we construct our social reality
generally and, in this instance, through which to utilize our phenomenological perspective. For Goffman, "framing" is a process by which culturally
determined definitions of reality shape, or frame, the way that we view, and
ultimately engage with, the people, objects, and events that we encounter on
a daily basis. To frame something is, for Goffman, the work that people do
in order to shape peoples' perceptions of the various elements inherent to
the world in which we live. Frame analysis has been employed in many sociological studies. Snow (see Benford & Snow, 2000; Snow & Benford, 1992;
Snow et al., 1986), most notably, has extended framing to analyses of social
movements in an effort to understand how such movements are successful
in galvanizing support and inspiring new membership.

While both Goffman (1974) and Snow (see Benford & Snow, 2000; Snow
& Benford, 1992; Snow et al., 1986) examined framing within contexts of
interpersonal interaction, I wish to extend frame analysis to American baseball museums as a way to understand the political meta-narrative that museums have crafted in order to define the meaning that baseball fans ascribe
to them relative to baseball heritage. Thus, while not originally specific to
place, framing can be applied to the built environment (see Dovey, 1999)
to conceptualize American baseball museums as phenomenological spaces
that have been designed to tell stories that situate them within baseball's
heritage narratives. Applying frame analysis to a few examples of American
baseball museums helps illustrate the meta-narratives at the root of American baseball museums' existence. These meta-narratives can be categorized
relative to a museum's intent to either stake a claim or make a claim relative
to baseball heritage.

The National Baseball Hall of Fame and Museum:
Situating America's Pastime

Perhaps the clearest example of a museum whose existence was intended to
frame baseball's meta-narrative is the Baseball Hall of Fame and Museum in

Cooperstown, New York. The Baseball Hall of Fame and Museum, and the meta-narrative it supports, is an excellent example of a museum's attempt to stake a claim relative to baseball heritage, and the museum has been critically examined previously. It owes its existence to the framing of, and attempt to legitimize, two important baseball-related myths: the Doubleday myth and the myth of the pastoral.

As professional baseball increased in popularity throughout the late 19th and early 20th centuries, the Mills Commission, largely initiated by former Major Leaguer and prominent sporting goods magnate Albert Goodwill Spalding was established to determine the game's origins (Seymour, 1960 [1989]). The Mills Commission determined, primarily through the uncorroborated testimony of one man, that Abner Doubleday, a longtime United States Army officer and Union General during the Civil War, invented baseball's rules in Cooperstown, New York, in 1839. This explanation was particularly satisfactory for Spalding, who, like many others involved with baseball, believed the sport to be deeply connected to, and reflective of, an emergent American culture that was distinct from that of the British (see, for example, Spalding, 1911 [1991]).

While the precise inventor of "America's pastime" remains in dispute, the notion that Doubleday invented baseball, and did so in Cooperstown, has been widely debunked by baseball historians. Nevertheless, Doubleday and Cooperstown remain at least superficially connected to the sport's heritage. In Doubleday's case, he has been featured in the Baseball Hall of Fame and Museum. A ball field that lies adjacent to the Hall of Fame and Museum where organized games are played, particularly by children, bears his name.

Entailed in the Doubleday myth is the myth that baseball's origins are a consequence of American pastoral life. The narrative of baseball as inherently pastoral may have served as a valuable counternarrative to perceived problems that were linked to cities, such as increased industrialization and immigration, that emerged before and during the Mills Commission in 1905. Quite the contrary; while baseball's precise inventor remains elusive, the sport's rules as they are generally known appear to be a consequence of the sport as played by ball clubs in and around New York City (Adelman, 1990). Thus, rather than being linked to American pastoral life, baseball was instead a direct outcome of the then-modern conditions inherent to city life.

These myths, when combined with the history of Cooperstown itself, make the impetus for the Baseball Hall of Fame and Museum, as well as its construction in 1939, particularly intriguing. The Hall of Fame and Museum was founded by Stephen Carlton Clark largely to spur tourism in

Cooperstown, which waned as a consequence of the Great Depression. The town itself, located on the southern edge of Otsego Lake in east central New York, was established by the father of noted American author and military serviceman James Fenimore Cooper. In fact, the Major Leagues celebrated baseball's centennial in 1939 by dedicating the Hall of Fame in Cooperstown and presenting a pageant that showcased Doubleday's supposed contribution to the game (Rader, 2009).

The meta-narrative of the Baseball Hall of Fame and Museum consequently contains interesting layers of place-based heritage. Cooper's most famous work, *The Last of the Mohicans,* while written in 1826, takes place during the French and Indian War in the mid-18th century in central New York. Cooper—whose most prominent work is linked to America's colonial history—is himself buried in Cooperstown and a statue erected in his honor remains a short walking distance from the Hall of Fame and Museum. The Hall of Fame and Museum, then, is located in a town whose own toponymic progeny is linked to literary representations of American heritage and the country's own meta-narrative of manifest destiny. It is within this place that baseball's origins have been linked and upon which the Hall of Fame and Museum was intended to capitalize. The Baseball Hall of Fame and Museum, and the meta-narrative it represents, is an excellent example of a museum's intended utility toward claim-staking: the attempt to use a museum to frame a multilayered American heritage meta-narrative that is linked to place.

Louisville Slugger Museum and Factory: A Brand's Alignment with Baseball Heritage

A second example of the use of a museum to frame a meta-narrative relative to baseball heritage is the Louisville Slugger Museum and Factory in Louisville, Kentucky. The venue opened in its current location in downtown Louisville in 1995. Its existence is an attempt to link a specific sporting goods brand to baseball's heritage through prominent hitters' use of the brand throughout the game's history.

The company began in 1856 as J. Frederick Hillerich's custom woodworking shop, where its primary products were bedposts, wood trim, butter churns, and wooden bowling balls and pins (Babal, 2008). According to company legend, Hillerich's seventeen-year-old son, John A. "Bud" Hillerich, went to Eclipse Park in the spring of 1884 to see his favorite player, Pete Browning, play. Browning, an outstanding hitter for the Louisville Eclipse, an American Association club, was dubbed the "Louisville Slugger." At this point in the season, however, Browning was experiencing a hitting slump. In an effort to help his favorite hitter, the young Hillerich offered to make him a bat at his father's woodworking shop while Browning watched. The new bat broke Browning out of his slump, the result of which aided Bud Hillerich in convincing his father to get into the batmaking business. This origin story, though, is in dispute (see Bailey, 2001).

The brand's marketing prowess, however, has never been contested. Bailey, for example, argued that Sam Severance, the company's former head of marketing, put forth the Browning story in company publications in 1939 in order to have a locally oriented "advent story" (2001, p. 2). Additional examples of the company's marketing savvy include their production of a bat endorsed by Honus Wagner in 1905, becoming the first sporting goods company to leverage celebrity endorsement. Also, since 1980, the company has given "Silver Slugger" awards to the best hitters at each position in each of the American and National Leagues. These are but a few examples of the company's innovative marketing practices throughout their history (for more evidence of recent campaigns, see MLB, 2014; Ryan, 2014).

The factory's expansion into a museum provides guests with the opportunity to hold game-used bats by well-known hitters throughout baseball history, who also happened to be Louisville Slugger clients, such as Mickey Mantle. The tour also consists of a visit to the museum's "bat vault," which includes bats made over the years for prominent clients. These bats and their constituent elements, such as the handle, knob, and barrel, have been numerically coded to serve as the template for current and future Louisville Slugger clients. Video testimonials of elite hitters under contract with the company play throughout the museum. Guests can take a tour of the factory floor, where they have the privilege of witnessing bats being made for the game's great hitters. The tour concludes with a visit to the merchandise shop, where guests receive a free Louisville Slugger "mini-bat."

Louisville Slugger has managed to leverage its contractual relationships with many of Major League Baseball's best hitters throughout the decades (Brown, 2013) in such a way as to align its brand with those players and their performances. The outcome of this marketing strategy, as exemplified in the museum and factory, is the framing of the brand as inherent to, if not the outright cause of, these elite hitters' success. Moreover, the brand's evolutionary meta-narrative—from its humble Kentucky craftsman beginnings as J. F. Hillerich's woodworking enterprise to the preferred choice among baseball's greatest hitters—parallels the meta-narrative of the Baseball Hall of Fame and Museum in Cooperstown in two ways.

First, the brand's origin story, though in dispute, depicts a chance encounter of a teenage boy offering a solution to his hometown hero's hitting woes in the form of elite American craftsmanship, handmade before the very eyes of the game's original "Louisville Slugger." The themes of boyhood, baseball, and innovation are in accordance with the American-centric origin story of baseball as put forth by Spalding's Mills Commission. Second, the sourcing of the Louisville Slugger's most prized raw material—northern white ash from the Pennsylvania-New York border—for their bat-making process further exemplifies the myth of the pastoral that is implicit within the sport's purported origin, as depicted in the Doubleday-Cooperstown myth. The Louisville Slugger brand may or may not be inherent to baseball history and the evolution of many of the game's greatest hitters. Regardless, the experience of attending the Louisville Slugger Museum and Factory has been designed to solidify the brand's relationship to baseball heritage through intentional marketing and framing of the brand so as to align its evolution with that of some of the game's greatest, all-time hitters.

Of particular, albeit implicit, value is the Louisville Slugger Museum and Factory's capacity to align itself with baseball heritage through its venue name. A growing body of literature within geography has explored the ways in which place-naming is used as a tool to exert power or influence (see Berg & Vuolteenaho, 2009; Light & Young, 2014; Rose-Redwood, 2011). While not nearly as embedded in the production of power through place-naming as exemplified elsewhere, the fact that "museum" is first and "factory" is second in the venue's name is meaningful. The presumably value-free and historically reverent associations with the word "museum" assists in sacralizing the museum's content (MacCannell, 1999), framing its subject matter as historically significant, even "shrine-like" (Babal, 2008). The Louisville Slugger Museum and Factory's meta-narrative provides an excellent example of a baseball-based brand's attempt to make the claim that it is inherent to the game's growth, responsible for its premiere performances, and positions the product as integral to successful competition in the "big leagues."

The Negro Leagues Baseball Museum: The Balance of the Public "Good" with Consumptive Relevance

While the previous two museums provide examples of place-framing toward material ends—be it to increase tourism and link baseball to a specific community in Cooperstown or to situate a sporting goods brand as inherent to baseball heritage in Louisville—the Negro Leagues Baseball Museum (NLBM) in Kansas City, Missouri, provides a unique example of a museum's use of place-framing to make a claim regarding its subject matter's contributions to baseball.

The NLBM was founded in 1990. It has preserved and taught African American baseball history from the late 1800s through the 1960s, and in 2006 the NLBM was designated as America's home for Negro Leagues baseball history by the United States Congress. The NLBM moved to its current address in Kansas City's historic 18th and Vine district in 1997 and has welcomed approximately 50,000 visitors there annually (Doswell, 2008). The museum shares a building with the American Jazz Museum, and both the NLBM and the neighborhood in which it resides have been targeted by community members and local leaders as a site of historical significance to the broader Kansas City community generally and African American culture specifically. The NLBM contains a variety of images, artifacts, and exhibitions that signify the contributions of prominent African American players, officials, administrators, owners, and media members.

In recent years, the museum acquired the Paseo YMCA, a historically significant structure that had been abandoned and is located a couple of city blocks from the NLBM. Built in 1914, the building was where Rube Foster formed the Negro National League in 1920. The multimillion-dollar renovation of the Paseo YMCA would allow the NLBM to expand and incorporate, among other things, the John "Buck" O'Neil Education and Research Center. O'Neil was a former Negro Leagues player and coach, the latter of which with the Kansas City Monarchs, and was the first African American coach in the Major Leagues when he joined the Chicago Cubs in 1962. In June 2018, though, vandals intentionally flooded the recently renovated building, the repairs for which were estimated to be $500,000 (Eliahou & Jackson, 2018).

The NLBM "is the world's only museum dedicated to preserving and celebrating the rich history of African American baseball and its impact on the social advancement of America" (About the NLBM, n.d.). Its intention is to educate the public as to the contributions of African Americans to

"America's pastime" and to highlight the role of baseball in African Americans' lives from the late 19th century to the demise of the Negro Leagues in the 1960s. As the vice president of Curatorial Services for the NLBM, Ray Doswell (2008), noted, the museum explores a variety of relevant themes with which younger generations, in particular, would benefit from engaging, such as race relations, economics, gender, labor, and military history. Despite the presumed social and personal benefits that engaging with the NLBM provides for its many visitors, it must actively engage in marketing strategies and practices to ensure its long-term viability as an enterprise (see Evans, 2019). This demonstrates that while the NLBM's meta-narrative may be considered objectively "good," it still does not exempt it from considerations of place-framing. The NLBM still exists to frame baseball heritage, even if the political intent underlying its existence might be considered noble.

In contrast to our first two museums, whose respective subject matter is continuously diachronic (Kligerman, 2007), the subject matter of the NLBM is fixed within a specific time frame and is thus more synchronic. Its most notable players, managers, and contributors have aged and many have passed away, leaving the NLBM to be the primary repository for African Americans' contributions to baseball through the 1960s. Furthermore, there is a dearth of artifacts and images from the Negro Leagues relative to those that are present in, for example, the Baseball Hall of Fame and Museum and the Louisville Slugger Museum and Factory. The primary sources that do exist have largely consisted of oral histories (Doswell, 2008). Consequently, the design and layout of the NLBM cannot rely as heavily on these visual and tactile stimuli as other museums might be able to do. Other elements that contribute to the museum's meta-narrative, then, increase in importance. To this end, a renovation that emphasized the introduction of electronically technologized elements was completed in 2018 to improve the attendee experience and facilitate repeat consumption.

The 2018 renovation and its consequent technological enhancements reflect a trend that appears to be present across a variety of museums. The focus of these spaces appears to have shifted from an emphasis on artifacts as valuable in and of themselves to artifacts as valuable to the degree that they contribute to a museum's intentionally crafted meta-narrative. This approach views the museum less as a space devoted to informing the guest on all things relevant to the museum's subject than paring down its material content in such a way as to transform the guest emotionally through a compelling, experiential narrative. The desired outcome of the latter is the "priming" of a guest so that she or he consumes the museum and its various product extensions through advocacy, word-of-mouth marketing, membership, the purchase of apparel, and other actions that indicate further consumption of the space and its subject matter (Doswell, 2008). The ubiquity of technology allows for a customized, yet replicable, narrative experience for guests. Museums, like any other business, are clearly "in the repeat business" too.

Selling the meta-narrative of the NLBM—the dual assertion of the relevance of the Negro Leagues to baseball heritage and African American history—to current and future guests, one could argue, reflects the challenge that the Negro Leagues themselves faced upon the integration of organized baseball shortly after Jackie Robinson signed with the Brooklyn Dodgers in 1947. As Lanctot explained, Black individuals at the time "valued the success of individuals within an integrated setting far more than the preservation of institutions" (2004, p. 312). This was widely felt across all Negro League teams, many of whom faced a dilemma in trying to market their product against the Robinson-led Dodgers when the latter happened to compete against a Major League team in a neighboring city. Moreover, Lanctot argued, separate, race-based businesses, including Black baseball, became increasingly irrelevant once successful integration occurred. That said, the social impact of separate businesses, including and especially the Negro Leagues, "helped build an irreplaceable sense of collective solidarity, identity, and self-esteem" (Lanctot, 2004, p. 312). Consumption of a museum dedicated to the Negro Leagues becomes even more complex when, as Nathan (2001) argued, contemporary white fans' engagement with the Negro Leagues is largely rooted in politically correct perceptions of an oppressed people's past. This demonstrates white privilege through a sanitized sense of nostalgia. For Nathan, white fans' indulgence with Black baseball history allows whites "to salve our guilt-ridden collective conscience" (2001, p. 469).

The challenges of the NLBM thus reflect the broader paradox of museums' existence. To denote a space as a museum frames its meta-narrative as significant and value-free. Museums, though, experience the constant challenge of asserting their relevance to consumers and competing for their discretionary dollar by presenting a past that is crafted to suit its needs in the present. The NLBM is no exception. As Acarin and Adams asserted, museums' "contribution to the construction of collective identity, memory, and imagination" are "haunted by the ever-increasing commodification of experience that contributes to the museum's struggle for relevance and viability in terms of the pedagogical, the political, and the ludic" (2015, p. 69).

In trying to assert the relevance and value of its meta-narrative, the NLBM sits at the intersection of the tension between providing content for the public good and the need to commodify its content to stay solvent in an increasingly crowded entertainment marketplace. The meta-narrative of the Negro Leagues Baseball Museum is an interesting, if not complex, example of the importance of a museum as the lone vehicle to make a claim regarding the valuable contributions of its subject matter to baseball heritage.

Conclusion

American baseball museums provide intriguing examples of framing sport heritage through place-based meta-narratives. Frame analysis allows us to deconstruct the meta-narrative that each of these three museums have employed. In so doing, we are able to understand what the meta-narrative for each museum is and how it situates its subject matter relative to baseball heritage. The meta-narrative of the Baseball Hall of Fame and Museum in Cooperstown, New York, for example, stakes a claim regarding that town's purported significance relative to baseball history. The meta-narrative of the Louisville Slugger Museum and Factory in Louisville, Kentucky, makes the claim that the Louisville Slugger brand is inherently linked to, if not the outright cause of, some of the game's elite hitters and hitting performances of all time. This meta-narrative runs parallel to nationalistic and pastoral notions of the game's history, both of which are themes within the Baseball Hall of Fame and Museum as well. The meta-narrative of the Negro Leagues Baseball Museum in Kansas City, Missouri, makes the claim of African Americans' contributions to baseball, while simultaneously highlighting the value of baseball to the Black experience in pre–Civil Rights Movement America. The meta-narrative of the NLBM, in contrast to the former two museums, demonstrates that meta-narrative is inherently political even if the intentions of that meta-narrative are "good"—that is, not solely to increase one's capitalistic footprint.

Suggestions for Future Research

The use of frame analysis could be applied in a variety of ways in future research. The frame-based dichotomy of "claim-making" and "claim-staking," for example, could be used as a framework to examine the perspectives of baseball museum attendees through quantitative or qualitative means. This dichotomy may serve as a useful starting point by which to develop nuanced, attendee-derived, conceptual frameworks of the baseball museum experience either through case studies of specific museums or through an attendee-centric typology of baseball museums. A phenomenologically derived approach to the baseball museum attendee's experience would be particularly valuable, considering that, as Wetherell et al. (2018) noted, the ways in which participants make meanings of the heritage situations in which they find themselves need to be explored.

References

About the NLBM (n.d.). https://nlbm.com/about-nlbm/ (accessed December 5, 2020).

Acarin, X., & Adams, B. (2015). Centers of experience: Bodies and objects in today's museums. In P. Benz (Ed.), *Experience design* (pp. 69–75). London: Bloomsbury.

Adelman, M. L. (1990). *A sporting time: New York City and the rise of modern athletics, 1820–70.* Champaign: University of Illinois Press.

Babal, M. (2008). Review: Louisville Slugger Museum & Factory, Louisville, Kentucky. *The Public Historian, 30*(4), 131–133.

Bailey, B. (2001). Hunting for the first Louisville Slugger: A look at the Browning myth. *The Baseball Research Journal, 30,* 96–98.

Benford, R. D., & Snow, D. A. (2000). Framing processes and social movements: An overview and assessment. *Annual Review of Sociology, 26,* 611–639.

Berg, L., & Vuolteenaho, J. (Eds.). (2009). *Critical toponymies: The contested politics of place naming.* London: Ashgate.

Brown, S. (2013). Louisville Slugger. *St. James encyclopedia of popular culture.* Detroit: St. James Press.

Carr, D. (2014). *Experience and history.* Oxford: Oxford University Press.

Conn, S. (2010). *Do museums still need objects?* Philadelphia: University of Pennsylvania Press.

Davies, S. M., Paton, R., & O'Sullivan, T. J. (2013). The museum values framework: A framework for understanding organisational culture in museums. *Museum Management and Curatorship, 28*(4), 345–361.

Doswell, R. (2008). *Evaluating educational value in museum exhibitions: Establishing an evaluation process for the Negro Leagues Baseball Museum* [Doctoral dissertation, Kansas State University].

Dovey, K (1999). *Framing places: Mediating power in built form.* London: Routledge.

Eliahou, M., & Jackson, A. (2018, August 9). Museum was vandalized, people from across the country stepped up to help. *CNN.* https://www.cnn.com/2018/08/09/us/negro-leagues-baseball-museum-vandalized-trnd/index.html (accessed December 5, 2020).

Evans, T. (2019). *Analyzing value propositions to understand consumer motivation: Increasing attendance at the Negro Leagues Baseball Museum* [Senior honors thesis, University of Missouri].

Gammon, S. (2004). Secular pilgrimage and sport tourism. In B. W. Ritchie & D. Adair (Eds.), *Sport tourism: Interrelationships, impacts and issues* (pp. 30–45). Bristol: Channel View.

Goffman, E. (1974). *Frame analysis: An essay on the organization of experience.* Boston: Northeastern University Press.

Gordon, K. O. (2013). Emotion and memory in nostalgia sport tourism: Examining the attraction to postmodern ballparks through an interdisciplinary lens. *Journal of Sport & Tourism, 18*(3), 217–239.

Grimaldi, S. (2015). Narrativity of object interaction experiences: A framework for designing products as narrative experiences. In P. Benz (Ed.), *Experience design* (pp. 56–68). London: Bloomsbury.

Harris, J. (2006). The science of research in sport and tourism: Some reflections upon the promise of the sociological imagination. *Journal of Sport & Tourism, 11*(2), 153–171.

Harrison, R. (2013). *Heritage: Critical approaches.* London: Routledge.

Hollinshead, K. (1997). Heritage tourism under post-modernity: Truth and the past. In C. Ryan (Ed.), *The tourism experience: A new introduction.* New York: Cassell.

Kirshenblatt-Gimblett, B. (1998). *Destination culture: Tourism, museums, and heritage.* Berkeley: University of California Press.

Kligerman, E. (2007). *Sites of the uncanny: Paul Celan, specularity, and the visual arts.* Berlin: De Gruyter.

Kulczycki, C., & Hyatt, C. (2005). Expanding the conceptualization of nostalgia sport tourism: Lessons learned from fans left behind after sport franchise relocation. *Journal of Sport Tourism, 10*(4), 273–293.

Lanctot, N. (2004). *Negro league baseball: The rise and ruin of a black institution.* Philadelphia: University of Pennsylvania Press.

Light, D., & Young, C. (2014). Toponymy as commodity: Exploring the economic dimensions of urban place names. *Urban Worlds,* 435–450.

MacCannell, D. (1999). *The tourist: A new theory of the leisure class.* Berkeley: University of California.

MLB News (2014, September 14). Louisville Slugger retires P72 bat model in honor of Derek Jeter. https://www.mlb.com/news/louisville-slugger-retires-p72-bat-model-in-honor-of-derek-jeter/c-96195366 (accessed December 5, 2020).

Nathan, D. (2001). Bearing witness to blackball: Buck O'Neil, the Negro Leagues, and the politics of the past. *Journal of American Studies, 35*(3), 453–469.

Norberg-Schulz, C. (1980). *Genius loci.* New York: Rizzoli.

Phillips, M. G. (2012). Introduction: Historians in sport museums. In M. G. Phillips (Ed.), *Representing the sporting past in museums and halls of fame* (pp. 1–26). London: Routledge.

Rader, B. G. (2009). *American sports: From the age of folk games to the age of televised sports, 6th ed.* New York: Pearson Prentice Hall.

Ramshaw, G. (2020). *Heritage and sport: An introduction.* Bristol: Channel View.

Redmond, G. (1973). A plethora of shrines: Sport in the museum and hall of fame. *Quest, 19,* 41–48.

Reference USA (n.d.). http://resource.referenceusa.com/ (accessed December 5, 2020).

Relph, E. (1976). *Place and placelessness.* London: Pion.

Relph, E. (1981). *Rational landscapes and humanistic geography.* New York: Barnes and Noble.

Riess, S. A. (1999). *Touching base: Professional baseball and American culture in the Progressive Era.* Champaign: University of Illinois Press.

Rose-Redwood, R. (2011). Rethinking the agenda of political toponymy. *ACME: An International E-Journal for Critical Geographies, 10*(1), 34–41.

Ryan, D. (2014). *The best digital marketing campaigns in the world II.* London: Kogan Page Ltd.

Seymour, H. (1960 [1989]). *Baseball: The early years.* Oxford: Oxford University Press.

Slowikowski, S. S. (1991). Burning desire: Nostalgia, ritual, and the sport-festival flame ceremony. *Sociology of Sport Journal, 8,* 239–257.

Smith, L. (2006). *Uses of heritage.* London: Routledge.

Snow, D. A., & Benford, R. D. (1992). Master frames and cycles of protest. In A. D. Morris and C. M. Mueller (Eds.), *Frontiers in social movement theory* (pp. 133–155). Dartmouth: Yale University Press.

Snow, D. A., Rochford, E. B., Worden, S. K., & Benford, R. D. (1986). Frame alignment processes, micromobilization, and movement participation. *American Sociological Review, 51*(4), 474–481.

Snyder, E. E. (1991). Sociology of nostalgia: Sport halls of fame and museums in America. *Sociology of Sport Journal, 8,* 228–238.

Spalding, A. G. (1911 [1991]). *Baseball: America's national game 1839–1915.* San Francisco: Halo.

Springwood, C. F. (1996). *Cooperstown and Dyersville: A geography of baseball nostalgia.* Boulder: Westview.

Tuan, Y. F. (1977). *Space and place: The perspective of experience.* Minneapolis: University of Minnesota Press.

Wertsch, J. V. (2002). *Voices of collective remembering.* Cambridge: Cambridge University Press.

Wetherell, M., Smith, L., & Campbell, G. (2018). Introduction: Affective heritage practices. In L. Smith, M. Wetherell, & G. Campbell (Eds.), *Emotion, affective practices, and the past in the present* (pp. 1–21). London: Routledge.

8

Baseball Heritage in Japan

A Case of the Masters Koshien

Eiji Ito, Kei Hikoji, and Makoto Chogahara

Baseball is one of the most popular sports in Japan. In 2016, the Japanese professional baseball league attracted the most spectators in Japan with an estimated 16.1 million (Sasakawa Sports Foundation, 2017). Surprisingly, the second-highest sport was high school baseball, with approximately 5.5 million spectators, as with the Japanese professional soccer league (Sasakawa Sports Foundation, 2017). This is because of the National High School Baseball Championships hosted at the Hanshin Koshien Stadium, which the Japan Broadcasting Corporation, NHK, provides uninterrupted live coverage of every game (Kawai & McDonald, 2012; Shimizu, 2012). Koshien is essentially a geographical name, but in Japan, people think of this ballpark in Hyogo when they hear the word *Koshien*. Every spring and summer, the winning high school baseball teams that qualify, a team from each prefecture, gather at the stadium and compete for the championship in Japan. For the 101st National High School Baseball Championship in August 2019, 49 representative teams from all the prefectures in Japan—two teams from Tokyo and Hokkaido—competed at the Hanshin Koshien Stadium for 16 days and attracted over 840,000 spectators (Japan High School Baseball Federation, n.d.).

While the Koshien baseball championship is an amateur sport, Japan considers it a national festival that brings excitement to baseball enthusiasts across the country (Komuku, 1995; Ariyama, 1997). Since many professional baseball players have participated in this national sporting event (Shimizu, 2012), many high school baseball players dream of playing at Koshien. Kelly (2011) highlighted the top five most resonant places in Japanese sports, one of them being the Hanshin Koshien Stadium based on such baseball heritage elements (the others include the Korakuen Baseball Stadium, Meiji Jingu Baseball Stadium, Nippon Budokan for marital arts, and Ryogoku Kokugikan for sumo). Reflecting the international view of sporting venues, the word *Koshien* has a similar meaning for Japanese people as *Wembley*, *Lord's*, *Wimbledon*, and *Heysel* (Kelly, 2011). The following description of the Koshien baseball championship encapsulates the heritage aspects of Koshien:

> In front of tens of thousands of stadium spectators and millions of television viewers around the country, the losing players crouch down on the edge of the infield, sweating and crying, to scoop up handfuls of the sacred soil of Kōshien Stadium into small cloth sacks. . . . They will bring this soil back to their own schools and spread it on their ball field to inspire future success. Tears, sweat, and soil mix in this heart-breaking gesture to express pride and disappointment. The emotional poignancy is heightened by the realization that many of the players have been [practicing] and playing baseball literally 350–60 days a year for five or six years—but from this moment on, most will never play organized baseball again for the rest of their lives. (Kelly, 2011, p. 482)

In this unique heritage ballpark, an annual masters sport event, called the Masters Koshien (MK), was launched in 2004 for people who used to be high school baseball players (Figure 8.1). Masters sport is adults' participation in competitive sport events (Young et al., 2015), which has become popular in Japan due to its aging population (Ito & Hikoji, 2021; Hikoji, 2018). More importantly for heritage sport tourism perspectives, Japanese people travel to participate in masters games (Ito & Hikoji, 2021; Ito & Kono, 2019; Hikoji, 2018), and heritage aspects of Koshien have attracted many Japanese people, especially ex-baseball players, to MK. MK provides them with an opportunity to compete and achieve their own youth goals at the Hanshin Koshien Stadium. They need to organize alumni baseball clubs (and win a qualifying round in each prefecture) to participate in MK. Therefore, MK also provides an opportunity for adults to form these alumni clubs in each prefecture, which promotes socialization among ex-baseball clubs. In fact, the number of high school alumni baseball clubs that have participated in MK has dramatically increased from 85 in 2004 to 678 in 2019 (Masters Koshien Organizing Committee, 2004, 2019).

With a keen focus on the unique allure of the Hanshin Koshien Stadium, the MK project intends to stimulate the dreams and longings of people who used to be high school baseball players, as well as the special emotional

Figure 8.1. A baseball game at the Masters Koshien. Photo courtesy of Kei Hikoji.

attachments they still embrace. Therefore, this masters sporting event also supports their sporting lives through baseball by connecting the impact of the Koshien heritage with masters sports. Additionally, as previously mentioned, participants travel to Koshien to participate in MK; therefore, it is reasonable to state that this masters event offers an interesting perspective of heritage sport tourism (Ramshaw & Gammon, 2005) in Japan. Ito and Hinch (2020) reviewed sport tourism research published in Japan and found that none out of 52 research papers examined heritage sport tourism—most of them focused on either active sport tourism or participant-based event sport tourism. This result led them to call for heritage sport tourism research in Japan and state that MK can be a suitable and unique case study for this research venue. In fact, MK can cover at least three categories of sport related heritage (Ramshaw & Gammon, 2005): tangible immovable (i.e., the Hanshin Koshien Stadium), intangibles (e.g., memories, nostalgia), and goods and services (e.g., participants' old school jerseys). Also, this ballpark has produced many national baseball heroes (e.g., Daisuke Matsuzaka, Hideki Matsui) who are considered to be both tangible (movable objects) and intangible (their achievements) heritages (Gammon, 2014). Another unique aspect of MK is that participants not only have authentic backstage stadium experiences (Gammon & Fear 2005; Ramshaw & Gammon, 2010; Ramshaw et al., 2013), but are able to play baseball at the heritage site. Therefore, MK has an integral heritage element and participation-based event sport tourism.

In summary, there is no doubt that the Hanshin Koshien Stadium contains unique baseball heritage elements in Japan (Kelly, 2011). The masters sporting event, MK, that leverages the powerful heritage elements has attracted many Koshien enthusiasts from all over the country for 18 years. As Ito and Hinch (2020) acknowledged, MK provides a unique case study of heritage sport tourism in Japan. Although Hikoji et al. (2012) identified individual, community, social, and educational benefits and Tani et al. (2012) examined event and sport promotion through printed media in the MK context, knowledge about Koshien heritage elements of this masters sporting event is limited. Therefore, the purpose of this chapter is to examine heritage aspects of the Hanshin Koshien Stadium from the perspectives of heritage sport tourism by using MK as a case study.

Method

The MK Organizing Committee has systematically collected newspaper articles, published on both national and local levels, that are specifically related to MK. We analyzed a total of 198 articles, published from 2004 to 2015. For data analysis, we employed thematic analysis, defined as "a method for identifying, [analyzing], and reporting patterns (themes) within data" (Braun & Clarke, 2006, p. 79), in an inductive manner. By referring to Braun and Clarke's (2006) procedure, we conducted the thematic analysis consisting of the following six steps: familiarizing the data, generating subthemes based on codes, searching for themes, reviewing themes, naming themes, and producing the report. The first author translated the direct quotes into English from the original Japanese articles.

Results and Discussion

Table 8.1 displays the results of the thematic analysis. Our thematic analysis identified three themes from the 198 articles: personal ($n = 201$), collective ($n = 74$), and MK-specific ($n = 46$) heritage. Heritage sport tourism has documented personal and collective heritage (e.g., Ramshaw & Gammon,

Table 8.1. Results of the Thematic Analyses

Subthemes	Codes	n
PERSONAL HERITAGE		201
Meaning-making	Fulfillment, eternal goal and dream, *ikigai* (life worthiness)	93
Positive Emotions	Fun, joy, impression	55
Nostalgia	Reminiscence, recollection, appreciation	40
Personal Identity	Self-respect, self-efficacy, self-perception, pride	13
COLLECTIVE HERITAGE		74
Socialization	Alumni, friend, and intergenerational bonding	37
Inspiration	Encouragement, dream, stimulation	32
Group Identity	Sense of belonging, sense of community	5
MASTERS KOSHIEN-SPECIFIC HERITAGE		46
Masters Culture	Lifelong sports culture, positive aging roles, baseball culture	23
Authenticity	Koshien	19
Social Benefits	Social contribution, restoring for community	4

2005), but MK-specific heritage is our unique contribution to the literature. The following sections explain and discuss each theme separately.

Personal Heritage

The most dominant theme, personal heritage, consists of the following four subthemes: meaning-making ($n = 93$), positive emotions ($n = 55$), nostalgia ($n = 40$), and personal identity ($n = 13$). MK seems to provide the participants with the feelings for meaning-making, which is defined as "the processes of gaining something important or valuable in life" (Iwasaki, 2008, p. 232). Heritage sport tourism has reported meaningful experiences that closely associate with nostalgia (e.g., Cho et al., 2014; Fairley & Gammon, 2005; Ramshaw, 2010). For example, Ramshaw (2010) highlighted that sport museum visitors seek the opportunities for interpretation and participation in the meaning-making process; MK is not exceptional. Our analysis identified the following codes of fulfillment (e.g., "I've fulfilled a lifetime dream"), eternal goal and dream (e.g., "Pursuing a dream I had when I was in high school"), and *ikigai*, or life worthiness (e.g., "Playing baseball with my ex-students is *ikigai*"). In particular, the last code is the Japanese eudaemonic concept of well-being that is a multifaceted construct including life affirmation, existential value, and meaning in life (Kono et al., 2019). Kono et al. (2019) emphasized the importance of a balance between leisure enjoyment and effort to enhance *ikigai* among Japanese university students. As discussed later, MK experiences seem enjoyable for the participants. However, at the same time, those experiences are also challenging since the MK participants need to negotiate various leisure constraints (e.g., interpersonal, time, and commitment constraints: Ito et al., 2020) for not only MK participation but also team management. Through both enjoyable and challenging experiences, MK participants may find meaningful values in this unique sporting event.

By participating in MK, people appeared to experience positive emotions including fun (e.g., "It was fun"), joy (e.g., "It was a joyful moment"), and impression (e.g., "I'm speechless with emotion"). It is not too surprising to find these positive emotions given that MK participation is considered a leisure activity. Leisure, defined as "activity chosen in relative freedom for its qualities of satisfaction" (Kelly, 1996, p. 8), has two critical elements: perceived freedom and intrinsic motivation (Iso-Ahola, 1980; Kelly, 1996; Neulinger, 1974). These two distinctive elements make leisure fun and provide people with various positive emotions that have been reported in heritage sport tourism contexts as follows: "Several football stadiums have achieved the status of places to be *enjoyed* through the perspective of the tourist or visitor than the fan" (Bale, 1993, p. 75, italics added). It seems that MK participants truly enjoy this participant-based sporting event held at the heritage ballpark.

Based on the following three codes, reminiscence (e.g., "I pursue my adolescent dream"), recollection (e.g., "My inexplicable passion for Koshien has never changed"), and appreciation (e.g., "I appreciate everyone who brought me to [Koshien]"), we identified the subtheme of nostalgia. This subtheme has been a central concept in heritage sport tourism since Gibson's (1998) seminal work. In the process of our thematic analysis, we purposefully distinguished this subtheme from the previous subtheme, positive emotions, because the nostalgia is a bittersweet, rather than positive, emotion (Cho et al., 2014). This distinction is particularly important for MK participants given that most of them were not able to make it to the Koshien baseball championship when they were high school students. It should be noted that, although we acknowledge the difference between nostalgia and reminiscence (the former is more complex than the latter; Cho et al., 2014), we decided to use nostalgia as an umbrella concept for reminiscence, recollection, and appreciation.

The last subtheme in personal heritage was personal identity, including self-efficacy (e.g., "This experience makes me feel confident"), self-perception (e.g., "By participating in [MK], I appreciate living 'in the now' as an elder"), and pride (e.g., "I want to boast to my children and grandchildren that I played in Koshien"). Sport tourists, such as fans, supporters, and event participants, aspire to identify themselves at sport events; therefore, personal identity is a prominent component of nostalgic sport tourism experiences (Cho et al., 2014; Fairley & Gammon, 2005). Fairley and Gammon (2005) stressed the role of nostalgia in personal identity by stating that "nostalgia is used by individuals as a form of identity maintenance" (p. 184). Additionally, MK involvement is considered to be serious leisure, which contributes to self-development, self-enrichment, self-expression, and enhancement of self-image (Stebbins, 2009), since the participants make substantial efforts in the leisure activity. Kono et al.'s (2020) findings support our interpretation, in which not only engaging in serious leisure but also recognizing personal rewards through such activities contribute to meaning in life among Japanese adults. Therefore, it is reasonable to state that the subthemes of meaning-making, positive emotions, and personal identity are closely linked in the MK contexts.

Collective Heritage

The second dominant theme, collective heritage, consists of three subthemes: socialization ($n = 37$), inspiration ($n = 32$), and group identity ($n = 5$). The first subtheme is socialization describing alumni (e.g., "[MK] is an alumni reunion"), friend (e.g., "I am happy to see my friends [through MK]"), and intergenerational (e.g., "MK enables us to socialize across generations") bonding among the MK participants. Socialization is a key concept to understand nostalgia sport tourism (Cho et al., 2014; Fairley, 2003), but it is interesting to find not only alumni and friend bonding but also bonding across generations. Fairley (2003), who examined nostalgic behaviors and experiences of group travelers following an Australian professional football team, reported socialization phenomena among newcomers. This finding is somewhat similar to intergenerational bonding in our MK context, as Fairley (2003) reported: "Through the socialization which occurs throughout the trip, with repeat group members sharing the group's folklore, first time trip participants are able to live past group experiences vicariously, thereby sharing the group's nostalgia" (p. 300). In terms of participant-based event sport tourism, Ryan and Trauer (2005) highlighted that social interaction motivates some masters game participants. In Japanese masters games contexts, Ito and Hikoji (2021) reported social bonding to be one aspect of leisure involvement positively related to interdependent happiness among Japanese participants in domestic masters events. Given that the nature of MK involves these two types of sport tourism (i.e., heritage and participant-based event sport tourism), it is not surprising that MK participants experienced various levels of socialization through the unique masters sporting event.

The second subtheme is inspiration, which consists of the following codes: encouragement (e.g., "I would like to encourage active baseball players of our high school"), dream (e.g., "I would like to pass on our [Koshien] dream to future generations"), and stimulation (e.g., "I would like to tell active high school baseball players how great Koshien is") to next generations. It is somewhat like the previous codes of socialization and nostalgia as personal heritage, but this code of inspiration emphasizes MK participants' positive and encouraging messages to younger generations and active high school baseball players (Hikoji et al., 2012). Although sporting knowledge itself is personal heritage, its transmission from one generation to another is a form of intrapersonal sporting heritage (Ramshaw, 2020). Moreover, one assumes that this subtheme represents a mixed nature of Koshien's educational aspects and MK participants' nostalgic feelings. The education system in Japan integrates the Koshien baseball championship and baseball club activities in the high school education system in Japan (Kawai & McDonald, 2012; Kelly, 2011). This education aspect was also identified in the MK context, as Hikoji et al. (2012) found educational benefits of MK (e.g., educational messages). In fact, Japanese adults (or society) seemingly expect to see ideal and educational values including fair play, teamwork, and supreme effort in the Koshien baseball championship and players (Kelly, 2011). Additionally, as MK appears to reinforce adults' nostalgic feelings as personal heritage, "the parents, teachers and national adult viewing audience who so nostalgically celebrate the efforts of the teenage players do this in an age of enormous gulfs between generational experiences and frictions between the generations in their own lives" (Kelly, 2011, p. 489). Therefore, the code of inspiration might reflect adults' educational expectations for young generations through their nostalgic feelings.

The last subtheme is group identity, which developed from a sense of belonging (e.g., "I want to play again with my high school jersey") and a sense of community (e.g., "I play for my high school's honor"). Sport heritage is closely linked to not only personal identity but also collective identity (Fairley & Gammon, 2005; Hinch & Ramshaw, 2014; Ramshaw & Gammon, 2010). Moreover, the following stadiums are examples of how regional/national identity can be constructed and/or heightened: Twickenham Stadium (the spiritual home of rugby in England) tours (Ramshaw & Gammon, 2010), Millennium Stadium (the home to Welsh rugby and football) tours (Gammon & Fear, 2005), and the Arctic Winter Games and the Canadian Football League (Hinch & Ramshaw, 2014). Koshien can also construct regional identity, as Kelly (2011) stated:

> It is intriguing, too, that the [Koshien] high school tournament has become such an expression of regional identity (the teams are prefectural representatives) when in fact, apart from some of the support groups, most of the fans who so enthusiastically cheer on their "hometown" team left their prefecture long ago, now live in Tokyo or Nagoya or Osaka, and rarely, if ever, return or want to return. (p. 489)

When discussing a lower level of group identity like this case study, Fairley's (2003) group-traveler study becomes very informative. She states that the norms and rituals of the groups through their group-based sport tourism experiences represent the group as a distinctive identity. It is reasonable to assume that this interpretation can apply to the development of group identity among the MK participants, as well, and that heritage aspects of Koshien may amplify this process.

MK-Specific Heritage

The last theme, MK-specific heritage, consists of three subthemes: masters culture ($n = 23$), authenticity ($n = 19$), and social benefits ($n = 4$). Although there were fewer articles coded into this theme than the two others, this theme involves Koshien's unique heritage elements. Recently, Ito et al. (2020) developed leisure-time physical activity constraints and constraint negotiation typologies. They included activity-specific categories in the typologies. This is due to the variability in constraints across various kinds of leisure activities (Godbey et al., 2010). Therefore, when examining constraints and constraint negotiation among active sport tourists who participated in masters games events, Ito and Kono (2019) also measured masters games-specific constraints and negotiation in addition to identifying meaningful differences between sport tourists and excursionists. Particularly in the context of the Koshien, Kelly's (2011) contention also supports our interpretation: "Sports may be highly standardized by codified rules of contests, but they are also strongly *place-specific,* and the association of sports actions and *place specificity* adds considerably to their power to generate collective memory" (p. 483, italics added). Given the variability in heritage sport tourism in terms of activities and places (e.g., museum tours, stadium tours, spectator behaviors), we propose that activity or place-specific heritage should be acknowledged in heritage sport tourism as well.

The first subtheme of MK-specific heritage is masters culture, which is described by lifelong sport culture (e.g., "I want to foster momentum for masters as lifelong sports"), positive aging roles (e.g., "Aging is not too bad"), and baseball culture (e.g., "I love baseball"). The first two codes are consistent with the masters sport's movement "in promoting 'sport for life' and an 'active healthy aging' agenda" (Young et al., 2015, p. 141), while the last one represents the form of sport (i.e., baseball) in MK. Our interpretation aligns with Ramshaw's (2020) proposition that sporting heritages can be practiced and performed at masters sporting events. The second subtheme is authenticity represented by narratives of Koshien (e.g., "Koshien is a mecca," "Koshien is a place I dreamed of for long time"). Given its history and background, the powerful and recognized symbolic heritage values of Koshien are not in question. Although the subtheme of authenticity overlaps with personal heritage (Ramshaw, 2020), authentic experiences are very activity- and place-specific for MK, in which participants actually play baseball in Koshien. Stadium tours allow visitors to experience the authentic backstage of the stadium (Gammon & Fear 2005; Ramshaw & Gammon, 2010; Ramshaw et al., 2013), but MK provides participants with an opportunity to become an actor on the stage. Moreover, as with the actual Koshien tournaments, audiences, friends, and families cheer on MK participants from the stands (Figure 8.2) and the same public-address announcer calls their names during games. All of these MK-specific sounds could be considered to be important intangible sensory sport heritages (Ramshaw, 2020). Wang's (1999) concept of existential authenticity, which involves personal or intersubjective feelings (a special state of being) and can have nothing to do with the authenticity of toured objects, associates with sporting heritages (Ramshaw, 2020) and appears to align with MK-specific heritage as well. Existential authenticity has two dimensions: intra-personal (e.g., self-making) and inter-personal (e.g., family ties) authenticity (Wang, 1999), both of which relate to personal and collective heritage. Furthermore, the fact that Koshien is a mecca of baseball in Japan supports the idea that "place matters in existential authenticity" (Rickly-Boyd, 2013, p. 683). Therefore, the three

Figure 8.2. Baseball players at the Masters Koshien. Photo courtesy of Kei Hikoji.

types of heritage might be interrelated to each other and might provide the MK participants with opportunities to experience existential authenticity.

The last subtheme is social benefits, which consist of social contributions (e.g., "We also engage in social action programs every year") and community restorations (e.g., "One of our main goals is to contribute to our high school and community"). Hikoji et al. (2012) particularly focused on the benefits of MK and reported individual, community, social, and educational benefits. Although our thematic analysis identified only community and social aspects, this seems to be due to our emphasis on heritage aspects in the coding process. For example, their individual and educational benefits somewhat overlap with our theme of personal heritage. Our results suggest that although active sport tourism initiatives promote *chiiki-saisei* (local revitalization) and *machizukuri* (place-based community development) in Japan (Hinch & Ito, 2018), heritage sport tourism also has the potential to achieve these practical implications.

Conclusion

The purpose of this chapter was to examine heritage aspects of the Hanshin Koshien Stadium from the perspective of heritage sport tourism by using MK as a case study. We analyzed 198 newspaper articles, published on both national and local levels, that are specifically related to MK. Our thematic analysis identified the following three themes: personal, collective, and MK-specific heritage. Most of the themes and subthemes were consistent with the literature of heritage sport tourism. Therefore, as Ito and Hinch (2020) speculated, MK can be considered a unique context of heritage sport tourism in Japan.

One of our theoretical and practical implications is the acknowledgment of MK-specific heritage—that is, an activity- and place-specific heritage to this masters sport event. Heritage sport tourism involves a variety of activities (e.g., stadium and museum tours) and places (e.g., Koshien, Wimbledon). While some heritage aspects are common, including personal and collective, others appear to be very specific and culturally informed. This type of heritage is particularly important to keep the unique appeal of tourist attractions and combat the threat of standardization and homogenization of sporting environments in the global era (Higham & Hinch, 2018). Stadium managers, sporting event organizers, and tourism practitioners should review and leverage the uniqueness of their heritage aspects. In this way, MK is one of the few exceptions in Japan. This masters sport event maximizes Koshien baseball heritage for its event management and the promotion of masters sport culture in Japan.

In conclusion, Japan hosted the Rugby World Cup in 2019 and the Tokyo Olympics and Paralympics in 2021. More importantly for this chapter, this country is also scheduled to host the World Masters Games Kansai in the near future (originally scheduled in 2021, but postponed due to the coronavirus pandemic). These events provide strong incentives for sport tourism research in Japan (Hinch & Ito, 2018), and we should acknowledge aspects of heritage sport tourism since this type of research is severely lacking in Japan (Ito & Hinch, 2020). These major sporting events have and will generate both tangible (e.g., the new national stadium) and intangible (e.g., nostalgia, memories) heritage elements. Our case study, MK, provides meaningful information to leverage these elements for not only sport promotion but also promotion of heritage sport tourism in Japan.

References

Ariyama, T. (1997). *Koshien yakyuu to nihonjin: Media no tsukutta ibento* [Koshien baseball and Japanese: The event made by media]. Tokyo: Yoshikawa Kobunkan.

Bale, J. (1993). *Sport, space and the city.* London: Routledge.

Braun, V., & Clarke, V. (2006). Using thematic analysis in psychology. *Qualitative Research in Psychology, 3*(2), 77–101. https://doi.org/10.1191/1478088706qp0630a

Cho, H., Ramshaw, G., & Norman, W. C. (2014). A conceptual model for nostalgia in the context of sport tourism: Re-classifying the sporting past. *Journal of Sport & Tourism, 19*(2), 145–167. https://doi.org/10.1080/14775085.2015.1033444

Fairley, S. (2003). In search of relived social experience: Group-based nostalgia sport tourism. *Journal of Sport Management, 17*(3), 284–304. https://doi.org/10.1123/jsm.17.3.284

Fairley, S., & Gammon, S. (2005). Something lived, something learned: Nostalgia's expanding role in sport tourism. *Sport in Society, 8*(2), 182–197. https://doi.org/10.1080/17430430500102002

Gammon, S. J. (2014). Heroes as heritage: The commoditization of sporting achievement. *Journal of Heritage Tourism, 9*(3), 246–256. https://doi.org/10.1080/1743873X.2014.904321

Gammon, S., & Fear, V. (2005). Stadia tours and the power of backstage. *Journal of Sport & Tourism, 10*(4), 243–252. https://doi.org/10.1080/14775080600805457

Gibson, H. J. (1998). Sport tourism: A critical analysis of research. *Sport Management Review, 1,* 45–76. https://doi.org/10.1016/S1441-3523(98)70099-3

Godbey, G., Crawford, D. W., & Shen, X. S. (2010). Assessing hierarchical leisure constraints theory after two decades. *Journal of Leisure Research, 42*(1), 111–134. https://doi.org/10.1080/00222216.2010.11950197

Higham, J., & Hinch, T. (2018). *Sport tourism development* (3rd ed.). Clevedon: Channel View Publications.

Hikoji, K. (2018). Masutazu supotsu [Masters sports]. In M. Kawanishi & H. Nogawa (Eds.), *Syougai supotsu jissenron* [Handbook of lifelong sport] (4th ed.) (pp. 185–189). Tokyo: Ichimura.

Hikoji, K., Chogahara, M., Tani, M., Sonoda, D., Matsumura, Y., Okada, A., Takada, Y., & Ishizawa, N. (2012). The multidimensional benefits of participation in masters sports: A case study of the "Masters Koshien." *International Journal of Sport and Health Science, 10,* 90–101. https://doi.org/10.5432/ijshs.201215

Hinch, T., & Ito, E. (2018). Sustainable sport tourism in Japan. *Tourism Planning and Development, 18*(1), 96–101. https://doi.org/10.1080/21568316.2017.1313773

Hinch, T., & Ramshaw, G. (2014). Heritage sport tourism in Canada. *Tourism Geographies, 16*(2), 237–251. https://doi.org/10.1080/14616688.2013.823234

Iso-Ahola, S. E. (1980). *The social psychology of leisure and recreation.* Dubuque, IA: Wm. C. Brown.

Ito, E., & Hikoji, K. (2021). Relationships of involvement and interdependent happiness between domestic and international Japanese masters games tourists. *Annals of Leisure Research, 24*(2), 262–268. https://doi.org/10.1080/11745398.2019.1610665

Ito, E., & Hinch, T. (2020). A systematic review of sport tourism research in Japan. In R. Sharpley & K. Kato, *Tourism development in Japan: Themes, issues and challenges* (pp. 82–101). London: Routledge.

Ito, E., & Kono, S. (2019). Similarities and differences in constraints and constraint negotiation among Japanese sport tourists: A case of masters games participants. *Journal of Sport & Tourism, 23*(2/3), 63–77. https://doi.org/10.1080/14775085.2019.1702582

Ito, E., Kono, S., & Walker, G. J. (2020). Development of cross-culturally informed leisure-time physical activity constraint and constraint negotiation typologies: The case of Japanese and Euro-Canadian adults. *Leisure Sciences, 42*(5/6), 411–429. https://doi.org/10.1080/01490400.2018.1446064

Iwasaki, Y. (2008). Pathways to meaning-making through leisure-like pursuits in global contexts. *Journal of Leisure Research, 40*(2), 231–249. https://doi.org/10.1080/00222216.2008.11950139

Japan High School Baseball Federation. (n.d.). Taikai nyuujyousha suu [The number of spectators]. Retrieved from http://www.jhbf.or.jp/sensyuken/spectators/

Kawai, K., & McDonald, B. (2012). Globalisation, individualism and scandal: New directions in Japanese baseball. *International Journal of the History of Sport, 29*(17), 2450–2464. https://doi.org/10.1080/09523367.2012.746831

Kelly, J. R. (1996). *Leisure.* Boston: Allyn & Bacon.

Kelly, W. W. (2011). Kōshien Stadium: Performing national virtues and regional rivalries in a 'theatre of sport.' *Sport in Society, 14*(4), 482–494. https://doi.org/10.1080/17430437.2011.565926

Komuku, H. (1995). Koshien to "nihonjin" no saiseisan [Re-creation of Koshien and "Japanese"]. In S. Esashi & H. Komuku (Eds.), *Koshien no shakaigaku: Koshien wo yomu* [Sociology of Koshien: Interpreting Koshien] (pp. 161–182). Tokyo: Sekai Shisosya.

Kono, S., Ito, E., & Gui, J. (2020). Empirical investigation of the relationship between serious leisure and meaning in life among Japanese and Euro-Canadians. *Leisure Studies, 39*(1), 131–145. https://doi.org/10.1080/02614367.2018.1555674

Kono, S., Walker, G. J., Ito, E., & Hagi, Y. (2019). Theorizing leisure's roles in the pursuit of ikigai (life worthiness): A mixed-methods approach. *Leisure Sciences, 41*(4), 237–259. https://doi.org/10.1080/01490400.2017.1356255

Masters Koshien Organizing Committee. (2004). *Masutazu Koshien gaido bukku 2004* [Masters Koshien Guide Book 2004]. Kobe.

Masters Koshien Organizing Committee. (2019). *Masutazu Koshien gaido bukku 2019* [Masters Koshien Guide Book 2019]. Kobe.

Neulinger, J. (1974). *The psychology of leisure.* Springfield, IL: Charles C. Thomas.

Ramshaw, G. (2010). Living heritage and the sports museum: Athletes, legacy and the Olympic Hall of Fame and Museum, Canada Olympic Park. *Journal of Sport & Tourism, 15*(1), 45–70. https://doi.org/10.1080/14775081003770983

Ramshaw, G. (2020). *Heritage and sport: An introduction.* Bristol: Channel View Publications.

Ramshaw, G., & Gammon, S. (2005). More than just nostalgia? Exploring the heritage/sport tourism nexus. *Journal of Sport Tourism, 10*(4), 229–241. https://doi.org/10.1080/14775080600805416

Ramshaw, G., & Gammon, S. (2010). On home ground? Twickenham Stadium Tours and the construction of sport heritage. *Journal of Heritage Tourism, 5*(2), 87–102. https://doi.org/10.1080/17438730903484184

Ramshaw, G., Gammon, S., & Huang, W. J. (2013). Acquired pasts and the commodification of borrowed heritage: The case of the Bank of America Stadium tour. *Journal of Sport & Tourism, 18*(1), 17–31. https://doi.org/10.1080/14775085.2013.799334

Rickly-Boyd, J. M. (2013). Existential authenticity: Place matters. *Tourism Geographies, 15*(4), 680–686. https://doi.org/10.1080/14616688.2012.762691

Ryan, C., & Trauer, B. (2005). Sport tourist behaviour: The example of the Masters games. In J. Higham (Ed.), *Sport tourism destinations: Issues, opportunities and analysis* (pp. 177–187). Oxford: Elsevier.

Sasakawa Sports Foundation. (2017). *Supotsu hakusho 2017: Supotsu ni yoru sosharu inobesyon* [The white paper of sports in 2017: Social innovation through sports]. Tokyo: Sasakawa Sports Foundation.

Shimizu, S. (2012). The significance of Koshien baseball in postwar Okinawa: A representation of 'Okinawa.' *International Journal of the History of Sport, 29*(17), 2421–2434. https://doi.org/10.1080/09523367.2012.751190

Stebbins, R. (2009). Serious leisure and work. *Sociology Compass, 3*(5), 764–774. https://doi.org/10.1111/j.1751-9020.2009.00233.x

Tani, M., Chogahara, M., Hikoji, K., Sonoda, D., & Matsumura, Y. (2012). Management evaluation of masters sports promotion using the print media: Action research of a masters baseball alumni event. *Journal of Asiania Sport for All, 12,* 32–53.

Wang, N. (1999). Rethinking authenticity in tourism experience. *Annals of Tourism Research, 26*(2), 349–370. https://doi.org/10.1016/S0160-7383(98)00103-0

Young, B. W., Bennett, A., & Séguin, B. (2015). Masters sport perspectives. In M. M. Parent & J-L Chappelet (Eds.), *Routledge handbook of sports event management: A stakeholder approach* (pp. 136–162). London: Routledge.

9

Exploring the Heritage of Baseball in South Korea

The Story of Regionalism and Nationalism

JUNGAH CHOI

Sport represents a country's social and cultural fabric, possessing both economic and social powers, which are vital tools in the promotion of national identity (Kwak et al., 2018). South Korea (henceforth, Korea) has traditional sports of its own—such as *Ssireum* (Korean wrestling) and *Taekwondo* (martial arts)—however, sports originating from different countries and cultures (such as soccer, baseball, and basketball) have also become popular sports in Korea. In particular, professional baseball is the most popular sporting event in Korea, attracting over eight million spectators per season through the 2016–2018 regular seasons.

Although the origins of baseball have been influenced by America and Japan, Korean baseball has accomplished a unique evolution and has its own characteristics based on distinctive Korean background and culture (Chiu et al., 2017). Since Korean society has suffered from war, Japanese colonial rule, and autocratic governments, baseball has become a symbol of expressing nationalism and patriotic sentiment; it is recognized as a tool offering Koreans relief from past political, economic, and cultural repression (Reaves, 2006). From the 1990s, the globalization of Korean baseball players who played abroad, especially in the United States, has contributed to a reconstruction of national identity and Korean nationalism (Cho, 2012c). While there was a downturn in the popularity of baseball during the late 1990s because of the Asian economic crisis, Korean baseball has once again become popular since 2006, along with the South Korean team's notable performance at international competitions such as the World Baseball

Classic, the WBSC Premier 12, the Olympics, and the Asian Games (Kim, 2008; Oh, 2009). The South Korean team came in third (2006) and second (2009) place in the World Baseball Classic, competed in the WBSC Premier 12 finals (2015, 2019), earned a gold medal at the Beijing Olympic Games (2008), and won at the Asian Games in 2010, 2014, and 2018. Today, Koreans enjoy the domestic contests between Korea Baseball Organization (KBO) League teams and enthusiastically cheer for their favorite squads. Further, Korean professional baseball has become a must-see cultural experience for international visitors who like baseball or sporting events in general, but particularly because of the cheering culture at KBO games (where audiences are much more enthusiastic than those in the United States), many of the between-inning games and contests, a variety of foods, and unique themed seats (Chiu et al., 2017). Stadiums offer skybox seats for VIPs and have various seating charts. For example, the Incheon SSG Landers Field (home of SSG Landers since 2021) includes 19 seating sections for fans to choose a preferable seat depending on their purpose. The Daejeon Hanwha Life Insurance Eagles Park (home of the Hanwha Eagles) and the Incheon SSG Landers Field have picnic areas where fans can build tents and enjoy watching the baseball games inside their tents.

Korean baseball has a long and rich heritage that, though influenced by both Japanese occupation and American baseball culture (Reaves, 2002), is distinctly Korean. Thus, this chapter examines the heritage of Korean baseball through a variety of perspectives in the light of sociopolitical issues that occurred in the Korean peninsula. Further, the chapter suggests future directions for Korean baseball heritage, including the potential development of a hall of fame and the preservation of historic stadia where, at present, Korean baseball heritage is underrepresented when compared to the Nippon Professional Baseball (NPB) and Major League Baseball (MLB).

American Influences on Korean Baseball

Baseball was first introduced to Korea at the time of the Korean Empire (1897–1910) by an American missionary, Philip L. Gillett, who established the first Young Men's Christian Association (YMCA) in Korea. The emergence of the YMCA was also an avenue for baseball, promoting the initial development of Korean baseball (Kim, 2008; Cho, 2012b; Reaves, 2002).

Although there was a decline in baseball as a result of Japanese control (1910–1945), Korean baseball players and teams had more opportunities to play with American players (Hirai, 2012). The top MLB players—including

Waite Hoyt (former pitcher for the New York Yankees), Herb Pennock (former pitcher for the Boston Red Sox), and George Kelly (former first baseman for the New York Giants)—came to Korea as part of an exhibition series with Korean amateur players in 1922. The visitation of future baseball Hall of Fame players contributed to the initial interest in baseball in Korea. After that, American baseball continued its influence on Korean baseball. The University of Chicago and the Philadelphia Bobbies (a professional women's baseball team comprising of young women ranging in age between 13 and 20) visited Korea in 1925 (Guthrie-Shimizu, 2012), and the Philadelphia Royal Giants of the Negro Leagues played Team Korea in 1927.

Although baseball almost disappeared in Korea during the Japanese occupation and during the Second World War, baseball in Korea was revived again with the support of American military forces (Kim, 2008). The KBA (Korea Baseball Association) was founded in the year following the U.S. military occupation to promote baseball in the Korean peninsula by staging friendly matches and providing baseball equipment. Several MLB teams, including the St. Louis Cardinals (1958) and Detroit Tigers (1964), competed against a Korean baseball team based in Seoul. A ticketing system was introduced in 1958 when the Cardinals visited Korea, thus beginning Korea's baseball spectating culture.

The Influence of Japanese Baseball in the Colonial Period

Although the emergence of baseball in Korea seems to have been highly influenced by American baseball, Korean baseball is also influenced by the Japanese style of baseball from that country's colonial era (Reaves, 2002). During the Japanese occupation (1910–1945), baseball in Korea was continued; however, it was controlled by the Japanese administration, and the majority of people who enjoyed baseball were Japanese residents living in Korea (Cho, 2012c). Koreans were limited in participating in team-based sports like baseball in order to undermine "team spirit" among Koreans (Ok, 2005). The Japanese government also passed the "baseball restriction law," which stated that Korean players were only able to play in Korean baseball tournaments that were sponsored by a Japanese company (Kim, 2008).

Although baseball was a symbol of colonialism, baseball also became a means for promoting nationalism and national identity for young Koreans opposed to the Japanese rule. In other words, victories against the Japanese on the ball field evoked nationalistic sentiments among colonized Koreans

(Cho, 2012a, 2012c, 2016a; Ok, 2007). Although baseball was controlled by Imperial Japan, baseball in Korea was resurrected after independence, in that playing baseball was an object of envy during the colonial period. Even Korean baseball maintained several characteristics of Japanese baseball after independence. For example, Korean baseball first began to flourish during the Korean high school tournament called *Chugryonggi*, mirroring the popularity of the Japanese league that started from the Japanese high school tournament *Koshien* (Cho, 2012a, 2012c; Lee, 2016).

Japanese baseball continued its influence on Korean baseball, producing numerous Korean-Japanese *zainichi* players, who played for the Japanese professional baseball league. After the *zainichi* baseball players began playing in Japan, these players imported advanced techniques from the Japanese leagues to Korea, such as the use of the curve ball in pitching, hitting for power, and the use of high-quality equipment. One of the most popular *zainichi* baseball players, Jang Hun—who is one of the greatest hitters in Japanese baseball history—made a considerable contribution in integrating Japanese baseball culture into Korean baseball. Further, the Korean baseball team won first place against the Japanese team at the 1963 Asian Baseball Championship (Lee, 2015; Lie, 2008). Under the first autocracy by President Park Chung-hee, baseball was often used as a political tool for communicating and strengthening the relationship with Japan. The first Korean professional baseball player, Baek In-Chon, was allowed to play in the Japanese league starting in 1962. Based on his experience playing in Japan, he served as a coach in Korea and focused on a Japanese style of baseball (Hirai, 2012).

When the Korean professional baseball league launched in 1982, many ethnic Korean *zainichi* players returned to their home countries to play in the Korean professional baseball league (Cho, 2016a). However, their athletic careers were difficult; they were a target of discrimination and pejoratively called *pan-jjokbari* (half-Japanese) due to anti-Japanese sentiment as a result of Japanese colonialism (Lie, 2008). In this context, the Korean professional baseball league seems more similar to the Japanese baseball culture than to American baseball, as it emphasizes team-based play, skills, and strategies instead of focusing on individual plays and muscular power (Kang, 2017). In addition, the Korean professional baseball league's governing system resembles Nippon Professional Baseball (NPB) in that both leagues are owned and funded by major companies (Hong & Lee, 2008; Walsh et al., 2015) such as Samsung, a Korean worldwide corporation, and the Yomiuri, a Japanese media conglomerate. This differs from MLB teams, which list the city with a team nickname (e.g., Los Angeles Dodgers). In this sense, Korean baseball was influenced by the Japanese version of baseball, *yakyu*, combining the characters for "field" and "ball," from the beginning of the Korean professional baseball league (Hirai, 2012; Reaves, 2002).

The 1980s and the Beginning of the Korean Professional Baseball League under Autocracy

The first Korean professional baseball league, called the Korea Baseball Organization (KBO) League, was founded in 1982 with six teams. The league was exploited for political propaganda in order to secure political powers under president Chun Doo-hwan's regime. The government initiative was to achieve political goals by distracting people's attention from larger political and socioeconomic issues (Kim, 2008; Kwak et al., 2017). In other words, the KBO League was used as a political tool at its inception in order to suppress the people's yearning for democracy and freedom (Kim, 2008; Reaves, 2002). The focus on professional sports, including the successful hosting of both the 1986 Asian Games and the 1988 Olympic Games, has also contributed to the development of elite sports in Korea (Ha & Mangan, 2002). Due to the popularity of professional baseball in Korea, the KBO League has expanded to ten teams (Korea Baseball Organization, 2019).

Although the beginnings of the KBO League were clearly political, professional baseball has become the most popular spectator sport in Korea (Hirai, 2012) because of the "home-based system" focusing on six regions of the Korean peninsula (Hong, 2011). Since a large number of Koreans left their hometowns to find a job in the 1980s, this regional approach inspired people to cheer for their home teams, which helped evoke nostalgic feelings (Cho, 2012c; Lee, 2016). Each KBO team represents specific regions, like Major League Baseball (MLB) and Nippon Professional Baseball (NPB), but the linkages between Korean teams and their home cities are stronger than other leagues. For example, in the past, each team could only select local players as their first-round draft picks. In other words, each team largely consisted of local players and coaches (Kim, 2008). The regional-based system has further intensified the competition between the southeast (Yongnam) and southwest (Honam) parts of Korea (Cho, 2008b). In this sense, baseball was not only a political proxy but also an outlet of resentment for people who lived in the Honam province, who experienced political and economic discrimination. Honam-region people enthusiastically cheered for the Haitai Tigers (renamed as the Kia Tigers in 2001) to distract from their sorrow caused by the Gwangju Uprising,* and the home stadium of Haitai was considered as a place of political resistance against government authorities. Other large rivalries include Seoul (the capital city) and Busan (the second-largest city), similar to the Real Madrid-FC Barcelona rivalry in Spanish football, as well as the Yomiuri Giants (Tokyo) and the Hanshin Tigers (Osaka) rivalry in Japanese baseball (Hong & Lee, 2008). The majority of Korean baseball fans stick to their regions in deciding which team to support. In particular, approximately 80 percent of respondents from the city of Busan support the Lotte Giants, a team representing their region (Lim & Lee, 2003). It is not only a baseball team in Busan, but also a symbol of Busan. The Sajik Stadium (home stadium of the Giants) has a unique and passionate atmosphere, along with the impressive supporters' unique forms of cheering culture. For example, the "Busan Galmaegi Song," which means "Busan Seagull," is the best-known baseball-cheering song in the KBO League. As a port city, the song is representative of the city itself, and the seagull became the team's emblem as well as its mascot (Hong & Lee, 2008). The combination of sport and commercialization also contributed to the development of the KBO League in the 1980s. Since all teams were owned by major corporations, each team has promoted the league with financial support and focused marketing efforts on TV broadcasts, as well as in venues and services (Cho, 2000; Hong & Lee, 2008).

Baseball Heroes, Postcolonial Legacies, and Globalization: 1990s to 2000s

The popularity of the KBO League constantly increased until 1995; however, the attendance decreased by 2.6 million in 1998 (Cho, 2008a). While the Asian financial crisis (IMF intervention: 1997–2001) influenced a downturn of spectating the KBO League, Korean baseball fans began to instead pay attention to Major League Baseball (MLB) and Nippon Professional Baseball (NPB), along with exporting Korean star players to bigger leagues (Cho, 2000; 2012a). During the dark economic period, nationalistic sentiments and emotional responses were ignited by elite sports players; thus, Korean athletes' glorious moments in the United States and Japan were the pride of the Korean nation (Cho, 2012a). Chan Ho Park was the first outstanding

---

* The Gwangju Uprising (happened in 1980, Gwang-ju) was a large-scale pro-democracy movement against the military junta led by Chun Doo-hwan. This movement resulted in hundreds of casualties and thousands of wounded and missing Gwangju citizens.

Korean player to gain prominence in the MLB, playing with the Los Angeles Dodgers from 1994 and being recognized as one of the league's best pitchers in 1997. The "Chan Ho Park Syndrome" transferred Koreans' attention to American baseball in 1990s. Park's glories promoted national pride and instilled Koreans with a spirit of patriotism during the period of national depression. Further, he has become a national hero and set a milestone by achieving 124 victories during his 17-year career to mark the most wins by an Asian-born pitcher (Kang, 2017). His successful debut in MLB inspired young Korean baseball players, many of whom want to be "like Chan Ho." Starting with Park, Korea became the largest provider of Asian players to the MLB (Cho, 2012a; Kang, 2017). There have since been various other Korean baseball players who left Korea for the MLB, including Shin-Soo Choo, who plays for the Texas Rangers, and Hyun-jin Ryu, who signed with the Toronto Blue Jays in 2020.

Along with Korean players' success in the MLB, a new sense of nostalgia and nationalism emerged among Korean baseball fans that was different from the feelings that occurred during the home-based rationalistic era. In other words, the role of professional teams as symbols of local identity still continues, but the strong sense of regionalism has been reduced (Cho, 2012c; Miller et al., 2001). Since Korean broadcasters began to air MLB games, there was a decrease in the demand for KBO League in the late 1990s. However, the Korean league regained popularity when Korea won a gold medal at the 2008 Beijing Olympic Games and did well at the 2009 World Baseball Classic (Cho, 2016b).

The globalization of Korean baseball has also fueled Korean nationalism, especially whenever the Korean national team meets a former colonial power, such as Japan and the United States, at an international baseball tournament (Cho, 2012c). Despite the globalization of baseball, a number of political discourses are still present in baseball, along with the memories of Japanese occupation in particular. As is the case with all types of sports, a victory against the Japanese team is similar to having "revenge" against Japan; it inspires nationalism, patriotic sentiments, and euphoria among Koreans (Cho, 2012c; Lee & Maguire, 2013; Ok, 2007). In terms of baseball, the World Baseball Classic has become a popular tournament among Korean baseball fans in that Korean and Japanese national teams meet and compete against each other. Defeating Japan again proved to be a moment that promoted nationalistic feelings (Cho, 2016b). Since Korean players have an intense rivalry against Japan, they planted Korean flags on the pitcher's mound after their victory against Japan at the 2006 World Baseball Classic

(Mangan et al., 2013; Oh, 2009). As such, both Korean players and fans always feel a strong sense of cohesion and belonging themselves when they play the Japanese team (Oh, 2009).

The postcolonial identity is more prominent among Korean immigrants who have settled in Japan for economic purposes and on the West Coast of the U.S. in order to avoid the discriminatory Japanese colonial policy. For example, the Angel Stadium of Anaheim became a cultural place where Korean residents in America could express and experience their postcolonial identity while they cheered on Team South Korea. Especially when South Korea beat Japan, a victory as well as a patriotic ritual—planting the national flag at the center of Angel Stadium—was regarded as a symbolic redemption of the postcolonial Korean identity (Lee & Maguire, 2013). In the case of immigrants to Japan, they also felt a great sense of achievement along with their postcolonial identity when the Korean national team received the championship title at the 2015 WBSC Premier 12, which is an international baseball championship sponsored by the World Baseball Softball Confederation (WBSC), by beating two sporting powerhouses, the U.S. and Japan, at the Tokyo Dome. In addition, Korean immigrants tend to keep their original and social ties to their ethnic communities; thus, the presence of Korean players in MLB and NPB becomes a means of retaining their ethnic identity by supporting Korean MLB and NPB players (Stodolska & Alexandris, 2004). The history of Korean diaspora still forms a significant feature of nationalism and national identity (nationalistic feeling among a diaspora) within the context of international sporting events. In this sense, the success of Korean players in MLB and NPB caused euphoria, nostalgia, and nationalism, in addition to further diasporic nationalism. Still, an anti-Japan antipathy, caused by colonial sentiment, exists and significantly accounts for Korean's nationalism and the sense of pride when the Korean national team encounters the Japanese team (Cho, 2012a; Lee & Maguire, 2013; Mangan et al., 2013).

Contemporary Intangible Heritage in Korean Baseball

Although the history of baseball in Korea is mainly influenced by American and Japanese baseball, Korean baseball has become a powerful symbol of Korean culture based on its unique characteristics. Korean baseball became a national pastime in that the development of Korean baseball corresponded to the nation's economic growth and the public's desire for more leisure activities (Cho, 2016a). Since its introduction in 1982, the KBO

League has drawn a total of more than 100 million spectators. What, then, brings baseball fans to Korean baseball parks?

First, the cheers and chants of Korean baseball spectators attract a sizable number of fans. Sporting events comprise a variety of stimuli that are taken in through an individual's sensory perception. The senses include the sound, smell, taste, visual, and touch components within the sporting event experience. Since auditory elements—including chants, cheers, music, and the sounds of the crowd—are an important part of the sport stadium experience (Lee et al., 2012), many baseball fans all around the world are impressed by Korean cheering culture, who enthusiastically cheer to support their teams and players. The concept of cheerleaders and a cheerleading captain began after the 1988 Olympic Games, while the leading of particular cheers began in the 1990s. The characteristics of Korean fan cheering culture include the sense of collective, enthusiastic, and empathetic aspects. Based on South Korea's collectivist cultures, Korean baseball fans tend to adhere to more group-disciplined chanting and cheering, while American baseball fans' cheering cultures are more self-oriented (Markus & Kitayama, 1991). Due to such a collectivistic culture, each team has their own team-based chanting, singing, and dancing, including cheerleaders who lead the crowd, make fans enthusiastic, and add entertainment factors during the games (Chiu et al., 2017). All the KBO teams are based on a particular region; the cheers and chants consist of songs related to specific locations and dialect words, creating a feeling of empathy and camaraderie with other fans who support the same regions and teams. Also, smells as well as tastes, including foods and beverages, are significant elements of the Korean baseball stadium experience. Each ballpark serves the representative food of the region where the ballpark is located, such as flat-grilled dumplings in Daegu Samsung Lions Park and smoked pork belly in Jamsil Baseball Stadium. Since Korean baseball fans visit baseball parks not only for watching the game itself but also for their leisure time with friends and family, a variety of specialty foods attract many fans who can enjoy the stadium atmosphere. The visual components are associated with the cheering traditions and rituals of Korean baseball. Each team also has its own color of balloon sticks. In the case of the Lotte Giants, there is a tradition for fans to inflate orange trash bags and strap them to their heads while they are cheering, and then they use them to pick up their trash after game is over (Choe, 2014). According to Lee and Ahn (2015), Korean baseball fans visit KBO League ballparks for eating, drinking, chanting, cheering, and dancing in the open air. The sensory perceptions further create intangible baseball heritage. For example, the sound has a positive impact on team identity and loyalty, which means that cheering makes the spectators feel connected to their teams (Lee et al., 2013). In particular, there are intense cheering battles, which make baseball fans feel a sense of identity and belonging more deeply, especially when the KBO teams play traditional rival teams (Chiu et al., 2017). Wearing a player's team jersey makes spectators feel a sense of belonging, solidarity, and pride.

Additionally, memories and nostalgia associated with attending baseball games in Korea are a form of intangible heritage as well in representative ballparks where international events are still held, such as Jamsil Baseball Stadium and Busan Sajik Baseball Stadium. In the case of Jamsil Baseball Stadium, there are collective forms of memories and nostalgia in terms of past players, teams, and events (Snyder, 1991). There are also personal or family-based nostalgic feelings associated with past baseball park experiences since the stadium hosted international scale events, such as baseball games during the 1988 Summer Olympics and the final game of the 2009 World Baseball Classic between Korea and Japan. Today, memories in relation to Korean baseball can be revived and dramatized through TV dramas and movies. Even Korean pop culture has produced a highly emotional regionalist and nationalistic discourse to young generations who have never experienced the colonial period or military dictatorship. For example, the movie *YMCA Baseball Team* (released in 2002) features the first Korean baseball team in 1905, covering the colonial past (Cho, 2012b). The film *Perfect Game* (released in 2011) is based on the story of two legendary pitchers between two rival teams, the Haitai Tigers and the Lotte Giants.

Baseball Stadiums and Baseball Halls of Fame and Museums in Korea

Although Korean baseball is on the world stage in terms of players' talent and fan support, the stadiums and facilities lag behind other baseball powerhouse countries such as Japan and the United States. Korean baseball heritage is particularly underestimated in comparison to that of Japan and the U.S., as there are no integrated Korean baseball museums or halls of fame to preserve and manage Korean baseball artifacts, memorabilia, and documents. Korean baseball heroes have emerged and the KBO League has grown rapidly, with an expanding number of fans visiting baseball stadiums since the foundation of the league. But the heritage value of stadiums has been disregarded, with many of the older stadiums with rich histories being completely destroyed. Baseball artifacts, memorabilia, and documents are being neglected, due to their being archived in multiple places and having no integrated baseball museum to house them.

In terms of baseball stadia, many of the outdated stadiums have been renovated to enhance the quality of baseball fans' experience. In this sense, the concept of a stadium is being transformed into a ballpark; it becomes not just a place for games but also a complex cultural space with a diverse range of entertainment, facilities, and foods. Although this transformation is in its early stages, Korean baseball stadiums appear to be following the developments in American ballparks—for example, the Daegu Samsung Lions Park, built in 2016, was based on the Citizens Bank Park (which is the home of the Philadelphia Phillies) (Kim, 2012).

Many KBO League teams largely renovated their stadiums with an increase in the number of attendances, including the Hanwha Eagles (2012), the KIA Tigers (2014), the SK Wyverns* (2015), followed by the KT Wiz (2015/2017). Some KBO teams have established new ballparks—for example, Daegu Samsung Lions Park (2016) for the Samsung Lions, and the Changwon NC Park (2019) for the NC Dinos. Also, a domed baseball stadium, the Gocheok Sky Dome (home of Kiwoom Heroes), was built in 2015 (Nam, 2015). Although newly built and renovated Korean baseball stadiums could improve the quality of facilities and services for spectators (Lee & Ahn, 2015), the Sajik Baseball Stadium and the Jamsil Baseball Stadium, built in the 1980s, still remain with a series of partial repairs (Chung, 2016). As such, many outdated Korean baseball stadiums have been renovated or completely demolished to build new ballparks, though this is not the best option in light of baseball heritage; stadiums are associated with both tangible and intangible values, local memory, social issues, and so on (Vecco, 2010).

On a personal level, fans can share and recall their own experiences with their parents as well as continue to create personal heritage with their children (Ramshaw & Gammon, 2015). When the KBO League kicked off with six teams in 1982, a membership program for kids gained enormous popularity, with approximately 300,000 child members in the first year, in the case of the OB Bears (now the Doosan Bears) (Choi, 2015). This membership has given kid fans a sense of belonging, in that they can bring their future children to a baseball stadium so as to remind themselves of their

---

* The SK Wyverns team was sold to Shinsegae Group and was officially renamed the SSG Landers in 2021.

pleasant childhood memories. In this sense, the former stadium is more valuable than new stadium in terms of providing nostalgic experiences, especially if a new venue fails to attract fans.

The Hanwha Life Insurance Eagles Park, built in 1964, is a case in point. It was chosen for renovation over demolition in 2012. In doing so, the baseball park still retains its historic and cultural symbolism as one of the first baseball stadiums in Korea and a place where some sporting heroes played, including Hyun-jin Ryu—the first ever KBO player to directly enter MLB. Several other older venues still exist, but they have been changed into different sites. For example, the old office building has been converted into the Hanwha Eagles' historical museum, and the old indoor practice field has become a practice field for social baseball club members to contribute to the local community.

Despite the cultural and heritage values, the Dongdaemun Baseball Stadium (DBS)—the country's first modern sporting venue, built in 1925, and the home of Korean amateur baseball for more than 30 years—was demolished in 2008 as part of urban regeneration plans. The demolition of the DBS not only indicates the stadium removal but also the disposal of the collective sporting memories and nostalgic sentiments linked to postcolonial Korean national identity (Lee, 2016). Although the original structure was demolished, the Dongdaemun Stadium Memorial Hall has been constructed in order to embrace and retain memories related to sporting events at the stadium (Lee, 2018).

Since KBO teams are affiliated with major companies, their name, the name of the ballpark, the logo, the emblem, and the uniform are all changed when a new corporation takes over a team. However, new companies take over their teams' history and reputation—for example, the SK Wyverns (the Incheon-based baseball team) were renamed SSG Landers following an ownership change, but they continue to maintain the heritage of Incheon baseball by displaying the all-time KBO championship emblems and symbols of glorious moments at the ballpark (Kim, 2021).

Thus, the retro-nostalgic baseball stadium design, started by Baltimore's Oriole Park at Camden Yards in 1992 (see Ramshaw & Gammon in this volume), has emphasized historical references and heritage-based designs (Friedman, 2007). Citi Field in New York has also preserved heritage by recreating historic elements of former stadiums (Pfleegor & Seifried, 2012). Although the retro stadium trend provides a meaningful cultural form, there are no retro stadiums in Korea yet. There are only retro-related events, including the Doosan Bears' "Player's Day" and the Lotte Giants' "Retro

Day," on which all players wear throwback jerseys. The Korean baseball parks built after 2010 have not been focused on nostalgia-inspired designs or celebrating baseball heritage. The Gwangju-Kia Champions Field includes the Gwangju-Kia Tigers' Baseball Museum, which provides the history of the Kia Tigers along with a number of uniforms and gears used by former players and memorabilia, including trophies and the championship flags. It is perhaps the only Korean ballpark with heritage displays.

The Jamsil Sports Complex, including the Jamsil Baseball Stadium, is in the process of reconstruction plan to establish a global MICE (Meetings, Incentives, Conferencing, Exhibitions) center that further extends to sport, concerts, and other leisure activities. It is clearly an ambitious plan, but the current stadium was built for Korea's first international sporting events, such as the 1986 Seoul Asian Games and the 1988 Seoul Olympic Games, representing a significant moment in Korea's modern sport history. Thus, it is important to consider the heritage values of old stadiums and the ways to incorporate the idea of Korean baseball heritage into the construction of new stadiums.

In terms of repositories of Korean baseball heritage, there is the Korean baseball hall of fame, located in the Kang Chang Hak Stadium at the southern part of Jeju island in Korea. It opened in 1998 with 3,000 items, though it is not affiliated with the KBO League (Lee, 2013). The Korean baseball hall of fame does not focus on individual players' records and achievements, preferring to exhibit a number of baseball heritage in the form of artifacts, memorabilia, and documents. In other words, it is different from the National Baseball Hall of Fame and Museum in Cooperstown, New York, which is a site of honoring individuals who made an outstanding contribution to baseball. Although there exist many Korean baseball heroes so far, including legendary pitchers Sun Dong-yol and Choi Dong-won, the current Korean hall of fame's artifacts and memorabilia is more on the KBO teams and league.

There is a plan for a Korean baseball hall of fame and museum (under the KBO League), which was supposed to be established in 2019, but construction was delayed due to conflicts with the local government. Still, there is no integrated place to house Korean baseball heritage; a number of donated collections and documents are located in the archive center at the KBO hall, some are in the current Korean baseball hall of fame, and others exist in the form of private collections. It seems to lag significantly behind the National Baseball Hall of Fame and Museum (built in 1939) in Cooperstown (Lee, 2013), and the Japanese Baseball Hall of Fame and Museum in Tokyo (established in 1959) ("Korea seeks to build baseball museum," 2011). As such, baseball heritage is underestimated in Korea in that many artifacts, memorabilia, and documents related to previous teams have been lost, especially when teams changed ownership. Establishing a Korean baseball of fame and museum would thus help to disseminate and develop Korean baseball as well as help others experience Korean baseball's past, present, and future by honoring the Korean baseball heroes and preserving Korean baseball heritage.

Also, future Korean baseball halls of fame and museums may attract Korean baseball fans by providing baseball heritage related to their favorite baseball teams and players (Wood, 2005). Since there has been significant global attention in Korean baseball as the 2020 KBO League was broadcast on ESPN, this may also attract foreign visitors who are interested in Korean baseball history and culture. Such Korean baseball halls of fame and museums may contribute to develop amateur and youth baseball, as they often can generate revenue by hosting programs and selling souvenirs (Ramshaw & Gammon, 2015).

Due to the continuing delays in establishing the Korean baseball hall of fame and museum, the Korean Digital Baseball Museum was inaugurated in 2020, making Korean baseball documents and records available to the general public. It is an appropriate way to collect and exhibit Korean baseball heritage during the era of COVID-19, as people can access this information without any restrictions. Such digitized information would be the cornerstone of a future Korean baseball hall of fame and museum and would help organize significant historical heritage related to Korean baseball (Digital Baseball Museum, 2020).

Conclusion

Baseball in Korea can be explained through the twin influences of Japanese baseball and American baseball. Throughout its history, the development of Korean baseball has been impacted by both regionalism and nationalism. Even though the KBO League was started for a political purpose—to foster national unity as well as to suppress the people's desire for democracy and distract people from political issues—professional baseball became a popular spectator sport in Korea (Cho, 2008a). The nationalistic sentiment among Korean baseball players and fans has become important, particularly when Korea plays Japan, as these matches are viewed in part through the lens of colonialism.

Despite the short history of the KBO compared to the MLB and the NPB, the KBO League has achieved a number of accomplishments and glorious moments, including producing many legendary players, receiving a gold medal at the Beijing Olympics in 2008, and winning the WBSC Premier 12 tournament in 2015. However, a new Korean baseball museum where people can recognize these achievements through heritage exhibitions does not yet exist. Along with these exhibits, a new museum would provide an opportunity for past Korean players to give public talks or hold autograph sessions, helping to create a form of "living" sport heritage (Ramshaw, 2010). In addition, displaying the feats of past sporting heroes could also include retiring players' numbers and naming events or awards after them (Reid, 2017). Many KBO teams built new baseball parks, and though these stadia may enhance the spectator experience, they come at a cost when it comes to preserving and recognizing Korea's baseball heritage. In this sense, the reconfiguration of stadiums into retro-style modern ballparks is recommended as a way of commemorating and preserving baseball heritage (Smith, 2008) as well a vehicle for commodifying the sporting past (Ramshaw & Gammon, 2017). Also, newly built ballparks can add heritage elements by displaying retired jerseys and pictures of famous past players and games inside of the stadium. In other words, sport heritage sites must balance both the preservation and commodification of the sporting past.

In summary, Korean baseball has generated a rich heritage formed by the unique background of Korean society, but exactly when a place of commemorating baseball heritage and history will be constructed is still in question. Although establishing a Korean baseball museum and hall of fame would celebrate Korean baseball heritage and help communicate the heritage of Korean baseball to future generations, there will likely be a conflict of interest between stakeholders. In particular, many museums were temporarily closed between 2020 and 2021 in response to the coronavirus pandemic. In this context, the Digital Baseball Museum has received much attention and is recognized as an online space where baseball fans can explore the history of the KBO League (see www.koreabaseballmuseum.com). Since COVID-19 accelerated the digitalization and visualization trends for museums, the KBO needs to provide, in addition to the online exhibitions, further creative initiatives and digital programs, such as virtual tours and VR games.

References

Chiu, W., Bae, J. S., & Won, D. (2017). The experience of watching baseball games in Korea: An analysis of user-generated content on social media using Leximancer. *Journal of Sport & Tourism, 21*(1), 33–47. doi:10.1080/14775085.2016.1255562

Cho, H. J. (2016, July 6). 58nyeon jeon 'hankuk choecho'ui seupocheu marketing [The first sports marketing before fifty years]. *Joy News.* http://inews24.com/view/966977 (accessed December 5, 2020).

Cho, Y. (2008a). Broadcasting Major League Baseball as a governmental instrument in South Korea. *Journal of Sport and Social Issues, 32*(3), 240–254. doi:10.1177/0193723508319721

Cho, Y. (2008b). The national crisis and de/reconstructing nationalism in South Korea during the IMF intervention. *Inter-Asia Cultural Studies, 9*(1), 82–96. doi:10.1080/14649370701789666

Cho, Y. (2012a). Baseball, Korea. In J. Nauright & C. Parrish (Eds.), *Sports around the world: History, culture, and practice* (Vol. 1, pp. 200–202). New York: Abc-Clio.

Cho, Y. (2012b). Colonial modernity matters? Debates on colonial past in South Korea. *Cultural Studies, 26*(5), 645–669. doi:10.1080/09502386.2012.697709

Cho, Y. (2012c). Major League Baseball as a forged national pastime: Constructing personalized national narratives in South Korea. *Inter-Asia Cultural Studies, 13*(4), 532–547. doi:10.1080/14649373.2012.717600

Cho, Y. (2016a). Double binding of Japanese colonialism: Trajectories of baseball in Japan, Taiwan, and Korea. *Cultural Studies, 30*(6), 926–948. doi:10.1080/09502386.2015.1094498

Cho, Y. (2016b). Toward the post-Westernization of baseball? The national-regional-global nexus of Korean Major League Baseball fans during the 2006 World Baseball Classic. *International Review for the Sociology of Sport, 51*(6), 752–769. doi:10.1177/1012690214552658

Cho, H. Y. (2000). The structure of the South Korean developmental regime and its transformation–statist mobilization and authoritarian integration in the anti-communist regimentation. *Inter-Asia Cultural Studies, 1*(3), 408–426. doi:10.1080/14649370020009915

Choe, S. (2014, November 2). In Korean Baseball, Louder Cheers and More Squid. *New York Times.* https://www.nytimes.com/2014/11/03/world/asia/to-understand-korean-baseball-head-to-the-stands.html (accessed December 5, 2020).

Choi, M. K. (2015, September 6). In early KBO days, Bears pioneered kids program. *Korea JoongAng Daily.* https://koreajoongangdaily.joins.com/2015/09/06/Baseball/In-early-KBO-days-Bears-pioneered-kids-program/3008842.html (accessed April 8, 2021).

Chung, H. (2016, April 3). Riverside location for proposed Jamsil baseball stadium. *Korea Times.* http://www.koreatimes.co.kr/www/news/nation/2016/04/116_201779.html (accessed December 5, 2020).

Digital Baseball Museum (2020). http://www.koreabaseballmuseum.com/Museum/Notice/view/5387 (accessed April 28, 2021).

Friedman, M. (2007). The spectacle of the past: Leveraging history in Fenway Park and Camden Yards. In S. Gammon & G. Ramshaw (Eds.), *Heritage, sport and tourism: Sporting pasts-tourist futures* (pp. 113–132). London: Routledge.

Ha, N. G., & Mangan, J. A. (2002). Ideology, politics, power: Korean sport-transformation, 1945–1992. *International Journal of the History of Sport, 19*(2–3), 213–242. doi:10.1080/714001746

Hirai, H. (2012). An indispensable but fragile geopolitical triangle: Baseball in Japan, Korea and Taiwan. *International Journal of the History of Sport, 29*(17), 2465–2477. doi:10.1080/095233672012746833

Hong, J., & Lee, C. (2008). New marketing challenge of the South Korean Professional Baseball League and the Lotte Giants. In S. Chadwick & D. Arthur (Eds.), *International cases in the business of sport* (pp. 389–403). London: Routledge.

Hong, E. (2011). Elite sport and nation-building in South Korea: South Korea as the dark horse in global elite sport. *International Journal of the History of Sport, 28*(7), 977–989. doi:10.1080/09523367.2011.563630

Kang, H. (2017, March 9). Korean baseball shifting to Major League style. *Korea Times.* https://www.koreatimes.co.kr/www/sports/2017/03/662_225360.html (accessed December 5, 2020).

Kim, B. (2008). Professional baseball in Korea: Origins, causes, consequences and implications. *International Journal of the History of Sport, 25*(3), 370–385. doi:10.1080/09523360701805811

Kim, H. T. (2012, December 26). hankuk choecho 'palgak yagoojang' Daegue deuleoseonda [The first eight angels ballparks in Daegu, Korea]. *Joy News.* http://inews24.com/view/713748 (accessed April 9, 2021).

Kim, H. J. (2021, March 25). SSG Landersfield saedanjang. SK yusan itgo SSG dama [SSG Landersfield renewal. Continue the SK legacy and take the SSG]. *Newsis.* https://newsis.com (accessed September 6, 2021).

Korea seeks to build baseball museum (2011, April 11). *Korea Times.* http://www.koreatimes.co.kr/www/sports/2018/09/600_85241.html (accessed December 5, 2020).

Korea Baseball Organization (2019). http://www.koreabaseball.com (accessed May 1, 2021).

Kwak, D., Ko, Y., Kang, I., & Rosentraub, M. (2017). *Sport in Korea: History, development, management.* Abingdon: Routledge.

Lee, C. J. (2015, March 16). Hankukyagooei ibangin [The stranger of Korean baseball]. *The Hankyoreh.* http://www.hani.co.kr/ (accessed December 5, 2020).

Lee, H. K. (2018). Recreating Dongdaemun Stadium in South Korea: Beyond Japanese colonial memories and towards a global city. *Seoul Journal of Korean Studies, 31*(1), 99–128. doi:10.1353/se0.2018.0005

Lee, J. W. (2016). Competing visions for urban space in Seoul: Understanding the demolition of Korea's Dongdaemun Baseball Stadium. In N. Koch (Eds.), *Critical geographies of sport: Space, power, and sport in global perspective* (pp. 142–156). Abingdon: Routledge.

Lee, J. W., & Maguire, J. (2013). The memory of colonialism and imagined unification: Two distinctive natures of South Korean sporting nationalism in the 21st century. In

K. Bromber, B. Krawietz, & J. Maguire (Eds.), *Sport across Asia: Politics, cultures, and identities* (pp. 77–94). Abingdon: Routledge.

Lee, K. H. (2013, March 23). 'Gugbogeub tusu' Sun Dong-yol myeongyeui jeondang heonaeg 1ho [The national treasure pitcher Sun Dong-yol will be entered the hall of fame first]. *Sportsdonga.* http://www.donga.com/ (accessed December 5, 2020).

Lee, S. H., & Ahn, S. Y. (2015, April 10). Upgraded baseball stadiums raise their game. *Korea JoongAng Daily.* https://koreajoongangdaily.joins.com/2015/04/10/features/Upgraded-baseball-stadiums-raise-their-game/3002968.html (accessed December 5, 2020).

Lee, S., Heere, B., & Chung, K. S. (2013). Which senses matter more? The impact of our senses on team identity and team loyalty. *Sport Marketing Quarterly, 22*(4), 203–213.

Lee, S., Lee, H. J., Seo, W. J., & Green, C. (2012). A new approach to stadium experience: The dynamics of the sensoryscape, social interaction, and sense of home. *Journal of Sport Management, 26,* 490–505. doi:10.1123/jsm.26.6.490

Lie, J. (2008). *Zainichi (Koreans in Japan): Diasporic nationalism and postcolonial identity.* Berkeley: University of California Press.

Lim, S. W., & Lee, K. M. (2003). The effects of professional baseball games between Youngnam and Honam Teams on regional emotion. *Korean Society for the Sociology of Sport, 16*(1), 73–92.

Mangan, J. A., Kim, H. D., Cruz, A., & Kang, G. H. (2013). Rivalries: China, Japan and South Korea–memory, modernity, politics, geopolitics–and sport. *International Journal of the History of Sport, 30*(10), 1130–1152. doi:10.1080/09523367.2013.800046

Markus, H. R., & Kitayama, S. (1991). Culture and the self: Implications for cognition, emotion, and motivation. *Psychological Review, 98*(2), 224–253. doi:10.1037/0033-295X.98.2.224

Miller, T., Lawrence, G. A., McKay, J., & Rowe, D. (2001). *Globalization and sport: Playing the world.* London: SAGE.

Nam, H. (2015, October 5). Nexen Heroes to play at domed baseball field. *Korea Times.* https://www.koreatimes.co.kr/www/sports/2020/08/600_188065.html (accessed December 5, 2020).

Oh, M. (2009). 'Eternal other' Japan: South Koreans' postcolonial identity. *International Journal of the History of Sport, 26*(3), 371–389. doi:10.1080/09523360802602257

Ok, G. (2005). The political significance of sport: An Asian case study—Sport, Japanese colonial policy and Korean national resistance, 1910–1945. *International Journal of the History of Sport, 22*(4), 649–670. doi:10.1080/09523360500123051

Ok, G. (2007). Coercion for Asian conquest: Japanese militarism and Korean sport, 1938–1945. *International Journal of the History of Sport, 24*(3), 338–356. doi:10.1080/09523360601101329

Pfleegor, A. G., & Seifried, C. S. (2012). Is building new the only option? A teaching approach to heritage management. *Sport Management Education Journal, 6*(1), 32–42. doi:10.1123/smej.6.1.32

Ramshaw, G. (2010). Living heritage and the sports museum: Athletes, legacy and the Olympic Hall of Fame and Museum, Canada Olympic Park. *Journal of Sport & Tourism, 15*(1), 45–70. doi:10.1080/14775081003770983

Ramshaw, G. (2020). *Heritage and sport: An introduction.* Bristol: Channel View Publications.

Ramshaw, G., & Gammon, S. (2005). More than just nostalgia? Exploring the heritage/sport tourism nexus. *Journal of Sport Tourism, 10*(4), 229–241. doi:10.1080/14775080600805416

Ramshaw, G., & Gammon, S. (2015). Heritage and sport. In E. Waterton & S. Watson (Eds.), *The Palgrave handbook of contemporary heritage research* (pp. 248–260). Basingstoke, Hampshire: Palgrave Macmillan.

Ramshaw, G., & Gammon, S. J. (2017). Towards a critical sport heritage: Implications for sport tourism. *Journal of Sport & Tourism, 21*(2), 115–131. doi:10.1080/14775085.2016.1262275

Ramshaw, G., Gammon, S., & Huang, W. J. (2013). Acquired pasts and the commodification of borrowed heritage: The case of the Bank of America Stadium tour. *Journal of Sport & Tourism, 18*(1), 17–31. doi:10.1080/14775085.2013.799334

Reaves, J. A. (2002). *Taking in a game: A history of baseball in Asia.* Lincoln: University of Nebraska Press.

Reaves, J. A. (2006). Korea: Straw scandals and strong arms. In G. Gmelch (Ed.), *Baseball without borders: The international pastime* (pp. 89–114). Lincoln: University of Nebraska Press.

Reid, H. (2017). Athletes as heroes and role models: An ancient model. *Sport, Ethics and Philosophy, 11*(1), 40–51. doi:10.1080/17511321.2016.1261931

Smith, M. M. (2008). From 'the finest ballpark in America' to 'the jewel of the waterfront': The construction of San Francisco's Major League Baseball stadiums. *International Journal of the History of Sport, 25*(11), 1529–1546. doi:10.1080/09523360802299278

Snyder, E. E. (1991). Sociology of nostalgia: Sport halls of fame and museums in America. *Sociology of Sport Journal, 8*(3), 228–238. doi:10.1123/ssj.8.3.228

Stodolska, M., & Alexandris, K. (2004). The role of recreational sport in the adaptation of first generation immigrants in the United States. *Journal of Leisure Research, 36*(3), 379–413. doi:10.1080/00222216.2004.11950029

Vecco, M. (2010). A definition of cultural heritage: From the tangible to the intangible. *Journal of Cultural Heritage, 11*(3), 321–324. doi:10.1016/j.culher.2010.01.006

Walsh, P., Hwang, H., Lim, C. H., & Pedersen, P. M. (2015). Examining the use of professional sport teams as a brand extension strategy in Korean professional baseball. *Sport Marketing Quarterly, 24*(4), 214–224.

Wood, J. (2005). Olympic opportunity: Realizing the value of sports heritage for tourism in the UK. *Journal of Sport Tourism, 10*(4), 307-321. doi:10.1080/14775080600805556

10

The "Gaijin Revolution" in Brazil

A Japanese Baseball Heritage at Risk?

FELIPE BERTAZZO TOBAR

Cultures, by their nature, are porous, and through historical interactions they can often be reshaped through a manifold of influences (Stewart, 1999). The heritage of immigration is one of the clear examples of this cultural phenomenon since it is a long-term product of a wide range of social relations and cultural manifestations—both tangible and intangible—experienced in the homeland and later at a new territory (Paiva, 2015). Usually, first-generation immigrants are willing to preserve their most valuable traditions and customs to pass on to future generations, especially those connected to social activities and people. Such behavior helps to explain why heritage can be a "dangerous concept" (Howard, 2003) since it has the potential to reproduce divisive intragroup nationalistic behaviors.

Sport has been used as a vehicle for informal cultural power where desired social behaviors, standards, and ideologies are exchanged within colonial populations (Stoddart, 1988). In Brazil, the first Japanese immigrants did not face resistance in maintaining their passion for baseball mainly due to Brazilians being unfamiliar with the sport. This chapter deals with historical and contemporary features of baseball in Brazil, where the sport became a symbol of Japanese collective identity. More specifically, it touches on the heritage facet, discussing how a form of isolation allowed the first immigrants and their descendants to preserve the Japanese baseball heritage until globalization forces gave rise to the beginning of the Gaijin Revolution, a process where non-Japanese descendants started to play and manage the sport through different ethnic influences.

As Ramshaw (2020) identified, sport heritage can be part of the existential self—in this case, through bloodlines—or by the only act of practicing the sport influenced by personal or cultural identities. Both dimensions are explored in this chapter, which considers Japanese baseball heritage as a discursive practice—in other words, as a process that attributes and shares meanings through language, sites, objects, contexts, and people, thus defining and constructing heritage representations (Harrison, 2012; Ramshaw, 2020). Through such a lens, it will be possible to better comprehend how baseball become a "Japanese sport," represented in Brazil's landscape in many of the heritage spheres—objects, displays, representations, engagements, locations, events, memories, commemorations, and places for cultural purposes and consumption—as described by Waterton and Watson (2015) in their definition of heritage.

Howard (2003) stated that "as heritage scholars; we depend on the quality of the information at our disposal" (p. 16). Since players and supporters of other mainstream sports in Brazil (such as football, basketball, and volleyball) have always overlooked baseball in Brazil due to its amateur status, few research explorations of baseball in Brazil exist in Brazilian academic literature. Therefore, the use of traditional scholarly sources such as peer-reviewed articles and book chapters; social media data from baseball amateur teams, mainly their Facebook pages; and sports websites, including their YouTube channels, which covers tournaments and friendly matches in different regions of the country, were all crucial in understanding the development of baseball in Brazil as well as its more recent transformations. Additionally, the digital archives of the Brazilian Digital Library and from the National Diet Library (NDL)—Japanese National Library—were accessed. As a result, rich historical and contextual data emerged, which contributed to a great extent to inform about the first years of baseball in Brazil.

The chapter is thematically and metaphorically divided into four topics, representing the four bases of the baseball diamond. First base examines the origin of the sport in Brazil, while second base highlights the cultural influence of Japanese colonies[*] over baseball in Brazil to the point where baseball was becoming known as the "Japanese sport." On third base, the Gaijin Revolution is explored, detailing the reasons for the revolution's emergence, as well as the contemporary circumstances in which understandings of the Brazilian baseball landscape are forcing changes in the way the sport is

---

[*] The terms "colony" or "colonies" in this chapter result from a direct translation (from the Portuguese to the English language) of historical documents. It is also self-referential since nowadays several baseball teams still proudly call themselves as teams that belong to the Japanese colonies. Both terms imply and can therefore be read as "community" or "communities" as well.

viewed by its practitioners and managers. Finally, the home plate discusses and analyzes whether this is a heritage at risk while also exploring avenues for sustainable and democratic development baseball in Brazil in the future.

First Base: Origins of Baseball in Brazil

The history of any sport cannot be separated from its geography. Researchers have differing views about who deserves credit for importing baseball to Brazil. For Rubio (2000), Godoy (2004), and Lore (2017), baseball was first introduced by the Japanese just after the ship *Kasato-maru* carrying the first set of 781 contracted emigrants arrived at the Port of Santos (coast of São Paulo State) on June 18, 1908. Historical documents describe that one of the ship's passengers, Mr. Samejima, brought the first baseball equipment with him to secure the perpetuation of the favorite sport of the Japanese (Fukuda & Stanganelli, 2006). On the other hand, documents from the archives of the Brazilian Digital Library as well as the NDL suggest that the birth of baseball in Brazil emerged with Americans who worked in companies like the Light Telephone Company, Armour Refrigerator, and for the U.S. consulate.

In this token, *Rio News*, launched in 1873 and originally published as *The South American Mail* and as *The British and American Mail*, registered the occurrence of baseball games in the cities of Rio de Janeiro and São Paulo before the arrival of the first Japanese immigrants in Brazil. This traditional newspaper for the British and American expatriate community living in Brazil reported that the first baseball game in Brazilian territory was played in a cricket ground in Rio de Janeiro on August 8, 1893, between the "Pie-eaters of Carson's" and the "Tart-raiders of Candido's" (*Rio News*, 1893). Beyond informing the public about the results of all games, *Rio News* contributed to highlighting how baseball was like football at the turn of the 20th century in Brazil: an exclusive leisure pastime—played only in English—by the white and urban upper-middle class (Tobar & Gusso, 2017).

The baseball archives of *Rio News* and the development of the sport in the following decades suggest that as the lower classes later appropriated football from the Brazilian aristocracy (Tobar & Gusso, 2017), Japanese immigrants followed the same path regarding baseball. Suzuki and Miranda (2008) indicated that the sport only survived in the following decades due to the efforts promoted by Japanese colonies to the extent that baseball is still considered a "Japanese sport" in Brazil (including by the Brazilian Olympic Committee on its official website). Fukuda and Stanganelli (2006) concurred, noting that Japanese descendants firmly adopted the game as their first sport and fundamental part of their culture in Brazil.

Alone on Second Base: The Long-Standing Cultural Influence of Japanese Communities on Baseball in Brazil

The largest Japanese population outside of Japan (approximately 1.5 million) resides in Brazil. Most Japanese immigrants initially arrived in Brazil to work in coffee cultivation following Brazil's outlawing of African slavery in the mid-19th century (Assembleia Legislativa do Estado de São Paulo, 2018). Until the start of the Second World War, approximately 188,000 Japanese immigrants (Motoyama, 2008) were allocated by the Imperial Company of Migration in house nuclei along the railroad tracks of the neighboring states of São Paulo (IBGE, n.d.) and Paraná (Rubio, 2000). Traditionally, while migration is normally precipitated for economic reasons, cultural traditions are also imported and often adapted by immigrants to the new territory (Sakurai, 1995). As described by Willems and Baldus (1942), to ensure adaptation in the new territory, the Japanese government and its Imperial Company of Migration exercised strict control, forcing the new Japanese immigrants to adapt to Western costumes (e.g., dress code) as well as to abandon Shinto and Buddhism as a form of public worship. It is essential to highlight that those concerns from the Japanese authorities occurred because of the fact that the first immigrants only arrived in Brazil due to business agreements with the Brazilian government, which needed workers to substitute the slavery force and populate specific regions of the country. In other words, there was a concern about preserving the migration agreement. Due to these cultural restrictions, kinesthetic activities such as music, dance, and sport, especially baseball, came to represent early manifestations of Japanese culture in Brazil.

According to the NDL (n.d.), within Japanese colonies, baseball was initially played on days off in empty lots or football fields with gloves from Japan and baseball bats made of Brazilian guava trees. In 1920, after the creation of the Mikado Undo Kurabu (Mikado Sports Club) in São Paulo by Kenji Sasahara, which was the first official baseball club of a Japanese community in Brazil, the sport would experience a period of expansion. Specifically, the period between 1925 to 1938 is considered the golden era of baseball in Brazil (Miranda & Portasio, 2010). During this era, an influx of 133,000 Japanese immigrants arrived in Brazil (Smith, 1979). In this context and following the enlargement of the coffee route in the countryside, several colony teams decided to launch the first three Japanese leagues in São Paulo State. In 1926, the names of the coffee railways were used for the leagues Noroeste, Paulista, and Sorocabana. Just under a decade later, in 1933, the first teams of the state of Paraná were created, namely Cornélio Procópio and Londrina (NDL, n.d.). As a result, baseball diamonds changed the local geographies and became a trademark part of any Japanese community in the countryside (Godoy, 2004).

In this expansionist environment in 1936, the first All-Brazil Baseball Tournament was held in São Paulo City (Olympic Brazilian Committee, n.d.). Covering its third edition in 1941, the *Brazil Asami Newspaper* called the tournament "the Intercolonial Baseball Championship," thus demonstrating that, despite its allegedly national dimension, baseball was largely restricted to the Japanese colonies (NDL, n.d.). This sport's isolation characteristic, though, was reinforced by former president Getúlio Vargas and his nationalism campaign, which advocated for an ethnic and culturally homogeneous country (Takeuchi, 2002). First, with the promulgation of the Decree-Law n.383 of 1938, any immigrant association was forbidden to accept membership of a Brazilian, either native-born or naturalized. Second, when Brazil abandoned a neutral position and declared war against the Axis powers, the attacks against the Japanese reached their peak. Considered suspects of espionage and subversion, Japanese immigrants and descendants could not speak their first language in public, assemble in any meeting, read Japanese newspapers, listen to Japanese radio broadcasts, or travel within the country without the police's permission. These actions contributed decisively to the complete interruption of social activities in Japanese communities, including baseball games (Takeuchi, 2002).

In 1947, with the constitution of the Baseball Federation of the São Paulo State, the first signals of an intended normalization of life in Japanese communities and the gradual integration into Brazilian society appeared. Intentionally or not, the first president was the Brazilian and non-Japanese-descendant sports journalist Olimpio da Silva Sá (Nicolini, 2013). Yet the strong Japanese influence over baseball in Brazil remained. Among the 28 teams gathered in the first assembly held at the São Paulo Young Men's Association, 23 representatives were *Issei* (first-generation) or *Nisei* (second-generation) Japanese. Nevertheless, as a consequence of the National Campaign, all clubs featured Brazilian (rather than Japanese) names based on the location of the Japanese colonies within Brazil (Serra, 2017). For Takeuchi (2002), the 1950s represented the beginning of the true reconciliation between Japanese and Brazilian societies. In 1958, during the celebrations

of the 50th anniversary of Japanese immigration, the first baseball sta-
dium in Latin America built with public resources was inaugurated. The
Mie Nish Baseball Stadium opened its gates with the presence of the Impe-
rial Japanese Family—Prince Takahito Mikasa made the ceremonial first
pitch—and the Waseda University baseball team from Tokyo (Cidade de
São Paulo, n.d.). In 1965, Japanese descendants launched the first Baseball
Federation of the Paraná State, and thirteen years later, its capital, Curitiba
City, hosted the inauguration of the second baseball municipal stadium in
Brazil, which in 2008 was renovated for the celebrations of the 100th anniversary of Japanese immigration (TribunaPr, 2013). Winter (2014)—who
interviewed Raylla Matusomori, a member of the Anhanguera Nikkey Club
from São Paulo—contends that for the first sixty years of Japanese immigrants arriving in Brazil, baseball was confined to the Japanese community,
which helped to foster the idea of baseball as a "Japanese sport" among the
Brazilian population. Aspects such as the ingrained prejudice and resistance
to a *Nisei* intermarriage (Smith, 1979; Kingsberg, 2015), or the preference
for football nurtured by Brazilians (Matz, 2017) explain why a successful
integration with the Brazilian society has never been achieved. Pictures of
baseball and softball squads of the 1930s, 1950s, and 1980s published at the
website of the São Paulo Giants baseball team confirm this scenario of sec-
tarianism (Giants, n.d.).

In this token, the experimented spatial isolation was fundamental for the
gradual naturalization of a proper and exclusive Japanese dynamic concerning managerial, tactical, technical, and disciplinary aspects toward the participants and the game itself (Batista Jr., 1998). Rubio (2000), in her one-year
ethnography study with 120 Japanese descendent-athletes and their families,
identified a well-organized familial structure in operating a baseball club.
She noticed that Japanese descendants were introduced to the game through
a natural inheritance transmission. A type of intergenerational transmission of sporting and civic values was led by male elders who performed
different tasks within the baseball club. As coaches, referees, or directors,
these highly experienced Japanese descendants transmitted the accumulated knowledge about training methods, style of play, dress codes, rules,
and behaviors imported from Japan since the first groups of immigrants to
Brazil. Rubio (2000) also noted that the discipline among the youth was reinforced continuously through various exercises that were intended to give
younger generations some sense of the adverse conditions experimented
by their *Issei* elders. In general, sports can be tools to teach a variety of
social, cultural, and political values metaphorically. Among the Japanese

descendants, there was a shared mentality that important intergenerational heritage transmissions should be passed through baseball. As a result, not only the Japanese descendants' worldviews, lifestyles, social behaviors, and cultural preferences were, to a certain extent, preserved for several decades, but their game style was also influenced by the way the sport was played in Japan.

During the games, the language used by players and referees also reflected a blend of cultural influences. On this point, Godoy (2004) referred to this language as "Japonglês"—a blend of Japanese, English, and Portuguese, explaining that the *Issei* arrived with a baseball vocabulary that only mixed English and Japanese. However, once players were more fully immersed in Brazilian cultural traditions (Rubio, 2000), the language was mixed with Portuguese and gradually adjusted to the accents and terminologies found in each state across Brazil. Similar to the popular appropriation that led the British pastime (football) to be called in the national idiom ("futebol"), in the baseball context, the ball ("bola" in Portuguese) became "bora"; the original bat ("bastão" in Portuguese) was named "bata"; the runner ("corredor" in Portuguese) changed to "lana"; and the pitcher ("lançador" in Portuguese) is called "pitcha." The generated cultural and social exclusiveness of the game, however, came to an end in the 1980s when baseball began to acquire a more "Brazilian DNA" (Matz, 2017). A series of events would reveal the beginning of the Gaijin Revolution, a process which would make the sport started to be considered a "mestizo modality" in Brazil (Rubio, 2000, p. 37). In the following years, Brazilian baseball would register the growing participation of non-Japanese descendants and the consequent emergence of new leagues, tournaments, and teams inspired—and sometimes formally linked—to a few Major League Baseball (MLB) franchises.

"I Want to Be Part Too": Heading for Third Base with *"Gaijins"*

In 1985, the *"dekassegui* movement," an expression used to refer to Japanese descendants who migrated to Japan for temporary work, became widely used during Brazil's economic bankruptcy (Motoyama, 2008). The Brazilian Consulate in Tokyo estimated that in 1989, 14,000 Brazilians were living in Japan, while by 2007 that number reached 313,000 (Fleury, 2018). Nowadays, approximately 191,000 *dekasseguis* are working in Japan (Consulate General of Brazil in Tokyo, n.d.). Jorge Otsuka, president of the Brazilian Baseball and Softball Federation (CBBS) since its foundation in 1990, pointed out that the exodus of third (*Sansei*) and fourth (*Yonsei*) generations as well as families prioritizing education over baseball were the leading causes of the downturn of Japanese descendants in baseball in Brazil (Matz, 2017). In 2006, Fukuda and Stanganelli (2006) identified 5,000 players registered in the CBBS (75 percent Japanese descendants), but in 2017 this number decreased to 3,000 (Matz, 2017). It is worth noting, however, that this number does not represent the totality of Japanese descendants currently playing baseball, since, according to the Brazilian Olympic Committee (n.d.), Brazil has 30,000 baseball players and no data are available to identify athletes' ethnicities. Nevertheless, for Márcio Irikura, director of the semi-professional baseball team Nippon Blue Jays in São Paulo, there is a consensus among the Japanese descendants about an unequivocal reduction of players in the past 20 years, which has poorly affected the game's quality (Ely, 2019a). Although there is an absence of precise numbers that would contribute to a broader understanding of baseball's current reality, the following facts reveal how the presence of gaijins is changing the game.

For Matz (2017), the Brazilian baseball DNA emerged in parallel to the *dekassegui* wave migration, with the initial symbol of Brazilian baseball development being the 16-year-old pitcher and non-Japanese descendant Jose Pett, who became the first Brazilian player in MLB's history after signing with the Toronto Blue Jays in 1992. Five years later, the Mitsubishi baseball team from Hiroshima hired the catcher, Luis Camargo, transforming him into the first "Brazilian *gaijin*" to play at the Nippon Professional Baseball Organization (NPB). Comparatively to the MLB, until that point, Japanese teams had signed 14 players from Brazil, all *Nisei, Sansei,* or *Yonsei* (Kimura, 1997). Internally, 1993 revealed the beginning of the fragmentation of Japanese descendants' exclusive control over Brazilian baseball. The CBBS, for the first time in its history, hired a foreign coach, Orlando Santana from Cuba, who brought new training techniques that—when combined with the discipline from the Japanese school—led Brazil to win the 1993 Baseball World Championship, Under-15 division. Celebration photos archived in the *Folha de Londrina* newspaper show how the entire Brazilian squad was formed of Japanese descendant players (Ogawa, 2018).

At that time, CBBS's directors realized that the Brazilian baseball DNA would eventually change and challenge Japanese descendants' historical domination within the sport. Simultaneously, there was a need to put Brazilian baseball on the map of world baseball. As a result, the CBBS implemented a series of transformations pushed to a great extent by two main factors: First, the CBBS and Japanese community teams began programs that introduced baseball to Brazilian youth in an attempt to attract new athletes after the *dekassegui* exodus. Second, and more decisively, international teams were seeking stronger and taller athletes, which thus placed Latino players in an advantageous position when compared with many Japanese descendant players (Pombo, 2007). In 2000, the search for Brazilian baseball prospects resulted in the construction of Brazil's top baseball school, the Yakult Academy. In its first year, the academy housed six Brazilians and 18 Japanese descendant players (Matz, 2017). In keeping with the increasing focus of MLB teams on Brazil (e.g., the opening of the Tampa Bay Rays Brazil Academy in 2009 [Espn, 2009] and the first MLB Elite Academy in 2017 [Pezzo, 2017]), by 2019 the National Team coached by the Cuban Rodolfo Puente had only 8 Japanese descendants out of 24 players for the qualification round of the 2019 Pan American Games (Henriques, 2019).

From a non-professional perspective, globalization forces increased the number of teams in Brazil. Through the increased advent and use of social media, fans who initially only consumed baseball through television (e.g., ESPN Brazil broadcasted the first MLB games in 1989) and the internet (at Orkut forums dedicated to the MLB) decided to launch baseball teams in regions of Brazil with little or no history of Japanese immigration. In contrast to *Nikkei* clubs, which only carried the names of their cities, colonies, or universities (e.g., Nikkey Marilia [1930], Atibaia Baseball [1952], Anhanguera Nikkei Club [1962], and the School of Economics, Business and Accounting baseball team of the University of São Paulo—FEA USP [1961]), the new teams employed American, Latin, and Brazilian influences. The first team that adopted a name free of any Japanese influence was curiously based in Rio de Janeiro, where baseball was played for the first time in Brazil. In 1993, a group of locals created the Arsenal Brazilian Baseball, which also became the first team of non-Japanese descendants to participate in a National Tournament organized by the CBBS (Ely, 2017). Within the northern part of Brazil, the states of Pernambuco, Ceará, Rio Grande do Norte, Bahia, and Maranhão registered the formation of Náutico Beisebol and Recife Mariners (2007), Beisebol Fortaleza (2012), Kangaços Maracanaú Beisebol (2016), Natal Solaris (2008), Seabra Carcara Beisebol (2015), Salvador Killers (2016), and João Pessoa Bravos Beisebol (2017), respectively (Ely, 2019b).

In the south of Brazil, the states of Santa Catarina and the Rio Grande do Sul created not only new teams but also independent leagues. Founded in 2006 by the extinct Pelotas, the Gaúcho Baseball League has teams such as the Porto Alegre Farrapos (2006), Ivoti Phoenix (2009), Porto Alegre White Tigers (2010), and Locones (2017) (Ely, 2019c). In addition, the Santa

Catarina Baseball League created in 2016 includes the Joinville Royals (2012), Brusque Brewers (2016), Blumenau Capivaras (2016), Itajai Sailors (2017), Jaraguá Shooters (2017), and Pomerode Eulen (2018), each of which pay homage to different heritage elements that represent their city's identities. For example, due to the German colonization in the Pomerode region, the Eulens innovated and created a uniform celebrating Oktoberfest (Liga Catarinense de Beisebol, n.d.). At the states where the Japanese communities were historically settled (e.g., São Paulo, Paraná, Mato Grosso do Sul, and Espírito Santo), new teams emerged either in opposition to the Japanese control of the game—as was the case of the Curitiba Lapwings (2008) coached by the Cuban Jose Inácio Santa Maria (Casal Travinha Esportes, 2018)—or to emphasize other, differing ethnicities. The Tomateros (2003), a Brazilian version of the Tomateros de Culiacán from Mexico, not only had as its first coach in Puerto Rican Miguel Reyes, but the red uniform was inspired by the Cuban National Team colors (Casal Travinha Esportes, 2017a).

Globalization outcomes have also produced an unexpected "cultural syncretism" (Stewart, 1999) among Japanese descendants who both create new baseball associations (e.g., Highlander Baseball & Beer [2014]; Londrina Red Sharks [2015]) and rename them by introducing an American influence (e.g., the former Rolândia Baseball Club [1935] became Rolândia Legends [2018]) (Casal Travinha Esportes, 2017b). In particular, the Porto Alegre White Tigers' case demonstrates how the incorporation of other cultural influences—especially American baseball culture—was essential to baseball teams' development. According to one of its founders, Thiago Kajiwara, the team initially had a Japanese name because of its relation with the Japanese-Brazilian Association of Rio Grande do Sul State but decided to adopt the nickname "White Tigers" to attract more Brazilians to the team (Borba, 2017).

Beyond names and nicknames, other heritage components of the game were introduced by the *gaijins*. At the ballparks where Japanese descendants still play, the game-day recipes include pastel—a fried snack created by the Japanese in 1940—and noodles (Jornal da Gazeta, 2016). However, the teams with more Brazilian players introduced barbecued meat and beer, two typical features of national culture that are also common in American ballparks. The discipline that was always part of baseball in Japanese communities and a vehicle to preserve the traditions and customs of previous generations was challenged by new players focusing more on an enjoyable leisure experience. This characteristic was found within the Highlanders Baseball & Beer team, which includes a majority of Japanese descendants.

Teams that are comprised of players who are in their forties and fifties and who played together during their childhood in Japanese community teams typically now embrace a more "Brazilian character" (i.e., a desire to make friends and enjoy a beer while playing baseball) (Ely, 2017).

Nonetheless, the most notable impact was detected within the diamond boundaries through changes in how the game is played and refereed. Even though the Brazilian Baseball and Softball Umpires and Annotators Association (1991) is almost entirely composed of Japanese descendants originating from the São Paulo Baseball Federation Umpire's Department (Blog da AABSB, 2011), the use of "Japonglês"—the blending of English, Japanese, and Portuguese terms—started to be commonly heard in baseball tournaments. A personal observation made at the second round of the 2019 Santa Catarina Baseball League during the game between the Joinville Royals and Itajaí Sailors included the umpire calling the runs using the Portuguese word "corridas" (fly balls) and not "Furai," as well as "home run" instead of "homoran." Additionally, *gaijins* brought further innovation to the sport with the first live broadcast games of amateur and semi-professional leagues, including CBBS's tournaments, through their YouTube channel "Travinha Esportes." As a result, *gaijins* not only secured their right to play baseball but also contributed to building a more accessible, democratic, and diverse "sportscape" (Bale, 2001).

Analysis and Discussion: Heading Home

As Parker and Manley (2016) stated, a broader range of issues relating to race/ethnicity, social class, and religion shapes our individual and collective identities. This view is aligned with Takatuzi's (2018) understanding of culture as constantly changing due to internal or external forces. In the case of the Japanese community in Brazil, baseball acquired a prominent role in reaffirming their collective identity, especially after the cultural restrictions imposed on first-generation immigrants. From the first ball games in Brazilian territory, in which the first immigrants strived to continue playing—to the point of creating baseball bats from guava trees—it was clear that the sport would become an important vehicle of Japanese heritage transmission. The first immigrants and their descendants valued baseball as a cornerstone of their heritage, and this heritage was considered important enough to pass along to their children. This connection between the Japanese community and baseball is representative of one of the concepts described by Ramshaw and Gammon (2005) in explaining the relationship between heritage and sport. The notion of "sport as heritage" encompasses scenarios in which the practices of a particular sport—including its traditions, rituals, and history—transcend the field of play and become representative of a people and part of a broader societal heritage (Ramshaw, 2020). The social, political, and cultural events experienced by Japanese immigrants and descendants in the 20th century contributed to building a discursive practice that defined, shaped, and legitimized the idea of baseball as a "Japanese sport," even though they weren't the first to bring the sport to Brazilian territory. The construction and renovation of baseball stadiums in the cities of São Paulo and Curitiba in conjunction with the 50th and 100th anniversaries of Japanese immigration was a powerful demonstration of this community's sociocultural relevance in Brazil. In other words, these public investments symbolized Brazilian authorities' views toward the ballparks as guardian places for the development and maintenance of Japanese culture and identity in Brazil.

The importance that the first Japanese immigrants attributed to baseball has always been strong due to its direct connection with the lived experience in the homeland. The sport acquired extreme value to these immigrants since it always functioned as a vehicle of cultural heritage transmission to the new generations. Although geographically situated in Brazil, the ballparks of Japanese communities represented an "imaginative" (Anderson, 2006) extension of life in Japan. During ball games, the rules, play calls, and on-field behaviors reflected Japanese customs, but other forms of heritage, such as the foods and beverages served to spectators, also reflected aspects of Japanese culture. In certain ways, the development of baseball within Japanese communities allows an understanding of the fabric of Japanese immigrants and descendants in Brazil—their traditions, values, and uses and senses of places. Since the Japanese community was the only ethnicity continuing to develop the sport in Brazilian territory after the British and Americans stopped playing it, Japanese baseball heritage went untouched for decades. Baseball's unpopularity in Brazil, largely motivated by political prohibitions and the population's preference for football, meant that Japanese immigrants and descendants had exclusive control of the sport. As such, baseball in Brazil became a "Japanese sport." These episodes legitimized viewpoints and perspectives that created an "authorized heritage discourse" (Smith, 2015) by linking the baseball past in Brazil solely to Japanese immigrants and their descendants, who unsurprisingly still manage the CBBS and the most important state federations. In a similar fashion to the opposition to *Nisei* intermarriage, Japanese communities feared losing the tangible and intangible traditions of baseball (such as the language and values of the game, the game-day habits, as well as the sport's administrative control in a national context) once mingled with other ethnicities. Precisely, the concern to preserve Japanese baseball heritage is one reason the Gaijin Revolution has emerged. Through a "dynamic intercultural and intracultural transactions" (Stewart, 1999, p. 55), the Gaijin Revolution was shaped by cultural syncretism involving Japanese, Brazilian, and American cultures, and was capable of transforming the structure of baseball in Brazil.

As demonstrated, the globalization forces that erupted at the end of the 1980s were revealed to be more potent than local sentiment. Unexpected external forces—the *dekassegui* wave, the interest of new markets to hire Brazilian players, and the arrival of Latin coaches—created conditions for a new baseball era in Brazil. When the Gaijin Revolution erupted, the CBBS—which, for decades, adopted the Japanese baseball methodology and facilitated a major exportation of Brazilian players to the NPB—could not control its effects. Instead, the entity recognized it and took advantage of the intercultural process that started to shape Brazilian baseball's DNA. The Brazilian intercultural process, which already had taken football and transformed it to one of the leading symbols of national identity, gradually created a new social space that was traditionally reserved for the Japanese community. It could be argued that this kind of transculturation process (Stewart, 1999) has been threatening to Japanese baseball heritage in Brazil. While there have undoubtedly been adaptations—such as the changing of the game's language at the Santa Catarina Baseball League—these new cultural relations should be viewed as a positive, as they have helped the sport to survive and thrive in Brazil. Likewise, the first immigrants contributed to the dissemination of the game when the Americans and the British abandoned its practice; nowadays, *gaijins* are contributing to propagating the sport to a different level which could not be reached by Japanese descendants alone. One player in particular illustrated how the openness of the Japanese community to *gaijins* produced positive effects. Paulo Orlando, a former pitcher for the Kansas City Royals 2015 World Championship campaign, only discovered baseball in 1997 when he was 12 years old, after his mother's boss—Hideo Ueno, who coached the youth baseball team of the Santo Amaro Club in São Paulo—invited him to a training session (Pereira, 2016).

As such, through new teams and leagues and different, innovative strategies to promote the game, new understandings of Brazilian baseball heritage have been taking place. This investigation did not reveal any intentions from *gaijins* to change the historical discourse concerning the Japanese influence in the development of the game. On the contrary, there has only been a sincere desire to share the field and their traditions, which can coexist with the ones that belong to Japanese descendants. The Allstars Legends organized at the Mie Nishi Stadium on July 2019—which reflects the "living sport heritage concept" discussed by Ramshaw (2010)—included the participation of both Japanese (e.g., Kleber Ojima, best pitcher at the 2003 World Championship in Cuba) and non-Japanese descendants (e.g., José Pett), illustrating a new approach to baseball culture at Brazilian ballparks. The configuration of this new social space suggests that if descendants are concerned with preserving Japanese baseball heritage, they should keep working for the growth of the sport, even if it means losing its management control. As Critchley (2017, p. 151) noted, "sport has the potential for the creation of new moments, a future heritage." The new baseball era has brought challenges to the maintenance of baseball in Brazil as a "Japanese sport" highly influenced by discipline and considered a vehicle for life lessons. However, a new discursive practice is being written, providing new chapters and meanings to baseball heritage in Brazil. Ironically, the greatest risk to the preservation of Japanese baseball heritage comes from Japan. More specifically, it concentrates on the behavior of the *dekasseguis* who returned to Brazil. As Kadia (2015) identified, for many, overseas experiences have infused a sense of "Brazilian-ness" represented by warm and friendly behavior (as opposed to the more formal behavior of many Japanese citizens). Highlanders Baseball & Beer is perhaps the best illustrative case of this scenario. In this sense, further research would be welcomed to identify whether this trend is strong enough to impact—and reshape—perceptions of baseball traditions in Brazil. Yet the events highlighted throughout this chapter indicate that descendants and *gaijins* can share home plate together and thus preserve their respective baseball heritages.

Conclusion

Baseball arrived in Brazil along with other sports such as football and cricket. While Brazilians made sports such as football their own, baseball was predominantly played for and by immigrants and, as such, reflected these communities' traditions and rules in terms of the way the game should be played and managed in a foreign territory. In particular, the Japanese community in Brazil—who viewed baseball as a fundamental element of their collective identity—demonstrated a decisive role to the sport's development despite the many adverse outcomes of World War II. Their desire to preserve the meanings and values of baseball created a Japanese baseball heritage, which led them to become the most prominent figures of the sport in Brazil—to the point that baseball became understood as a "Japanese sport." However, similar to what the *Issei* had experienced after their arrival when they slowly appropriated the game from the British and Americans, globalization forces in the 1980s contributed to baseball acquiring a more "Brazilian DNA." Employing the baseball diamond metaphor mentioned in the introduction, this chapter revealed that Americans and British influences initially occupied first base while Japanese immigrants and descendants remained alone at second base for many "innings" (decades). In the run for the third base, however, they were challenged by *gaijins* who sought the right to play the sport. Presently, both Japanese descendants and *gaijins*—who had not demonstrated any intention to steal third base, but rather to share it—must work together to keep the game alive through attracting new players. As described, both traditions do not necessarily exclude one another, which provides hope that they will "run home" together and therefore preserve both old and new baseball heritages in Brazil.

References

Anderson, B. (2006). *Imagined communities: Reflections on the origin and spread of nationalism.* New York: Verso.

Assembleia Legislativa do Estado de São Paulo (2018, July 19). Autoridades da província de Fukui visitam a Alesp [Fukui Japanese province officials visit Alesp]. https://www.al.sp.gov.br/noticia/?id=393466 (accessed January 30, 2022).

Bale, J. (2001). *Sportscapes.* Sheffield: Geographical Association.

Batista Jr., M. (1998). *Beisebol no Brasil: Breve histórico e perspectiva [Baseball in Brazil: Brief history and perspective].* São Paulo, SP: Mimeo.

Blog da Aaabsb (2011, January 09). Nossa Associação [Our Association] [Blog post]. http://beisebolesoftbolbrasil.blogspot.com/2011/01/nossa-associacao.html (accessed December 5, 2020).

Borba, T. (2017, September 08). Beisebol em Porto Alegre? Temos, sim senhor! [Baseball in Porto Alegre? Yes Sir, we do have it!]. https://medium.com/betaredacao/beisebol-em-porto-alegre-temos-sim-senhor-3196c79eba8a (accessed December 5, 2020).

Brazilian Olympic Committee (n.d.). Baseball / Softball. https://www.cob.org.br/pt/cob/time-brasil/esportes/beisebol—softbol/ (accessed December 5, 2020).

Casal Travinha Esportes (2017a, July 31). Conheça o Tomateros Baseball Club (SP) [Find out about the Tomateros Baseball Club (SP)]. [Video file]. https://www.youtube.com/watch?v=kkWR1dlQVjQ (accessed December 5, 2020).

Casal Travinha Esportes (2017b, November 09). Torneio Nacional de Beisebol: Highlanders busca título em nova categoria [Baseball National Tournament: Highlanders competing for a title in a new category]. [Video file]. http://travinha.com.br/2017/11/09/torneio-nacional-beisebol-highlanders/ (accessed December 5, 2020).

Casal Travinha Esportes (2018, March 13). Lapwings Baseball Curitiba (PR). [Video file]. https://www.youtube.com/watch?v=A4hqbZIYCX0 (accessed December 5, 2020).

Cidade de São Paulo (n.d.). Estádio Municipal Beisebol Mie Nishi. [Mie Nish Municipal Baseball Stadium]. http://www.capital.sp.gov.br/turista/atracoes/ar-livre/estadio-municipal-de-beisebol-mie-nishi (accessed December 5, 2020).

Consulate General of Brazil in Tokyo (n.d.). Consulate General of Brazil in Tokyo. http://cgtoquio.itamaraty.gov.br/en-us/ (accessed December 5, 2020).

Critchley, S. (2017). *What we think about when we think about football*. New York: Penguin Books.

Ely, N. (2019a, March 24). Paulista de Beisebol 2019: Nippon Blue Jays é o recordista de títulos. [Paulista Baseball tournament 2019: Nippon Blue Jays holds the record for most titles]. http://travinha.com.br/2019/03/24/paulista-beisebol-2019-nippon-blue-jays/ (accessed December 5, 2020).

Ely, N. (2019b, January 31). Liga Nordeste de Beisebol 2019 iniciará no dia 17 de fevereiro. [The Northeast Baseball League 2019 will start on February 17th]. http://travinha.com.br/2019/01/31/liga-nordeste-de-beisebol-2019/ (accessed December 5, 2020).

Ely, N. (2019c, July 17). Domingo tem Torneio Gaúcho de Beisebol. [On Sunday, there is the Gaúcho Baseball Tournament.] https://travinha.com.br/2019/07/12/torneio-gaucho-de-beisebol-2019/ (accessed December 5, 2020).

Ely, N. (2017, November 28). Torneio Nacional de Beisebol: Cariocas—time do organizador da competição. [National Baseball Tournament: Cariocas—competition organizer team]. http://travinha.com.br/2017/11/27/nacional-de-beisebol-cariocas-time-do-organizador/ (accessed December 5, 2020).

ESPN (2009, April 18). Rays looking for new talent in Brazil. https://www.espn.com/mlb/news/story?id=4079550 (accessed December 5, 2020).

Fleury, F. (2018, August 26). Imigração brasileira para o Japão volta a crescer após dez anos [Brazilian immigration to Japan grows again after ten years]. https://noticias.r7.com/internacional/imigracao-brasileira-para-o-japao-volta-a-crescer-apos-dez-anos-26082018 (accessed December 5, 2020).

Fukuda, O., & Stanganelli, J. (n.d.). Beisebol. http://www.atlasesportebrasil.org.br/textos/33.pdf (accessed December 5, 2020).

Fukuda, O., & Stanganelli, J. (2006). Beisebol. In DaCosta, Lamartine (Ed.), *Atlas Do Esporte No Brasil* (pp. 8.99–8.100). Rio de Janeiro: CONFEF.

Giants (n.d.). TÚNEL DO TEMPO. [Blog post]. https://www.giants.com.br/tunel-do-tempo/ (accessed December 5, 2020).

Godoy, L. (2004, July 21). Brasil adota o "japonglês" para tentar entender o beisebol [Brazil adopts the "japonglês" in an attempt to understand baseball]. https://esporte.uol.com.br/olimpiadas/ultimas/2004/07/21/ult2250u4.jhtm (accessed December 5, 2020).

Harrison, R. (2012). *Heritage: Critical approaches*. New York: Routledge.

Henriques, G. (2019, January 29). Pré-Pan 2019: Saiba tudo sobre a seleção brasileira de beisebol masculino [Pre-Pan 2019: Learn all about the Men's Brazil baseball team]. https://www.torcedores.com/noticias/2019/01/pre-pan-selecao-brasileira (accessed December 5, 2020).

Howard, P. (2003). *Heritage: Management, interpretation, identity.* London: Continuum.

IBGE (n.d.). Japoneses: Destino dos imigrantes [The Japanese: the destiny of immigrants]. https://brasil500anos.ibge.gov.br/territorio-brasileiro-e-povoamento/japoneses/destino-dos-imigrantes (accessed December 5, 2020).

Jornal da Gazeta (2016, January 01). O beisebol conquista espaço no país do futebol [Baseball gains ground in the country of football]. https://www.youtube.com/watch?v=bTN5c19utI8 (accessed December 5, 2020).

Kadia, M. K. (2015). Repatriation but not "return": A Japanese Brazilian dekasegi goes back to Brazil. *The Asia-Pacific Journal, 13*(14), 1–18.

Kimura, M. (1997, October 19). Japão assina com o primeiro 'brasileiro' [Japan signs with the first 'Brazilian']. https://www1.folha.uol.com.br/fsp/esporte/fk191025.htm.

Liga Catarinense de Beisebol (n.d.). Facebook [Fan Page]. https://www.facebook.com/beisebolsc/ (accessed December 5, 2020).

Liga Catarinense de Beisebol (2019, May 23rd). Friendly game—Pomerode vs. Navegantes. [Facebook status update]. Retrieved from https://www.facebook.com/beisebolsc/posts.

Matz, E. (2017, December 26). Best of 2017—Meet 16-year-old Eric Pardinho, Brazil's first million-dollar arm. http://www.espn.com/espn/feature/story/_/id/19668967/eric-pardhino-brazil-first-million-dollar-arm (accessed December 5, 2020).

Miranda, M. P., & Portasio, R. P. (2010). MADE IN USA: Os "esportes americanos" na imprensa brasileira [The 'American Sports' in the Brazilian press] (Unpublished master's thesis). São Paulo / Paulista University. https://en.calameo.com/read/000091377 f02bb7e304c9 (accessed December 5, 2020).

Motoyama, S. (2008). O Museu Histórico da Imigração Japonesa no Brasil [The Historic Museum of the Japanese Immigration in Brazil]. *Comunicação & Educação, 13*(3), 133–138.

National Diet Library (n.d.). Brazilian baseball. https://www.ndl.go.jp/brasil/e/column/baseball.html (accessed December 5, 2020).

Nicolini, H. (2013, June 11). Perdemos Olímpio Sá [We have lost Olímpio Sá]. https://blogs.gazetaesportiva.com/henriquenicolini/2013/06/10/perdemos-olimpio-sa/ (accessed December 5, 2020).

Ogawa, V. (2018, July 27). Quando éramos reis [When we were kings]. https://www.folhadelondrina.com.br/esporte/quando-eramos-reis-1011451.html (accessed December 5, 2020).

Paiva, O. D. (2015). Imigração, patrimônio cultural e turismo no Brasil [Immigration, cultural heritage and tourism in Brazil]. *Anais Do Museu Paulista: História E Cultura Material, 23*(2), 211–237. doi:10.1590/1982–02672015v23n0208

Parker, A., & Manley, A. (2016). Identity. In E. Cashmore & K. Dixon (Eds.), *Studying football* (pp. 97–112). New York: Routledge.

Pereira, J. (2016, February 22). Beisebol com DNA brasileiro [Baseball with Brazilian

DNA]. https://www.otempo.com.br/superfc/beisebol-com-dna-brasileiro-1.1239707 (accessed December 5, 2020).

Pezzo, R. (2017, November 02). Barry Larkin e Steve Finley ajudarão garotos da Academia MLB Brasil em Novembro [Barry Larkin and Steve Finley will help boys at the MLB Brazil Academy in November]. https://www.theplayoffs.com.br/mlb/barry-larkin-e-steve-finley-ajudarao-garotos-da-academia-mlb-brasil-em-novembro/ (accessed December 5, 2020).

Pombo, C. (2007, December 26). Beisebol muda cara e exporta [Baseball changes its face and exports]. https://www1.folha.uol.com.br/fsp/esporte/fk2612200710.htm (accessed December 5, 2020).

Ramshaw, G. (2010). Living heritage and the sports museum: Athletes, legacy and the Olympic Hall of Fame and Museum, Canada Olympic Park. *Journal of Sport & Tourism, 15*(1), 45–70.

Ramshaw, G. (2020). *Heritage and sport: An introduction.* Bristol: Channel View Publications.

Ramshaw, G., & Gammon, S. (2005). More than just nostalgia? Exploring the heritage/sport tourism nexus. *Journal of Sport & Tourism, 10*(4), 229–241.

Rio News (1893, August 8). Local Notes. Rio News, p. 4. http://memoria.bn.br/docreader/DocReader.aspx?bib=349070&Pesq=base-ball&pagfis=3920 (accessed December 5, 2020).

Rubio, K. (2000). Tradição, família e prática esportiva: a cultura japonesa e o beisebol no Brasil [Tradition, family, and sporting practice: The Japanese culture and baseball in Brazil]. *Movimento Journal, 6*(12), 37–44.

Sakurai, C. (1995). Primeiros pólos da imigração japonesa no o Brasil [First groups of the Japanese immigration to Brazil]. *USP Journal, 27*, 32–45.

Serra, M. (2017, September 11). São Paulo F.C. http://www.saopaulofc.net/noticias/noticias/spfcpedia/2017/9/11/time-de-beisebol-do-sao-paulo (accessed December 5, 2020).

Smith, R. J. (1979). The ethnic Japanese in Brazil. *Journal of Japanese Studies, 5*(1), 53–70.

Smith, L. (2015). Intangible heritage: A challenge to the authorised heritage discourse? *Revista d'etnologia de Catalunya, 40*, 133–142.

Stewart, C. (1999). Syncretism and its synonyms: Reflections on cultural mixture. *Diacritics, 29*(3), 40–62.

Stoddart, B. (1988). Sport, cultural imperialism, and colonial response in the British Empire. *Comparative Studies in Society and History, 30*(4), 649–673.

Suzuki, F. S., & Miranda, M. D. (2008). A história da imigração japonesa e seus descendentes: Prática de atividade física e aspectos sócio-culturais [The history of Japanese immigration and its descendants: Physical activity and socio-cultural aspects]. *Conexões: Revista Da Faculdade De Educação Física Da Unicamp, 6*, 408–419.

Takatuzi, T. (2018, March 05). Arigatô: Os japoneses no Paraná [Arigato: The Japanese in Paraná]. http://www.revistaideias.com.br/2018/03/05/arigato-os-japoneses-no-parana/ (accessed December 5, 2020).

Takeuchi, M. Y. (2002). O perigo amarelo em tempos de guerra (1939–1945) [The yellow danger in war times (1939–1945)]. São Paulo, SP: IMESP.

Tobar, F., & Gusso, L. (2017). Becoming Brazilian: The making of national identity through football. *International Journal of Sport and Society, 8*(2), 37–49.

TribunaPr. (2013, January 20). Reinaguração do estádio de beisebol na Solitude será hoje: De Letra. [The reopening of the baseball stadium at Solitude will be today: De Letra]. https://www.tribunapr.com.br/esportes/reinaguracao-do-estadio-de-beisebol-na-solitude-sera-hoje/ (accessed December 5, 2020).

Willems, E., & Baldus, H. (1942). Cultural change among Japanese immigrants in Brazil. *Sociology and Social Research: An International Journal, 26*(6), 525–537.

Winter, B. (2014, February 13). Baseball in Brazil? U.S. sports rise in the land of soccer. https://www.reuters.com/article/us-brazil-worldcup-baseball/baseball-in-brazil-u-s-sports-rise-in-the-land-of-soccer-idUSBREA1C1EZ20140213(accessed December 5, 2020).

11

Caribbean Series Baseball Heritage with Diasporic, Economic, and Political Implications

Thomas E. Van Hyning

Few regions of the world have as strong a link to baseball heritage as the Caribbean. Various tournaments, players, locations, and traditions highlight the enduring baseball-heritage relationship in the region. In particular, one of the main Caribbean regional sources of pride is the Caribbean Series (a.k.a. Caribbean World Series [CARWS]), held initially from February 20–25, 1949, in Havana, Cuba—and which continues to the present. It reflects a broader form of heritage, as proposed by Bagnall (2003), with an emphasis on interaction between actors (e.g., fans) and sites and objects (e.g., stadiums and museums). Players from non-host Caribbean countries and players from the United States in these Winter Leagues are imports, as opposed to host country natives. Imports may include Dominicans who play in Colombia, or Panamanians and Cubans on a Dominican team. Fletcher (2012) noted that "areas of fandom become even more complex and layered for diasporic communities, where competing national loyalties, heritages, and traditions may be articulated through sport" (p. 9). The author covered the February 1–7, 2020, CARWS in San Juan's Hiram Bithorn Stadium—a venue named after the island's first light-skinned big leaguer (1942 Chicago Cubs). José "Gacho" Torres, 1926 Newark Stars, Eastern Colored League, is Puerto Rico's first big leaguer, per a December 16, 2020, ruling by Major League Baseball (MLB) adding 1920–1948 Negro Leagues to official MLB records (Kepner, 2020). The author noticed a large contingent of Dominican fans at games, most of whom live in Puerto Rico. There were also Venezuelan fans—most of whom reside in Puerto Rico or Florida—cheering for the

Lara Cardinals, their "home country's" entry. Some fans rooting for Mexico lived in Texas or California, but most flew in from Mexico.

Utilizing personal observations, interviews, notes, and archival research, this chapter focuses on 1) CARWS games, records, and achievements; 2) the sense of national and regional pride in honoring CARWS heroes via their induction into the Caribbean Series Hall of Fame (CARSHF); 3) the role played by museums in Puerto Rico, Mexico, Venezuela, and the Dominican Republic in honoring CARWS stars, among other luminaries, with notable MLB careers (e.g., Martín Dihigo, Roberto Clemente, Luis Aparicio, Fernando Valenzuela, and Juan Marichal); 4) the complex diasporic, economic, and political challenges affecting baseball heritage in Cuba, Puerto Rico, Venezuela, and the Dominican Republic; 5) the past and present virtual halls of fame, including the Puerto Rico Professional Baseball Hall of Fame (PRPBHOF), the Latino Baseball Hall of Fame (LBHF), and the Hispanic Heritage Baseball Museum Hall of Fame (HHBMHOF); and 6) the respect that Caribbean baseball fans have for U.S.-based players/managers representing their country in CARWS. Through these observations, interviews, and archival research—and through focusing on different eras of baseball events and heritage in the Caribbean—this chapter aims to demonstrate the differing meanings, understandings, and uses of baseball heritage in the region.

Pre-CARWS, 1923 to 1948

Prior to the formation of the CARWS, Caribbean baseball hosted many of greatest names in baseball history. These players—and the impact they brought to the region—formed the groundwork of baseball heritage to come. For example, teams such as the 1923–24 Santa Clara Scorpions in Cuba's Winter League included National Baseball Hall of Fame (NBHF) inductees Oscar Charleston and José de la Caridad Méndez; the Concordia (Venezuela) 1934 team with NBHF inductees Josh Gibson and Johnny Mize; and the 1937 Ciudad Trujillo Dragons (Dominican Republic) had NBHF inductees Satchel Paige, Josh Gibson, and Cool Papa Bell, plus Puerto Rico baseball legend Perucho Cepeda, on their roster. NBHF inductee Martín Dihigo from Cuba played for the Águilas Cibaeñas in the three-team Dominican Republic League in 1937 (which, unfortunately, bankrupted baseball on the island for 14 years due to lucrative player salaries). Regional baseball legends also featured on these early teams. Tetelo Vargas, one of several Dominican players on the Estrellas Orientales, was subsequently inducted in three Caribbean Baseball Islands' halls of fame: Dominican Republic (1967), Puerto Rico (1992), and Cuba (1998). Legendary pitcher Satchel Paige's 1939–40 season included 208 strikeouts for the league champion Guayama Witches and remains Puerto Rico's single-season record (Crescioni, 1997). Venezuelan baseball historians, in particular, cherish Jackie Robinson's barnstorming trip to Venezuela between November 18 and December 23, 1945, as part of the American All-Stars team, which included baseball greats Roy Campanella and Gene Benson. Benson stated: "I roomed with Jackie . . . that series helped Jackie a lot" (personal communication, June 15, 1992). Dupouy (2019) further noted that the tour "was an unforgettable experience for all baseball fanatics in our country" (p. 6). Many of the great players in the Caribbean of this era have been recognized in museums and halls of fame in the region. For example, the Francisco "Pancho" Coímbre Museum (Figure 11.1) opened in Ponce, Puerto Rico, on January 21, 1992, after Coímbre—one of the great players in Puerto Rico's history—perished in a 1989 house fire at the age of 80. This museum further serves as Ponce's Sports Hall of Fame. From a sport heritage perspective, this era of baseball in the region therefore has both tangible movable (halls of fame and museums) and intangible (memories of great players) qualities that continue to the present day (Ramshaw & Gammon, 2017). Furthermore, these pre-CARWS teams, players, and tours helped to develop much of the event-based heritage to come.

Phase I: The Genesis of CARWS, Roberto Clemente, and Pete Rose

The creation of the CARWS highlights the next phase of this region's baseball history and became one of the most important catalysts in the development of baseball heritage in the region. The four-team CARWS between Cuba, Panama, Puerto Rico, and Venezuela (1949–60) was the brainchild of Venezuelans' Oscar Prieto Ortiz and Pablo Morales. As Hernández (2016) explained, an "accord was created between officials from Cuba, Panama, and Puerto Rico, to establish *La Confederación de Béisbol Profesional del Caribe* (Caribbean Professional Baseball Confederation), with an initiative to join, which [Venezuela] shortly thereafter accepted" (p. 1). Credit is due to George Trautman, president of the National Association of Professional Baseball Leagues (NAPBL), for putting four Caribbean Winter Leagues (Cuba, Panama, Puerto Rico, Venezuela) under the NAPBL during the December 1947 Minor Leagues' convention in Miami, Florida. Venezuela's impetus for a CARWS was confirmed by Mario Emilio Guerrero (M.E.

Figure 11.1. The Francisco "Pancho" Coímbre Museum. Photo by Héctor Ortiz Rivera.

Guerrero, personal communication, February 1, 2020). Guerrero (2009) cited the 1946–50 Inter-American Series (a.k.a. the Pan American Semi-Pro Tournament) between the Monterrey Sultans from Mexico, the All Cubans, semi-pro Brooklyn Bushwick, and Venezuela's Cervecería Caracas as the impetus for proposing a four-team CARWS.

A 1961–64 Inter-American Series between Nicaragua, Panama, Puerto Rico, and Venezuela took place. One of the lasting heritage legacies of this series was the involvement of baseball legend Roberto Clemente, who played for San Juan in Venezuela (1961), and Managua, Nicaragua (1964). During the latter series, a fan even tossed an iguana toward Clemente in right field—a shaken Clemente ran away (Van Hyning, 1995, p. 66). Art López, playing for Cinco Estrellas (Nicaragua) witnessed this (A. López, personal communication, March 15, 2021). López was a Puerto Rico–born player who moved to the South Bronx at age 12 and later played throughout the Caribbean. Beyond his legendary baseball career, Clemente is perhaps best known for perishing in a plane crash on a mercy mission to Managua on December 31, 1972, after Nicaragua's devastating earthquake. Several heritage markers honoring Clemente remain to this day, including the Roberto

Figure 11.2. Clemente Mural at Bithorn Stadium. Photo by Thomas E. Van Hyning.

Clemente Stadium in Masaya, Nicaragua, and a mural is in front of Bithorn Stadium in Puerto Rico (Figure 11.2) where he played and managed the San Juan team. Coincidentally, Museo del Deporte de Puerto Rico (Sports Museum of Puerto Rico), located in Guaynabo, in San Juan's Metropolitan Statistical Area (MSA), held a February 21 to April 30, 2020, exhibition of Clemente memorabilia, but the exhibition prematurely closed in late March 2020 due to lockdowns as a result of the coronavirus pandemic. The exhibitions included memorabilia, photos, documents, and artwork loaned by the Clemente Museum in Pittsburgh. Beyond sharing the material culture of Clemente's life and career with the people of Puerto Rico, the exhibition was also meant to entice a form of heritage sport tourism (Ramshaw, 2020) to, in particular, attract mainland U.S. tourists who are interested in Clemente's life and legacy to Puerto Rico. The exhibition was to conclude April 30, 2020, the last day of a scheduled three-game Miami Marlins and New York Mets MLB series at Hiram Bithorn Stadium, but that series was cancelled due to COVID-19.

While many players who were born, raised, and/or had much of their early baseball career in the region came back to play and manage in their home countries, teams also attracted American stars as well. Most notably, Pete Rose—who is MLB's career hits leader and played much of his career with the Cincinnati Reds—played early in his career (1964–65) with the Caracas Lions. Rose is held in high esteem by "béisbol aficionados" in Venezuela with a .351 regular season and .455 post-season average during his stint with the Lions. While Rose's heritage legacy in the United States is complex (see Ramshaw & Gammon, 2020), Venezuelans speak highly of Rose's baseball hustle and are proud he plied his trade there. Art López, who reinforced the Águilas Cibaeñas entry from the Dominican Republic, in a four-team Inter-American (Phase III) Series, in Caracas, February 4–9, 1965, between two Dominican and two Venezuelan clubs, was voted Series MVP, over Rose, by the sportswriters (A. López, personal communication, March 24, 2021). López was impressed by Rose's "constant hustle." The development of the CARWS, as well as the many legendary players who played in the tournament, helped to solidify the tournament as part of the baseball heritage in the region. Many heritages—particularly in sport—require strong historical foundations in order to continue for decades to come. The fact that two of baseball's greatest and most legendary players—Roberto Clemente and Pete Rose—were part of the tournament's development gave the CARWS both a strong heritage and an ongoing legitimacy in the baseball world.

Phase II: CARWS, 1970 to 1989

Building on its history and heritage from its initial phase, the CARWS changed and evolved during its second phase of development, and featured additional star players, teams, and performances. A three-team CARWS between Magallanes, Licey, and Ponce, took place in Caracas, February 5–10, 1970. Guigo Otero Suro, Puerto Rico League president, helped resurrect it (Van Hyning, 1995). Host Magallanes (7–1) prevailed over Ponce (4–4) and Licey (1–7). A. Saer Gómez (personal communication, March 3, 2020) covered this 1970 series. "It was a very special celebration," and "first one in our history." Saer broadcast 25 CARWS in 50 years as a broadcaster. In addition to top players, three NBHF managers—whose involvement began just prior to this phase and continued into this era—are part of Venezuelan League history, including Sparky Anderson (1964–65 Magallanes), Earl Weaver (1962–63 Lara), and Bobby Cox (1974–77 Lara).

A few notable highlights included the 1974 CARWS, won by Caguas, in the first one hosted by Mexico. Mike Schmidt (1995 NBHF inductee) and Jay Johnstone played chess en route to Mexico from Puerto Rico (Barea, 1997). Héctor Espino, 1974 Series MVP and All-Star 1B with a .429 average, is Mexico's Babe Ruth: 783 career homers, a record 484 in the Minor Leagues (summer); and 299 in his 24 Mexican Pacific League (winter) seasons (Hughson, 2010). His father owned dump trucks; Héctor developed strong wrists, a powerful chest, and solid work ethic while helping his dad. Héctor Espino Stadium in Hermosillo hosted the 1982 CARWS, won by Caracas. Legendary pitcher Fernando Valenzuela pitched a shutout over Ponce, after becoming 1981 NL Cy Young Winner, Rookie of the Year, and 1981 World Series champ with the Los Angeles Dodgers. Dennis Lewallyn stated, "Fernando was impressive in the CARWS" (personal communication, June 29, 2019). Lewallyn pitched for the Zulia Eagles in Maracaibo, managed by Luis Ernesto Aparicio Montiel. "Travel was tough—eight-hour bus trips; we would fly to Caracas. We were paid in U.S. dollars, but could exchange them." Venezuela's economy was driven by its oil economy and owners paid good salaries to players. Maracaibo hosted the 1986 Caribbean Series at Luis Aparicio Ortega "El Grande de Maracaibo" Stadium. Águilas de Mexicali won it. The senior Aparicio ("El Grande") was the father of Venezuela's only (1984) NBHF inductee—shortstop Luis Ernesto Aparicio Montiel. Landino's (2018) SABR bio noted that Aparicio Jr. "was the symbol of the growth and development of the game of baseball in Latin America— in Venezuela and hometown of Maracaibo. His place among the greatest players in baseball signified the climax of a cycle of progress for baseball, the national sport of Venezuela and an intrinsic part of its cultural heritage" (Landino, 2018, para. 2). This era of development not only helped solidify the tournament as an important part of baseball culture; the success of other national teams during this phase also helped make it an integral part of the region's sport heritage.

Detour to Miami, Florida (1990–91), through 1995

By the 1990s, the CARWS could be considered a type of sport heritage event, given both its history and symbolic capital in regional baseball culture. However, following Pinson's (2017) discussion, many heritage sporting events are intrinsically tied to particular locations and, if they become portable, lose much of their heritage appeal. Such was the case when the CARWS took place at the Orange Bowl in Miami in 1990–91. The events were financial flops with lack of Caribbean fan support and indifference by Miami residents. In fact, only 50,000 spectators total showed up over six days in February 1990 to see Escogido, managed by the legendary Felipe Alou, win five of six games. The 1991 event was won by Licey.

The event moved back to Mexico (1992–93), Dominican Republic (1994), and Puerto Rico (1995) after the Miami experiment, with greater success. The 1994–95 San Juan Senators put together a "Dream Team," and finished 6–0, as the first CARWS team with "Puerto Rico" on uniforms instead of the league champion's name. Their two NBHF inductees, 2B Roberto Alomar (2011) and DH Edgar Martínez (2019), plus a constellation of other MLB stars—catcher Carlos Delgado, 1B Carmelo Martínez, 3B Carlos Baerga, SS Rey Sánchez, Juan González (LF), Bernie Williams (CF), and Rubén Sierra (RF)—pulverized the Toros del Este starters, who included NBHF inductee Pedro Martínez (February 6) and José Rijo (February 9, 1995). Roberto Alomar (14 hits, .560 AVG and 10 RBIs) was MVP, while Puerto Rican Bernie Williams's three HR led all batters. Twenty-five years later, Williams expressed that he has fond memories playing in the CARWS: "Playing winter ball for Caguas and Arecibo and my CARWS experiences [1995 and 1996] were very helpful" (B. Williams, personal communication, February 1, 2020). This statement further highlights the intrinsic ties between heritage and place, as well as some of the limitations on heritage mobilities. On the surface, "growing" the CARWS by playing in the United States seemed to be a good idea. Yet, as is demonstrated by this era, the CARWS needed to be connected to the places in which it was most meaningful, lest it lose its heritage and cultural value.

Founding the Caribbean Baseball Hall of Fame and the 2020 CARWS

Much of the heritage recognition of Caribbean baseball and the CARWS came in the mid-1990s. In 1996, Juan Francisco Puello Herrera, an attorney in the Dominican Republic and commissioner of the Caribbean Professional Baseball Confederation, established the Caribbean Baseball Hall of Fame, a virtual hall of fame that honors the great players of the CARWS and builders who contributed to the development of Caribbean baseball. Puello Herrera also ensured the CARWS returned to the Caribbean after its unsuccessful sojourn to the United States in the early 1990s; the CARWS has been played in the Caribbean ever since. The first four 1996 CARSHF inductees were U.S. import Willard Brown, Puerto Rico, MVP, 1953 series; Rico Carty, Dominican Republic, MVP, 1977 series; Héctor Espino, Mexico, MVP, 1974 and 1976 events; and Camilo Pascual, Cuba. J. F. Puello Herrera shared insights on three decades leading the Confederation, and ensuring its historical legacy and financial solvency. "We do this [Induction] every year and invite family and friends. This year [2020] we inducted ex-players, executives, and broadcasters from Venezuela since they were unable to host the 2019 event, plus five players who represented Puerto Rico" (personal communication, February 6, 2020).

The 2020 CARWS featured several existential sport heritages (Ramshaw, 2014) in which family connections between past and present series were realized. Most notably, Ozney Guillén, the youngest manager in CARWS history, managed in the tournament (Figure 11.3). His father, Ozzie Guillén, was the first Latino MLB manager to win a World Series (2005 Chicago White Sox), and Ozney was their batboy. Bilingual Ozney inserted this on his lineup card: "ten un plan" (have a plan); "breathe" and "have fun." His squad took a 3–0 lead over Lara after five innings, behind six-foot-eight Edgar de la Rosa, a Dominican hurler, the tallest player on all six rosters. Eight Colombia players were Dominicans, five were Venezuelans, and 15 were Colombians. Lara scored six in the seventh; the game-winner was a two-run single by five-foot-six 2B Alexi Amarista, the series' smallest player. "I took advantage of a pitch which didn't break" (A. Amarista, personal communication, February 1, 2020). Their Game One starter—Logan Darnell, Nashville, Tennessee—was their only U.S. import.

The 2:30 p.m. contest was between Mexico, managed by Benji Gil, and Toros del Este, whose skipper was Puerto Rico native Lino Rivera. Yunesky Maya, from Pinar del Río, Cuba, bested Mexico 2–1. Maya answered why many Cuban baseball players from his generation have first names starting with Y. "Because of the Russians!" (Y. Maya, personal communication, February 1, 2020), perhaps suggesting further existential heritages. Santurce won the ten-inning nightcap over Panama 4–3. Pre-game ceremonies honored the 1995 undefeated Puerto Rico "Dream Team," further demonstrating the importance of heritage in the tournament's ongoing operations. Super Bowl Sunday (February 2) included a 2:30 p.m. Santurce-Culiacán game, so Puerto Rico's fans could enjoy Super Bowl parties and the football game, suggesting that the connections with U.S. sporting cultures remain intact.

Figure 11.3. Ozney Guillén (*left*) stands next to Ozzie Guillén, his father, at the 2020 CARWS press conference. Photo by Thomas E. Van Hyning.

Many of the participants in the 2020 CARWS described their uses and understandings of baseball heritages in the region, as well as integrating wider strategies and tactics—particularly from the United States. Ozney Guillén has a photo of Willie Mays from the 1955 CARWS. He picked the brains of former MLB managers Bobby Cox, Jack McKeon, and Alex Cora. Ozney used the "shift" (an on-field defensive tactic) in managing 2019 Tri-City Valley Cats, Houston's short-season affiliate, NY-Penn League, but not in the 2020 CARWS. He expressed concern over low Minor-League salaries: "$1,000/month is not enough; should pay us more. Some of my players had to be Uber drivers to make it." Ozney felt that winter ball remains a great showcase for players (O. Guillén, personal communication, February 3, 2020).

Other players expressed forms of personal heritage connections to the series and baseball in the region. Peter O'Brien, 2020 CARWS MVP, noted, "My mom is Cuban and I'm perfectly bilingual, comfortable in either [English or Spanish] language" (P. O'Brien, personal communication, February 3, 2020). Two days later, he got the key hit versus Santurce, and answered media questions in Spanish. He was invited to the 2020 spring training by the Atlanta Braves. This MVP of the 2019–20 Dominican Winter League was called "Caballete" by Lino Rivera, translated to "the guy" or "show horse." L.

Figure 11.4. Luis Sojo
with his CARSHF plaque.
Photo by Thomas E. Van
Hyning.

Rivera (personal communication, February 6, 2020) opined that the Toros
would not be in the title game without O'Brien's clutch hitting.

The current CARWS is also creating new heritage legacies, particularly
on the management side of the game. Loriam Argumedo Dau, the first female general manager in CARWS history, chose Ozney to manage her 2019–
20 Montería Cowboys in the six-team Colombian Winter League, noting
in particular his pedigree: "for baseball know-how . . . metrics ability, 2019
minor-league managing, family name . . . Ozzie (dad) recommended him"
(L.A. Dau, personal communication, February 3, 2020). Argumedo Dau is
from Montería, a cattle-producing area. She was certified in Cuba (physical
trainer) and has 25 years of experience in baseball, starting as a trainer. She
enjoys her GM role, and looks forward to Barranquilla, Colombia, hosting
a CARWS.

Heritage was also part of the 2020 pre-game festivities and traditions.
David "Big Papi" Ortiz—former star player with the Boston Red Sox—
threw out the ceremonial first pitch at the February 5, 2020, contest between

Toros del Este and Santurce. Ortiz (2022 NBHF inductee) has a personal connection to the tournament, having played for the Dominican Republic in the 1999–2001 and 2003–2004 CARWS. Ortiz noted: "It is a great honor to throw the first pitch at Bithorn, where I hit the series-winning homer in 1999; helped Aguilas Cibaeñas win it in 2003. These are precious memories; when you play in front of Caribbean fans, it is special and helpful. I came through in key situations and I'm very appreciative of the CARWS, and winter ball" (personal communication, February 5, 2020). Two years later, Ortiz was inducted into the CARSHF, in Santo Domingo, February 2, 2022 (Vicioso 2021). One main event of the 2020 CARWS was the induction ceremony into the CARSHF, hosted by the Sports Museum of Puerto Rico. Twelve members were inducted, including Venezuelan infielder and former MLB player Luis Sojo. He gave a heartfelt speech and was all smiles while holding his hall of fame plaque (Figure 11.4).

Additional Baseball Heritages in the Caribbean

Beyond the CARWS, other baseball heritages in the Caribbean are flourishing, particularly in the establishment of baseball halls of fame and museums. On November 18, 2017, El Museo del Béisbol Zuliano (Museum of the Zulia Eagles) opened to the public at Luis Aparicio Ortega Stadium in Maracaibo, Venezuela. Fifteen former players and managers were inducted in Zulia's Hall of Fame, including Aparicio ("El Grande") and son (Aparicio Montiel). The museum was established using private funds. La Casa Museo del Pelotero Profesional Dominicano (Dominican Professional Baseball Players Museum) is a five-story structure in front of Quisqueya Stadium Juan Marichal, their only stadium to host two pro baseball teams—Licey Tigers and Escogido Lions (Guerrero, 2015). The National Federation of Dominican Baseball Players inaugurated the Dominican Pro Baseball Players Museum, October 17, 2015, in Santo Domingo, the oldest city in the Americas (founded in 1496). The ceremony was led by Mario Melvin Soto, former MLB pitcher. This museum honors players from their Winter League and MLB, with wide-screen TVs, wall exhibits, photos, videos, vignettes, murals, postcards, and exhibits of bats, baseballs, uniforms, and other memorabilia. Funding came via private donations from past and present Dominican MLB players. The Salón de la Fama del Béisbol Latino (LBHF) was inaugurated in La Romana, Dominican Republic, on May 23–30, 2010. It recognizes the contribution of Latin American players to baseball. Twenty-four inductees were part of the inaugural class, divided into three groups: Latin American members of NBHF (includes Latin American recipients of the Ford Frick Award), the veterans; and contemporary players since 1959.

LBHF gives out the Tommy Lasorda Award, dedicated to non-Latino personalities who promote baseball development in Latin America. The first recipient was Peter O'Malley, former owner of the Los Angeles Dodgers (2010). Many inductees have been enshrined in other baseball museums both in the region and in the United States, demonstrating the depth of baseball heritage in the country.

Final Thoughts

The heritage of the CARWS—and baseball heritage in the Caribbean as a whole—is flourishing, particularly if the 2020 tournament is any indication. The Toros del Este bested Santurce, 4–3, in the semis, and Lara, 9–3, in the February 7, 2020, title game, to finish 6–1. Winning starters for the Toros, semi-finals and finals, were Yunesky Maya from Cuba and Paolo Espino from Panama. The author sat in a box seat during the Toros-Lara game, next to Omayra, spouse of Santurce's team mascot. Omayra's physician, Luis Molinary, is Santurce's team doctor. L. Molinary said that CARWS teams must have MLB-sanctioned trainers (personal communication, February 6, 2020). Most of the 15,000 fans on February 7 were Dominicans residing in Puerto Rico. Many stormed the field after the last out. Caribbean baseball fans are more passionate, demonstrative, and knowledgeable than U.S. fans, for example, chanting, "MVP" when Peter O'Brien stepped to the plate. Dancers entertained fans between innings, common in the CARWS. Camaraderie existed between media members representing each country. Rums of Puerto Rico and Discover Puerto Rico were visible corporate sponsors, and alcoholic beverages were served at concessions. A protest against Nicolás Maduro—with signs—was held by Venezuelan fans during a Lara game. Edwin Hernández, executive director of the Sports Museum of Puerto Rico, umpired in this CARWS.

The Toros del Este 2020 title was sweet for their skipper Lino Rivera, who was runner-up, 2018 CARWS, Guadalajara, Mexico, with Águilas Cibaeñas, behind Caguas. Opening Ceremonies in that 2018 series, February 2, featured an appearance by former U.S. president Bill Clinton, seen in Puerto Rico's dugout, shaking hands and inquiring about players' families' post-Hurricane Maria. Guadalajara native Saúl "Canelo" Alvarez, world middleweight boxing champ, threw the first pitch (Van Hyning, Spring 2018, p. 14). These aspects—the players, games, fan traditions, recognition of the tournament's past, and the links to regional cultural heritage—all point to the CARWS being a cornerstone of baseball heritage for decades to come.

More than this, however, the CARWS has broad heritage, along with diasporic, economic, and political implications, due to the political realities in Cuba and Venezuela, economic challenges facing Puerto Rico, and the relations between MLB (and Minor Leagues) vis-à-vis Winter League clubs, among others. The observations, interviews, and research in this chapter—which helped illuminate the eras of the CARWS, how its heritage has been used and interpreted, as well as the ways in which baseball heritage continues to be recognized today—demonstrate the important and unique value that heritage has for baseball in the Caribbean. The heritage of baseball in the region is maintained and enhanced not only by this event but also through the establishment of many baseball-themed museums and halls of fame, which should be maintained and developed both for local and visiting audiences. Baseball heritage in the Caribbean is strong and appears to continue to be recognized and celebrated in the years to come. Further research from baseball and heritage scholars could look at the uses of heritage as a way of differentiation both intra-regionally and with the United States, how (and whether) baseball heritage—including at the CARWS—could be used in regional tourism development. There is also potential for further heritage recognition, particularly through museums and halls of fame, as well as through in-stadium heritage markers, plaques, and displays.

References

Bagnall, G. (2003). Performance and productivity at heritage sites. *Museum and Society*, *1*(2), 87–103.

Barea, H. (1997). Historia de los Criollos. San Juan, PR: Ana G. Méndez University System.

Crescioni Benítez, J. A. (1997). El Béisbol Profesional Boricua. San Juan, PR: First Book Publishing.

Dupouy Gómez, M. (2019, August 21). *Las Estrellas Americanas visitan Venezuela*. Béisbol Inmortal. http://beisbolinmortal.blogspot.com/2019/08/las-estrellas-americanas-visitan.html (accessed December 7, 2020).

Fletcher, T. (2012). Who do '"they cheer for?"' Cricket, diaspora, hybridity and divided loyalties Amongst British Asians. *International Review for the Sociology of Sport*, *47*(5), 612–631.

Guerrero, M. (2009, February 1). La Serie Interamericana fue precursora de Serie Caribe. *Listín Diario*. https://listindiario.com/el-deporte/2009/02/01/89646/la-serie-interamericana-fue-precursora-de-serie-caribe (accessed December 7, 2020).

Hernández, L. (2016). NAPBL gathering in Miami gave birth to the Caribbean Series. *The National Pastime,* Vol. 36. https://sabr.org/research/2016-national-pastime (accessed December 7, 2020).

Hughson, C. (2010, July 27). *The "Mexican Babe Ruth" Héctor Espino.* Mop-Up Duty. https://mopupduty.com/the-mexican-babe-ruth-hector-espino/ (accessed December 7, 2020).

Kepner, T. (2020, December 16). "Baseball rights a wrong by adding Negro Leagues to official records. *New York Times.* https://www.nytimes.com/2020/12/16/sports/baseball/mlb-negro-leagues.html (accessed January 14, 2022).

Landino, L. (2018, January 23). Luis Aparicio SABR bio. https://sabr.org/bioproj/person/87c077f1 (accessed December 7, 2020).

Pinson, J. (2017). Heritage sporting events: Theoretical development and configurations. *Journal of Sport & Tourism, 21*(2), 133–152.

Ramshaw, G. (2014). A Canterbury tale: Imaginative genealogies and existential heritage tourism at the St. Lawrence ground. *Journal of Heritage Tourism, 9*(3), 257–269.

Ramshaw, G. (2020). *Heritage and sport: An introduction.* Bristol: Channel View.

Ramshaw, G., & Gammon, S. J. (2017). Towards a critical sport heritage: Implications for sport tourism. *Journal of Sport & Tourism, 21*(2), 115–131.

Ramshaw, G., & Gammon, S. (2020). Difference, dissonance, and redemption in sport heritage: Interpreting the tangled legacy of Pete Rose at two museums. *Journal of Heritage Tourism, 15*(2), 217–227.

Van Hyning, T. E. (1995). Puerto Rico's winter league: A history of Major League Baseball's launching pad. London: McFarland.

Van Hyning, T. E. (Spring 2018). Caguas Criollos. *The Baseball Research Journal,* Vol. 47 No. 1. Phoenix: SABR, 7–16.

Vicioso, Dolores (2021, November 25). David Ortiz named to Caribbean Series Hall of Fame. https://drl.com/wordpress/2021/11/25/david-ortiz-named-to-caribbean-series-hall-of-fame/ (accessed January 26, 2022).

12

"Our Very Own 'Field of Dreams' in England's Green and Pleasant Land"

Baseball Heritage in Britain

Brett Lashua

This chapter presents a potted cultural history of baseball in Britain and considers its heritage in practice, particularly in relation to my experiences playing baseball (as an expat American*) "over here." Despite recent scholarly attention to the British origins of baseball (Block, 2019; Hise, 2010), its early formations and attempts to popularize the pastime in the United Kingdom have been largely forgotten or ignored. Baseball remains marginal within the British sport heritage landscape, both tangibly and in the popular sport imagination (Capon, 2003).

I lead off with the opening of a new baseball facility at Farnham Park, Surrey, in 2013, to begin to contextualize the concrete and imagined terrain of British baseball heritage. Farnham Park was purportedly the first purpose-built baseball and softball complex in the United Kingdom. Unpacking this claim, the second part of this chapter is grounded in historical scholarship on British baseball and antecedent baseball activities and facilities in the U.K., pre-1940. Third, the chapter adds ethnographic "field" notes from my experiences playing baseball (2012–2015) in the northern division of the British Baseball Federation (BBF). Particular emphasis is placed on the challenges of developing fields and facilities within the cultural "sportscape" of British baseball. Finally, the chapter comes "home" by linking British baseball to questions of cultural history and heritage. For

---

* Originally from northeastern Ohio in the U.S., I grew up playing baseball. After moving to the U.K. in 2005, I played softball for a couple of seasons in Cardiff and only "discovered" baseball in Yorkshire in 2012.

Burke (2012), "cultural history is best regarded not as a field with a fence around it but rather as a history written from a particular angle or viewpoint, concentrating on the symbolic element in all human activities" (p. 7). These symbolic elements "privilege encounters, dialogues, viewpoints, conflicts, misunderstandings and translations (including mistranslations)" (p. 9). Accordingly, the next section of this chapter highlights symbolic encounters, viewpoints, and (mis)translations at the opening of Farnham Park.

Background: "Our Very Own 'Field of Dreams' in England's Green and Pleasant Land"?

In 2013, I was playing recreational baseball in the BBF when my club qualified for the league's national championship tournament. This event took place at the brand-new Farnham Park Baseball Ground. These new fields at Farnham Park* were heralded as a watershed moment in British baseball, "the UK's first baseball and softball complex" (BaseballSoftballUK, 2013). John Walmsley, chair of BaseballSoftballUK (BSUK), celebrated the opening of the site with a hotchpotch of quixotic iconography: "This is a sporting landmark; our very own 'field of dreams' in England's green and pleasant land" (BSUK, 2013). The imagery in the phrase "England's green and pleasant land" is from William Blake's poem *And did those feet in ancient time* (c. 1808), more famously known—after being set to music in 1916 by Hubert Parry—as the anthem "Jerusalem." "Jerusalem" serves as an unofficial national song for England.** Blake's lines recount the apocryphal tale of Jesus visiting England (and specifically Glastonbury) and a moment when England became heaven on earth. The poem laments the industrializing landscape (transformed by "Satan's dark mills"), in which England's pastoral landscape should be viewed as a kind of heavenly paradise. Walmsley's statement implies that a British baseball field is its own kind of heaven on earth. The phrasing achieves this also by connecting England's pastoral "green and pleasant land" to the baseball film, *Field of Dreams* (Robinson, 1989). In *Field of Dreams*, the film's central character, played by Kevin Costner, is compelled to build a baseball diamond in an Iowa cornfield after

---

* Farnham Park was built by BaseballSoftballUK with support from Sport England and Major League Baseball's Baseball Tomorrow Fund. The facility features a full-size international-standard baseball field and three smaller softball/youth baseball fields.

** "Jerusalem" is for England what "God Save the Queen" is for the United Kingdom; neither England nor the United Kingdom has an official national song.

being visited by the ghost of a legendary player ("Shoeless" Joe Jackson) and hearing a voice tell him "If you build it, he will come" (widely recirculated as "if you build it, *they* will come"). The film has become something of a cult classic for baseball aficionados, and also serving, more widely, as a metaphor for architects, planners, politicians, and managers who deploy its wistful optimism in the face of adversity (Crawford, 1998; Snyder & McCullogh, 2000; Webb, 2003).

This brief account of Farnham Park as a "field of dreams" begins to illustrate the curious terrain of the history and heritage of British baseball. If cultural landscapes mirror the societies that construct them, then the interest in sport heritage landscapes can reflect "what a people feel they had, wish they had and, perhaps, what they would like to have again" (Ramshaw, 2005, p. 5). While Walmsley's comments draw upon a repertoire of baseball symbolism combined with English nationalism, this symbolic "encounter" at Farnham Park was selectively mythogenic—actively producing myths (see Silk, 2015)—in order to forge links between baseball and Britain. However, a longer historical view illustrates that the odd pairing of phrases is not as unusual as it may seem, and the opening of Farnham Park was not as much of a "first" as it was made out to be.*

A Potted History of Baseball in Britain

Far from being "America's game" (per Walt Whitman**), baseball is a derivative sport. Many scholars argue that baseball originated in Britain, where versions of the game had been played since at least the middle of the 18th century (Block, 2019; Bloyce, 2008; Hise, 2010; Majumdar & Brown, 2007). Block (2005) wrote of an antecedent ball game from 1672, noting it traveled to America during early waves of British colonial migration to North America. In another example, Bloyce (2008) reported that Jane Austen referred to a game called "base ball" in the late 18th century. Other early moments chronicled by Hise (2010) include the first recorded game of "Bass-Ball" in 1749 in Surrey, England, and an account of "Base Ball" recorded in 1755 in the diary of English lawyer William Bray. Hise (2010) also acknowledged the

---

* There are other, earlier fields; Richmond Baseball Club, founded in 1992, plays at Connare Field—built in 2003.

** "It's our game; that's the chief fact in connection with it: America's game; it has the snap, go, fling of the American atmosphere; it belongs as much to our institutions, fits into them as significantly as our Constitution's laws; is just as important in the sum total of our historic life" (Walt Whitman, 1889; in Schmidgall, 2001, p. 261).

1744 publication of *A Little Pretty Pocket-Book*, which included a woodcut showing "stool ball" along with a rhyme entitled "Base-ball." Block (2019) noted one of the first "fathers" of American baseball, the English sportswriter and ardent baseball promoter Henry Chadwick, had in 1860, "proclaimed that baseball was of 'British origin' and 'derived from the game of rounders'" (p. 3). While during the last 160 years many Americans would dispute its origins and relationship to rounders (and cricket), even Major League Baseball (2013's "Baseball Discovered" project) acknowledged the longer historical arc of the game (i.e., predating its 1839 "invention"), and historians have asserted its British "paternity" (as Block [2019] put it*). Block (2019) asserted that in fact "base ball" pre-dated rounders, but by the 1870s most Britons "had forgotten, or had never known, the game's original name" (p. 28). Whether baseball evolved from rounders, or vice versa, the argument is clear: baseball's origins are British.

Another body of scholarship has focused on the modern game (c. 1874 to present) in the United Kingdom, vis-à-vis its positioning as an American pastime. Research has focused in particular on baseball exhibition tours of Britain, 1874–1924 (Bloyce, 1997, 2005, 2008; Bloyce & Murphy, 2008; Chetwynd, 2006; Johnes, 2000; Moore, 1994; Zeiler, 2006). Others have researched regional leagues (Bloyce, 2006, 2007; Chetwynd & Belton, 2007) and geographic-specific histories of baseball in Yorkshire, Liverpool, and southeast Wales (Johnes, 2000; Smyth, 1993; Weltch, 2008).

The first of several exhibition "world tours" of professional American baseball players visited Britain in 1874, bringing an expression of American values, ideals, and growing imperialism amid shifting global interdependencies (Bloyce & Murphy, 2008; Moore, 1994). For Bloyce (1997), the 1874 tour was "an attempt to illustrate to the rest of the world that the Americans were a unified, advanced and scientific nation" (p. 208). Harry Wright, a British-born son of a cricketer, was a leading baseball player and manager with the Boston Red Stockings. As he witnessed baseball superseding cricket in the rest of America, he was certain that British sportsmen would embrace the sport in a similar fashion. Enlisting the help of A. G. Spalding, Wright arranged for the Red Stockings and Philadelphia Athletics to play a series of exhibition games in England in 1874. Minimal press coverage treated baseball as little more than "glorified rounders" and "poor man's cricket" (Johnes, 2000). Others considered the game antithetical to English

---

* Block's (2019) history is, in my view, among the best treatments of the disputed origins of the game.

sportsmanship, which in turn perpetuated the notion that baseball was inherently an American pastime (Bloyce, 2008; Voigt, 1976).

Fourteen years later, with continued interest in developing baseball in Britain, Spalding organized another world tour in 1888–1889 (Moore, 1994; Zeiler, 2006). During this tour ("The Great Base Ball Trip Around the World"*), players arrived in England in late winter; matches were played in terrible weather and restricted to county cricket grounds. Despite the conditions, crowds were recorded of up to 8,000 spectators (in London, March 8, 1889; and Leighton, March 16, 1889). Although most games were well attended, connotations of social class and amateurism coupled with condescending commentaries in the English press (as with the previous tour) to reinforce nationalistic ideologies that reflected Britain's resistance to any American cultural "invasion" via the commercialization and professionalization of sport (Bloyce, 1997, 2005, 2008; Bloyce & Murphy, 2008). Bloyce and Murphy (2008, p. 127) noted the "minimal" and derisive media coverage, such as in the *Times*:

> We are not prepared to say that it is altogether possible to judge without prejudice a game which the Americans have presumptuously preferred to cricket. . . . As for the essentials of the game, it would be singular if they did not strike some chords of sympathy in the English breast, considering that they are the same as those of "rounders." . . . Consequently, we must have latent affinities for baseball. (March 18, 1889, p. 9)

Perhaps owing to these affinities, baseball was established on a minor scale with the creation of the National Baseball League of Great Britain (1889)** (Bloyce, 1997).

At this time—rather than Farnham Park—the "first" documented baseball facility in England was built in Derby. There, Derby County's football stadium (demolished in 2003) was named the Baseball Ground, as it was first used, from 1890 to 1898, as the home field for the Derby County Baseball Club, before its conversion into a football pitch. Originally named Ley's Baseball Ground, the field was part of sports facilities (Ley's Recreation Ground) built by industrialist Sir Francis Ley for workers at his ironworks. The Baseball Ground was the focal point of the complex, part of a personal

---

* This tour featured stops in the "Sandwich Islands" (Hawai'i), New Zealand, Australia, Ceylon (Sri Lanka), India, Arabia (Saudi Arabia), Egypt, Italy, France, England, Scotland, and Ireland.

** This league was dissolved after just one season due to excessive "rowdiness"; it was followed by the Baseball Association of Great Britain, in 1890.

quest by Ley to introduce baseball to the United Kingdom. Ley embraced the "rational recreation" movement to link baseball to football (soccer) as alternating, seasonal, health-promoting working-class sports in Britain. Other notable events at this time include the establishment of five London baseball teams, such as the Thespians, in 1894. Led by R. G. Knowles, an American musician and comedian, the Thespians were comprised primarily of American entertainers working in London's theatres. Other ballclubs, such as the London Remingtons, were supported by American businesses— that is, Remington Typewriter. The British league survived at an amateur level, until "with the paucity of [press] coverage, the game went into decline and, to all intents and purposes, disappeared some time after the 1900 season" (Bloyce & Murphy, 2008, p. 129).

The baseball tours were part of wider attempts by American entrepreneurs to unfasten baseball from its British heritage. Gems (2011, p. 107) argued that, for many, baseball exemplified Americans' perceptions of themselves as a decent, wholesome, and independent people. During these early tours, Spalding claimed he was so struck by the differences between baseball and rounders that he was convinced that baseball had to have originated in America (Block, 2019). In 1905, Spalding organized the Mills Commission, a group of former baseball administrators and associates, and two United States senators, to determine the origins of the game (Block, 2019; Gems, 2011; Gems et al., 2008). The commission enshrined Abner Doubleday's 1839 "invention" of the game at Cooperstown, New York. With this mythogenic distancing of the game from its British antecedents, Americans sought to construct a distinct national identity via sport (Gems, 2011).

Two additional baseball world tours—one prior to World War I (1913), and another in its aftermath (1924)—represented further attempts by American baseball entrepreneurs to embed the game in the British sporting landscape. Met once again with negative press, British disinterest in baseball was in part a response to fears over the professionalization of cricket, and also "an arena in which they [the British] could give less risky vent to their anxieties about Britain's decline as a world power in the face of American expansionism" (Bloyce & Murphy, 2008, p. 136). Through a coolness toward baseball, dominant media discourses reflected how the British "feared that they were losing ground culturally, politically and economically to the former colony" (Bloyce, 2005, p. 94). The 1924 exhibition tour represented "the last high-profile attempt by American entrepreneurs to establish the game" in Britain (Bloyce & Murphy, 2008, p. 137).

Perhaps surprisingly, although the four tours (1874–1924) failed to spark widespread interest, there followed a "golden age" of British baseball during the 1930s. The English entrepreneur Sir John Moores became interested in baseball after observing it being played during his visits to America. Moores thought baseball had potential to rival cricket, and he helped establish the National Baseball Association in 1933. His financial contributions also ensured greater media coverage of baseball in Britain than had been afforded previously to the game.

At the other end of the social hierarchy, Smyth (1993) examined media coverage of baseball in the 1930s to explore how the working classes, locality, and the Americanization of British popular culture helped explain the development of baseball in the north of England. Paying particular attention to the Yorkshire League (1936–1937) and the Yorkshire-Lancashire League (1938–1939), Smyth charted baseball's (re)configuration in the north. In Leeds, professional baseball made an impressive "debut" in July 1935, drawing a crowd of over 10,000 people. Smyth (1993) explained that the Leeds baseball club featured local celebrity rugby players in the hopes of attracting existing working-class rugby fans to baseball, and also noted that many rugby athletes participated in baseball in the off-season to keep fit. In Leeds, baseball was viewed therefore as a growth sport that could thrive in local Yorkshire community leagues, schools, and summer programs too (Smyth, 1993). Professional Yorkshire League teams recruited expat American and Canadian players to strengthen their squads, but with the creation of the Yorkshire-Lancashire League in 1938, teams began limiting foreign professionals to allow greater development opportunities for British players. The outbreak of World War II brought an abrupt end to the league.

The moderate success of baseball in northern Britain during the 1930s was accompanied by further resistance in some areas, including southeastern Wales (Cardiff and Newport) and on Merseyside (Liverpool) (Guttmann, 1995; Weltch, 2008). Moores met opposition to setting up an American-style baseball league in Liverpool, not only because of its American associations but also because an earlier version of "British baseball" was still being played there. This version, also known as "Welsh baseball," more closely resembles rounders. It differs from the American game with a dissimilar number of players (11), scoring scheme (one point per base reached), innings structure (two innings), with no foul areas, underhand pitching, and players outfitted in rugby- or football-style uniforms (Weltch, 2008). Johnes (2000) suggested that this version of baseball emerged in working-class areas of

Newport and Liverpool in the early 1900s, where there was weak interest in cricket (as an upper-class sport) and an underlying regional anti-English sentiment. Although there was pressure on the Welsh game to adopt American rules in order to make it more attractive, it maintained its unique identity in working-class communities (Johnes, 2000). Bloyce (2007) argued that "British/Welsh baseball" endured where it fostered "belonging and identity, reminiscent of [resistance to] earlier attempts made to establish American baseball during the exhibition tours" (p. 66). Media coverage also reinforced distinctions between American baseball as an "outsider" sport and "British baseball" as an established national sport. However, due to its unique regional inflections, this version of the game has remained marginal in southeast Wales and Merseyside.

According to Chetwynd (2008), despite its extensive history in Britain, "baseball had too many low tides of interest when there was nobody to carry the tale of the British game" (p. 264). Drawing from ethnographic experiences playing for the Great Britain National Team in the 1990s, Chetwynd (2006) also observed that most players did not have much sense of British baseball history. While some scholarly historical attention has focused on the lack of (or negative) media coverage, for Chetwynd (2006) another significant factor in the idiosyncratic and stagnant status of baseball in Britain has been the shortage of places to play. In the next section I also draw from ethnographic observations—that is, "field" notes—to spotlight some of the challenges of playing baseball in Britain, specifically the difficulties of creating places to play.

"Field" Notes: Playing Baseball in Britain

The British Baseball Federation (BBF), founded in 1987, is the current national governing body for baseball in the United Kingdom. During the 2013 season, there were approximately 40 clubs with 58 league teams in the BBF, split by player ability and geographical location into four divisions with north/south regions. These divisions ranged from the highly competitive National Baseball League, to less competitive AAA and AA divisions, to recreational beginner-level Single-A baseball. This third section of the chapter locates my experiences as a player in the BBF's AA Northern Division (2012–2015); during our successful 2013 season my team competed in the national playoffs at this level, at Farnham Park.

My home club was established in Yorkshire in 2009. From over 200 club members (from varying nationalities), in 2013 the club fielded just one team consisting of approximately 40 active players, of whom only a dozen or so were available on most game days. This team was comprised of about 20 Americans, many employed at a nearby American military installation. The rest of the team consisted mostly of British players (ranging from absolute beginners to talented veteran players), who all expressed to me an appreciation for the "Americanness" of the game. The club also attracted a small number of Japanese players (predominantly students at U.K. universities) and a handful of players from within the European Union (e.g., Dutch, Italians, Poles) living in the United Kingdom. In what follows, I share two field notes, first describing a typical game day at our home field, and then the 2013 playoffs at Farnham Park. The emphasis in these observations, like other ethnographies of baseball and home ballparks (Krizek, 2003; Trujillo, 1992), rests on the fields, facilities, and baseball sportscape. These fields are significant manifestations of the symbolic "place" of baseball in Britain.

Field Notes: April 28, 2013—Building the "Field"

There is no field here, just a huge expanse of boggy grass far behind a secondary school. There is an area that has been designated for baseball—at the extreme corner of the plot, abutting the railroad line—but it currently has football (soccer) goalposts in the middle of what should be our left field. We have to lift the goalposts out of the ground and set them aside (left fielder, beware of those open postholes!). Although a new club and only established here since 2009, there is an earthen pitcher's mound (most teams use a portable, homemade, Astroturf-covered wooden platform as a temporary mound) and base cutouts where there's no grass. There's nothing else, as far as baseball facilities, and this is one of the best I've seen so far in the U.K.! Dropping a ball field on top of other sports grounds seems the norm: in one team's park, the lanes of an athletics track cut into and across the first base line (tempting me to "stay in lane" and peel off to the right instead of proceeding down the baseline to first!). Elsewhere we play atop cricket pitches, with their defined bowling creases etched across the outfield. No club (at least not in the north) has a permanent field.*

To temporarily create our field, we transport everything, in wheelbarrows and on our backs down to the ball field area—kit bags, bases,

---

* In 2018, the Hull Scorpions Baseball Club built an enclosed park at Alderman Kneeshaw Park with bleacher seating and a batting cage, near the site of the ballpark used by the Hull Aces in the 1960s and 1970s.

fencing, flag poles and netting used for a backstop, rakes, sledgehammers, shovels, and all our personal equipment—from a shipping container beside the school's carpark. On Sunday game days, we arrive for nine in the morning, three hours before first pitch, to set up the field. The most laborious part is putting up all the fencing, with hundreds of meters of orange plastic mesh barrier/"snow" fencing, strung on metal poles every three meters or so around the perimeter of foul territory and as a home-run fence across the outfield; our "backstop" takes as many as six of us to erect, by attaching a huge expanse of netting to four flag poles, then raising them (against the wind!) behind home plate (see Figure 12.1). Sometimes, we also drag an old lawnmower down to cut the infield grass, too, when the school's groundskeepers have not recently mown or did not cut the grass short enough—most places we play are dangerously lively for grounders, rutted and bumpy from other sports. After also raking weeds from the patches of dirt that serve as base cutouts, we line the batter's boxes and base lines, and a field takes shape. All of this takes place (almost always) in a spitting rain, with temperatures around 10 °C (50 °F) with the wind whipping across the expansive open space. I'm half-frozen and completely

Figure 12.1. Brett Lashua prepares to strike out. Note the temporary backstop, plastic fencing around the field, marquee, and seating. Photo by Debra Lashua.

*knackered before we even start to play ball. Then—after a customary dou-
ble-header (because of the distances, often over 80 miles, that teams have
to travel in the north of England; there simply aren't enough teams in any
local area for single games)—we have to disassemble everything, unpeg
and roll up all the fencing, draw down the backstop netting and poles, fold
chairs set out for players, pack up all the kit bags and other equipment,
and haul everything back to our storage container. After two ball games
(noon until two, and three until five), and then deconstructing the field,
it's often seven o'clock before I start for home—unless we want a celebra-
tory pint at the pub up the road. In total, it's a long day—around 10
hours—for two ball games, outside in near-constant drizzle. I'm soaked,
bone-chilled, and, like most of the middle-aged players on these teams,
feeling physically ruined. I chuckle every time I see mention of the Field of
Dreams cliché "If you build it . . ."; we had to build it every Sunday.*

Field Notes: September 1, 2013—BBF playoffs, Farnham Park

*I was looking forward to playing at Farnham Park for the National
playoffs, mostly because we wouldn't have to struggle with setting up the
field! Because of distance involved, we drove down (five hours on the
motorway) the day before and stayed overnight in a nearby hotel. Unfortunately, my pre-game excitement was tempered by an underwhelming
first impression of Farnham Park; it didn't look much more than any of
the Little League facilities I experienced growing up in Ohio in the 1970s
and 1980s, let alone the multi-venue baseball/softball mega-complexes
that sprung up later. Farnham's three small youth baseball/adult softball fields had to be adapted for adult baseball games by extending
the infield across the grass line into the outfield and using temporary
wooden pitching mounds. Our first game on one of these smaller fields
felt rather familiarly ad hoc for a "permanent" facility. That said, it was
great to have working bathrooms nearby for the first time all season. For
our second game, we shifted to the international full-size field, although
this felt strange then too; it was vast, with massive, foul territories that
made the gameplay peculiarly distant, especially while watching from
our dugout (see Figure 12.2). After losing and being eliminated, we stayed
to watch another game. The teams were outstanding, but—for me—the
fields were basic and (because of the three smaller fields) not as well
equipped as I expected, without bleacher seating, no batting cages, and no
food available for purchase on site (food concessions were not established
until 2017). Yes, it was a relief to simply pack up my own kit bag and*

walk back to the car when we were done, but then there was a long drive home from the U.K.'s "first" purpose-built ballpark. Yes, to repurpose the famous line, "they built it and we came"; however, for me it still lacked something of the magical atmosphere that is key to ballpark culture. One teammate (originally from Georgia) and I joked about our memories of Little League. I mentioned that, win or lose, we always went for ice cream cones after games. "Ice cream?" he scoffed. "We always went for a hot dog and a Coke!" Unfortunately, neither was to be had at Farnham Park. This facility may be a(nother) "first" (of sorts) for British baseball, but it seems a small first step.

These ethnographic observations evoke some of the (dis)connections between baseball and the physical landscape in Britain. It was almost as if baseball had been dropped "fully formed" (from the U.S.) into the British sportscape. The history of the game in Britain is virtually unknown outside of a small circle of British baseball clubs, players, fans, and scholars. *It is only in an absence of this history that Farnham Park can be considered a "first" for British baseball. My observations also begin to characterize some of the relationships between history, heritage, and landscape for baseball players in Britain. In discussions with teammates, I found that most Americans in the ballclub played to maintain links to their cultural roots; conversations, such as with my Georgian teammate, centered on baseball memories, nostalgia, and comparisons to earlier experiences of playing (often in childhood or youth leagues) in the United States. As expats, we were generally "looking back" at America—at "home"—through our shared sense of American baseball heritage. In contrast, many British teammates spoke of the associations they made between baseball and an imagined sense of "Americanness," or what Chambers (1985) referred to as "Americanicity"—the desire to adopt or imitate American culture and style. British players on the baseball club participated to forge connections with American popular culture, embracing baseball (actively) in similar ways to their mediated consumption of American popular music, televised sport, and Hollywood films. When we weren't playing baseball, during lulls in practice or during long drives on game days, we were often talking about these mediated representations of America and Americanness. My British teammates expressed that they enjoyed baseball because*

---

* One British baseball history resource is "Project Cobb" (http://projectcobb.org.uk), operated by BBF lifetime member Joe Gray (although, from October 2019, it appears this site is no longer being maintained).

Figure 12.2. A view of the main field at Farnham Park. Note the permanent backstop and fencing, dugouts, and vast foul territory. Photo by Brett Lashua.

they perceived it as a distinctly American pastime (eschewing its British heritage altogether). Through these lenses—popular media and popular memory—baseball's imagined heritage offered a resource for (re)constructing and negotiating cultural identities (Smith, 2006) for British and American ballplayers. The "ballpark"—or the vicissitudes of creating one—provided a territory for many of these meanings to play out.

Conclusions: Baseball in Britain, Cultural History, and Cultural Heritage

This chapter has traced a few lines of baseball's history and heritage in Britain. I opened with the invocation of an iconographic reimagining of the British cultural sportscape ("England's green and pleasant land") fused with American baseball popular culture (the film *Field of Dreams* [Robinson, 1989]) at the 2013 opening of the Farnham Park baseball facility. This symbolism attempted to embed the game within the British landscape but arguably ignored both the origins and antecedents of baseball in Britain. Therefore, the chapter mapped out cultural historical scholarship, particularly noting the baseball tours of Britain 1874–1939, to help explain the "prolonged resistance" to the game, especially in British media (Bloyce &

Murphy, 2008, p. 120). Then, drawn from my experiences as a ballplayer, I shifted to ethnographic observations to illustrate how the game operates in practice "on the ground." In these observations, an almost complete absence of facilities was compounded by little awareness of baseball's heritage in Britain.

In the case of British baseball heritage, the remaking of the past is both "symbolic" (in Burke's [2012] terms) and mythogenic—captured in the phrase "our very own 'field of dreams' in England's green and pleasant land" (BaseballSoftballUK, 2012). Smith (2006) described heritage as "a process of engagement, an act of communication and an act of making meaning in and for the present" (p. 1). In this, heritage encompasses "memory and remembering, performance, place, and dissonance" (p. 3). It not only offers a resource for negotiating or contesting cultural meanings, values, and identity constructions (Smith 2006), but it also facilitates "collective amnesia" or social forgetting (Misztal, 2003), in the (re)construction of new meanings and myths. In this, heritage becomes an active process: *to heritage.* This process, as Smith (2006) noted, has fluidity and changeability; it is as much about preserving the past as "reworking the meanings of the past as the cultural, social and political needs of the present change and develop" (p. 4). The impetus to describe Farnham Park as a kind of "first" in the U.K. illustrates a kind of selective remembering, or forgetting, in processes of (re)constructing a "new" baseball heritage—what may be summed up as an amnesiac, ahistorical "mistranslation" of baseball's British cultural heritage (Block, 2019).

And on it goes. In 2019, again ignoring the history of baseball in the U.K., another "first" for baseball in Britain was celebrated with Major League Baseball's "MLB London series." These mid-season games (June 29–30, 2019, featuring the Boston Red Sox against the New York Yankees[*]) were noted in British media (recounting the start of the game) as "the first ever inning of London's first ever game" (Engel, 2019, para. 4). So much for history, then. It is perhaps unsurprising that journalists ignore the British origins of the game, its longer presence in the U.K., and the historical scholarship on baseball in Britain (Block, 2019). And yet, as Engel (2019) concluded, "before baseball can really take hold in Britain it will need some unique traditions of its own" (para. 13). British baseball traditions? If only there were.

---

[*] A second set of games were scheduled for June 13–14, 2020, with the St. Louis Cardinals facing the Chicago Cubs. However, these games were cancelled due to the coronavirus pandemic.

Acknowledgment

I'm grateful to Dr. Gabby Riches for her assistance developing an earlier version of the literature review.

References

BaseballSoftballUK (2013). UK's first baseball and softball complex opened in Farnham Park. http://www.baseballsoftballuk.com/news/view/uks-first-baseball-and-softball-complex-opened-in-farnham-park (accessed December 6, 2020).

Block, D. (2005). *Baseball before we knew it: A search for the roots of the game.* Lincoln: University of Nebraska Press.

Block, D. (2019). *Pastime lost: The humble, original, and now completely forgotten game of English Baseball.* Lincoln: University of Nebraska Press.

Bloyce, D. (1997). "Just not cricket": Baseball in England, 1874–1900. *International Journal of the History of Sport, 14*(2), 207–218.

Bloyce, D. (2005). "That's your way of playing rounders, isn't it?" The response of the English press to American baseball tours to England, 1874–1924. *Sporting Traditions, 22*(1), 81–98.

Bloyce, D. (2006). A very peculiar practice: The London Baseball League, 1906–1911. *NINE: A Journal of Baseball History and Culture, 14*(2), 118–128.

Bloyce, D. (2007). John Moores and the 'professional' baseball leagues in 1930s England. *Sport in History, 27*(1), 64–87.

Bloyce, D. (2008). "Glorious rounders": The American baseball invasion of England in Two World Wars—unappealing American exceptionalism. *International Journal of the History of Sport, 25*(4), 387–405.

Bloyce, D., & Murphy, P. (2008). Baseball in England: A case of prolonged cultural resistance. *Journal of Historical Sociology, 21*(1), 120–142.

Burke, P. (2012). Strengths and weaknesses of Cultural History. *Cultural History, 1*(1), 1–13.

Capon, D. (2003). *Print-media strategies and Internet fan tactics: Articulating Scott Gomez, an emerging hero, across the popular sport imaginary* [Master's thesis, University of Alberta].

Chambers, I. (1985). *Urban rhythms: Pop music and popular culture.* Basingstoke: Macmillan.

Chetwynd, J. (2006). Great Britain: Baseball's battle for respect in the land of cricket, rugby, and soccer. In G. Gmelch (Ed.), *Baseball without borders: The international pastime* (pp. 263–287). Lincoln: University of Nebraska Press.

Chetwynd, J. (2008). *Baseball in Europe: A country by country history.* London: McFarland & Company.

Chetwynd, J., & Belton, B. A. (2007). *British baseball and the West Ham Club: History of a 1930s professional team in East London.* London: McFarland & Company.

Crawford, S. A. (1998). Field of dreams. *International Journal of the History of Sport,* *15*(3), 150–153.

Engel, M. (2019, July 1). London's MLB crowd offers baseball a new land of opportunity. *The Guardian* [online]. https://www.theguardian.com/sport/blog/2019/jul/01/london-mlb-red-sox-yankees (accessed December 6, 2020).

Gems, G. R. (2011). Baseball, invented tradition and nationalistic spirit. In S. Wagg (Ed.), *Myth and milestones in the history of sport* (pp. 86–121). Basingstoke: Palgrave Macmillan.

Gems, G. R., Borish, L. J., & Pfister, G. (Eds.). (2008). *Sports in American history: From colonization to globalization.* Champaign, IL: Human Kinetics.

Guttmann, A. (1995). *Games and empires: Modern sports and cultural imperialism.* New York: Columbia University Press.

Hise, B. (2010). *Swinging away: How cricket and baseball connect.* London: Scala Publishers.

Johnes, M. (2000). 'Poor man's cricket': Baseball, class and community in South Wales, c. 1880–1950. *International Journal of the History of Sport, 17*(4), 153–166.

Krizek, R. (2003). Baseball ethnography: Finding our way home. *American Communication Association, 6*(2), 1–9.

Major League Baseball (2013). *Baseball discovered.* http://mlb.mlb.com/mlb/mediacenter/baseball_discovered/ (accessed December 6, 2020).

Majumdar, B., & Brown, S. (2007). Why baseball, why cricket? Differing nationalisms, differing challenges. *International Journal of the History of Sport, 24*(2), 139–156.

Misztal, B. (2003). *Theories of social remembering.* Maidenhead: Open University Press.

Moore, G. (1994). The great baseball tour of 1888–89: A tale of image-making, intrigue, and labour relations in the Gilded Age. *International Journal of the History of Sport, 11*(3), 431–456.

Ramshaw, G. (2005, April). *Nostalgia, heritage, and imaginative sports geographies: Sport and cultural landscapes.* Paper Presented at the Forum UNESCO University and Heritage 10th International Seminar "Cultural Landscapes in the 21st Century," Newcastle upon Tyne, UK. https://www.researchgate.net/profile/Gregory_Ramshaw/publication/281624806_Nostalgia_Heritage_and_Imaginative_Sports_Geographies_Sport_and_Cultural_Landscapes/links/55f048f008ae199d47c1fb74.pdf (accessed December 6, 2020).

Robinson, P. (Director). (1989). *Field of Dreams* [Motion picture]. United States. Universal Pictures.

Silk, M. (2015). 'Isles of Wonder': Performing the mythopoeia of utopic multi-ethnic Britain. *Media, Culture & Society, 37*(1), 68–84.

Schmidgall, G. (Ed.) (2001). *Intimate with Walt: Selections from Whitman's conversations with Horace Traubel 1888–1892.* Des Moines: University of Iowa Press.

Smith, L. J. (2006). *Uses of heritage.* London: Routledge.

Smyth, I. (1993). The development of baseball in Northern England, 1935–1939. *International Journal of the History of Sport, 10*(2), 252–258.

Snyder, C. R., & McCullough, M. E. (2000). A positive psychology field of dreams: "If you build it, they will come . . ." *Journal of Social and Clinical Psychology, 19*(1), 151–160.

Trujillo, N. (1992). Interpreting (the work and the talk of) baseball: Perspectives on ballpark culture. *Western Journal of Communication, 56*(4), 350–371.

Voigt, D. Q. (1976). *America through baseball.* Lanham, MD: Taylor Trade Publications.

Webb, R. (2003). Field of Dreams. *School Planning & Management, 42*(7), 24–26.

Weltch, A. (2008). British baseball: How a curious version of the game survives in parts of England and Wales. *National Pastime: A Review of Baseball History, 28,* 30–33.

Zeiler, T. W. (2006). *Ambassadors in pinstripes: The Spalding world baseball tour and the birth of the American Empire.* Lanham, MD: Rowman & Littlefield.

13

Movable, Removable, or Immovable?

Baseball Statues and Ballpark Relocation

CHRIS STRIDE

Baseball's Bronze Age

In the last three decades, public sculptures of sporting heroes have grown exponentially. Statues depicting soccer players stand in over 70 countries (Stride & Thomas, 2011). Other sports with more localized or niche appeal have likewise been celebrated through figurative monuments, be it surfers in Hawaii or speed skaters in Norway (Osmond et al., 2006, Slotnik, 2013). U.S. baseball franchises have been particularly active in this regard. By April 2021, there were 257 subject specific statues of baseball players, coaches, owners, broadcasters, and even fans, in situ across the U.S., of which 184 were sited at Major or Minor League ballparks. These were joined by 27 statues of anonymous hitters and pitchers (Stride & Thomas, 2011).

Statues are associated with permanence. Upon unveiling, headline-writers use clichés as to how the subjects or moments depicted are "immortalized" or "preserved." Affixed atop a solid plinth of brick or stone, and most typically cast in hard-wearing bronze, a statue's construction only adds to its sense of durability. Yet bronze and stone gradually deteriorate when exposed to the elements, and statues are prone to damage, be it through vandalism or vehicle strikes. Declining resources and fading memories may result in the poor maintenance and general neglect of a monument. Occasionally, society's view of the statue subject or their legacy may change so dramatically that the sculpture becomes an awkward reminder best removed, a scenario illustrated by the felling of numerous Confederate statues across the United States since 2015.

Sports statues face a further challenge to the notion of "immortality in bronze"—specifically the loss (or change in use) of a statue's original location. Many sport statues stand at sports stadia and venues. Sometimes these locations are pragmatic choices based on ease of planning permission or availability of space. More often, the statue's very *raison d'être* is to brand the host organization and its stadium, conferring a sense of authenticity and tradition, or to evoke nostalgia among fans—in turn enhancing the fans' bond with their team and its home venue (Holbrook & Schindler, 2003; Seifried & Meyer, 2010). A statue of a past hero may also serve to connect a sports team's history with a new or heavily refurbished venue. This process helps create a sacred space for supporters, thus enhancing the often-feature-less concourse or exterior of what Bale (1993) termed the "tradium"—the rationalized and commodified modern sports arena.

Just as a statue influences the stadium environment and becomes part of a team's heritage, the stadium, too, will influence interpretations and meanings ascribed to a statue. The statue's physical location at the stadium links the subject of the statue to the venue, the team using it, and to the supporters who attend. Assuming that the subject of the statue actually played or performed at the stadium, the statue's presence at the venue will encourage supporters to reengage with the player's specific moments and achievements, and to enable older fans to share memories of the player with friends and family. The stadium also provides an emotive visual backdrop, placing the subject alongside colors, images, and supporters of the team they represented.

On the other hand, stadia are not eternal, nor always particularly venerable. Sports teams build new homes for many reasons: to exploit new fan bases and commercial opportunities, improve spectator access and transport, upgrade facilities, gain income from the sale of real estate, and address safety and security legislation, because of political pressure or incentives, or simply when their competitors appear to have benefited from a move. Major and Minor League Baseball welcomed a plethora of new venues in the 1990s and 2000s, a trend shared by other North American sports such as basketball, hockey, and football (Barr, 2012; Freedman, 2013; Reichard, 2017). Over these two decades, 21 of 30 MLB franchises moved to new venues, often from "concrete donut" style multi-sport stadia to retro-styled downtown/city-center ballparks with quirky layouts and individual heritage-referencing touches (Goldberger, 2019; Enders, 2018). Many of the U.S.'s baseball statues were commissioned to decorate these new venues and complement their nostalgia-themed concourses and exteriors, as well as aid in broader urban regeneration projects of which these stadia (and their surroundings) are anchor developments. However, several ballpark statues predate the retro-ballpark boom (Stride & Thomas, 2011).

When a sports organization vacates an old stadium in favor of a newer model, the fate of any statue sited around it is uncertain. Building on the definitions of Ramshaw (2020), heritage connected with a sports venue—the structure itself, the field, and the fixtures and fittings—can be defined as either immovable, movable (to the new stadium), or removable (to a new owner or indefinite storage). While much of an abandoned stadium falls into the former category, at least until it meets the wrecking ball, a migrating franchise can uproot adornments such as statues and relocate them to their latest venue. This would be the expected course of action, given that the desire to evoke nostalgia and celebrate authenticity, continuity, and tradition will be even more apposite at a new stadium. In this way, a sports organization can use their past to directly support the present, bringing an established heritage identity to the blank canvas of a new home (Ramshaw et al., 2013).

However, there are instances when a statue may not be relocated at the new venue due to the subject of the statue (i.e., who or what the statue depicts or represents), the moment depicted by the statue, or the lack of a suitable location to re-erect the statue. Alternatively, a statue's ownership may be contested. Beyond sports organizations, statues are sometimes funded by fans, local residents, or local authorities, giving these groups a stake in the sculpture's fate. Where stadiums stand in residential districts, a statue sited outside the stadium can be both venue infrastructure *and* a civic landmark. If a sports organization were to depart a location and attempt to take any statues with them to their new venue, they might face resistance from numerous stakeholders—for example, local residents, campaign groups, or the civic authority—thus rendering the statue "morally" immovable even while the adjacent arena lies empty or demolished.

As such, a statue situated at a venue which is about to be demolished may potentially be immovable, movable, or removable, with its eventual status—and how that decision was arrived at—saying much about how the organization, its fans, local residents, and public bodies interact with their heritage and each other. Statues reflect their host's, funder's, or creator's heritage through the subject or moment depicted, the way that he, she, or it is presented—and even become heritage objects themselves (Savage, 1994; Dupre, 2007). Therefore, a statue's history and geography can be used to further probe "societal ideas and ideals of . . . American life" (Schein, 2006).

Arguments over who or what a sports statue belongs to—and hence where it should reside—encapsulate, and can be used to examine, wider ownership debates, regarding both the intangible "identity" of a sport's team, the tangible stadium environment and surrounding land, and the power to shape perceptions of these spaces.

In this chapter I investigate the Atlanta Braves' move from Turner Field, in the city's downtown core, to Truist (originally Sun Trust) Park in the northern suburbs of Cobb County in 2017. I focus on the relocation of the Turner Field statues depicting Hank Aaron and Ty Cobb, which together illustrate the immovable and removable typologies described previously. By examining the very different disputes that erupted around these statues— and the reactions of fans, the franchise, and local communities—I hope to illuminate the issues and tensions surrounding statue ownership, and demonstrate how they reflect wider ongoing debates regarding the legacy of the players depicted and Atlanta's sport heritage and history. Sports statues are "hollow icons" that can absorb and project more than one meaning (Osmond et al., 2006): this multivalence appeals to clubs, fans, and civic authorities alike. However, because a sports statue allows the different communities that coalesce around a sports organization to each perceive ownership of the team's heritage, identity, and territory, moving that statue highlights these multiple claims and disrupts assumptions, often reopening divisions and creating conflict. Further, I assess how moving—or not moving—these statues has changed their meanings. With sports statues now ubiquitous across the world's stadia, the issues raised by the parochial dispute described in this chapter are likely to resonate far more widely in the future.

The Bronzed Braves

Table 13.1 lists the subject-specific and anonymous statues of players, managers, founders, and fans, originally erected at MLB venues, that have faced the upheaval of a stadium move as of April 2021. As the table illustrates, for 27 of 32 potential statue moves where a franchise was vacating a ballpark, they took the statue with them, classifying the majority of these bronze ballplayers as movable monuments.

Beyond maintaining franchise identity and promoting its heritage in a new setting, this movability reflects a franchise-centric pattern of baseball statue instigation, funding, and legal ownership (Stride & Thomas, 2017). In fact, 87 percent of the monuments were commissioned and funded directly by the franchise concerned, their owners, or their sponsors (Stride &

Table 13.1. Baseball Statues at Subsequently Vacated Major League Ballparks

Statue Subject	Year first unveiled	Original Location	Franchise playing at original location when statue erected	Year franchise vacated ballpark	Statue moved	Second Location	Year franchise vacated ballpark	Statue moved	Third Location
Christian von der Ahe	1885	Sportsman's Park	St. Louis Browns	1892	Yes	New Sportsman's Park	1919*	Yes*	Bellefontaine Cemetery, St. Louis
Honus Wagner	1955	Forbes Field	Pittsburgh Pirates	1970	Yes	Three Rivers Stadium	2001	Yes	PNC Park
Connie Mack	1957	Shibe Park	Philadelphia Phillies	1970	Yes	Veterans Stadium	2003	Yes	Citizens Bank Park
Dickie Kerr	1966	Houston Astrodome	Houston Astros	1999	Yes**	Fingers Baseball Museum, Houston	NA	Yes	Constellation Field, Sugar Land, Texas
Stan Musial	1968	Busch Memorial Stadium	St. Louis Cardinals	2005	Yes	Busch Stadium			
Anonymous "The Batter"	1975	Veterans Stadium	Philadelphia Phillies	2003	Yes	Citizens Bank Park			
Anonymous "The Play at Second"	1977	Veterans Stadium	Philadelphia Phillies	2003	Yes	Citizens Bank Park			
Ty Cobb	1977	Atlanta-Fulton County Stadium	Atlanta Braves	1996	Yes	Turner Field	2016	Yes**	Royston Museum
Hank Aaron	1982	Atlanta-Fulton County Stadium	Atlanta Braves	1996	Yes	Turner Field	2016	No	
Phil Niekro	1986	Atlanta-Fulton County Stadium	Atlanta Braves	1996	Yes	Turner Field	2016	Yes	Truist Park, Cobb County
Jackie Robinson	1987	Montreal Olympic Stadium	Montreal Expos	2004	No				

Roberto Clemente	1994	Three Rivers Stadium	Pittsburgh Pirates	2000	Yes	PNC Park
Bob Gibson	1998	Busch Memorial Stadium	St. Louis Cardinals	2005	Yes	Busch Stadium
Jack Buck	1998	Busch Memorial Stadium	St. Louis Cardinals	2005	Yes	Busch Stadium
Stan Musial	1998	Busch Memorial Stadium	St. Louis Cardinals	2005	Yes	Busch Stadium
Red Schoendienst	1999	Busch Memorial Stadium	St. Louis Cardinals	2005	Yes	Busch Stadium
Enos Slaughter	1999	Busch Memorial Stadium	St. Louis Cardinals	2005	Yes	Busch Stadium
Lou Brock	1999	Busch Memorial Stadium	St. Louis Cardinals	2005	Yes	Busch Stadium
Dizzy Dean	2000	Busch Memorial Stadium	St. Louis Cardinals	2005	Yes	Busch Stadium
Rogers Hornsby	2000	Busch Memorial Stadium	St. Louis Cardinals	2005	Yes	Busch Stadium
George Sisler	2001	Busch Memorial Stadium	St. Louis Cardinals	2005	Yes	Busch Stadium
Cool Papa Bell	2002	Busch Memorial Stadium	St. Louis Cardinals	2005	Yes	Busch Stadium
Ozzie Smith	2002	Busch Memorial Stadium	St. Louis Cardinals	2005	Yes	Busch Stadium
Warren Spahn	2003	Turner Field	Atlanta Braves	2016	Yes	Truist Park, Cobb County

* The statue moved before the franchise vacated the ballpark, and was in situ at Bellefontaine Cemetery before von der Ahe's death in 1913.
** The statue didn't move with the franchise.

Thomas, 2011). Even when fans or local media have organized or funded a statue project, the statue has typically been gifted to the franchise, such as in the cases of the statue of Stan Musial of the St. Louis Cardinals and of Harry Kalas of the Philadelphia Phillies (Donnellon, 2011; Stanton, 2012). Furthermore, in the 1960s and 1970s, multi-use stadiums were mostly built on city fringes or at inner-city brownfield sites in former industrial districts. The handful of statues erected outside these concrete coliseums—notably at Pittsburgh's Three Rivers Stadium and Philadelphia's Veterans Stadium— were, like their host venues, part of the game-day experience but physically separate from residential districts, reducing their impact as a landmark. When a departing franchise wished to transplant its statues to its new ball-park, there were unlikely to be local objections or barriers.

However, two ballpark-sited statues that did not move with their franchise stood outside the Braves' Turner Field in Atlanta, Georgia, which was vacated in 2017 in favor of a new venue, Sun Trust Park (now renamed as Truist Park), in Cobb County, 10 miles northwest into the sprawling suburbs. This migration was the first where a franchise left a modern (i.e., post-1990 downtown) ballpark for a less central location, reversing the trend of the past quarter-century (Goldberger, 2019).

Major League sport arrived in Atlanta in 1966, with the Braves baseball franchise (formerly of Boston and then Milwaukee) and an NFL expansion team (Falcons) lured by a new stadium, as well as an expanding population and television market in a previously untapped region. Atlanta's mayor Ivan Allen, the driving political force behind the stadium project, had campaigned for office on a desegregation ticket. Allen saw Major League Baseball—in which the color barrier had been broken for almost two decades— as key in promoting wider racial integration, displaying Atlanta's "urban maturity" and status, and thus boosting business within his city (Bisher, 1966; Anderson, 2000). The Atlanta-Fulton County Stadium was in many ways typical of the era, a concrete bowl catering for both baseball and football. However, it was just a mile south of downtown, next to a freeway but close to residential areas.

In 1990, Atlanta won the right to host the 1996 Olympic Games. The games committee chose to build the Olympic stadium immediately adjacent to the Fulton County Stadium, attracted by its transport access and relatively central location (French & Disher, 1997). The stadium was designed to be reconfigured into a new ballpark after the Olympics, which was then leased to the Braves. This arrangement suited both the Olympic committee, who could demonstrate a city legacy, and the Braves, who had already been exploring options for a new ballpark (French & Disher, 1997). The ballpark was named Turner Field after Ted Turner, media magnate, philanthropist, and the Braves' owner at the time. So by 1997, the Braves had a modern, centrally located stadium, albeit not quite in the same buzzy, gentrified, signature locations that some of their rivals were moving to.

At the time of their move to Turner Field, the Braves had already accumulated three baseball statues. Native-born Georgian Ty Cobb (unveiled 1977) was an all-time great of the game—though never a Brave, his playing career pre-dating, by several decades, the Braves franchise in Atlanta. Former home-run record holder Hank Aaron was unveiled in 1982 and the knuckleball pitcher Phil Niekro in 1986. The Braves were ahead of the curve: at the time of Niekro's statue unveiling, these were three of only six ballpark-sited statues, and Aaron and Niekro were the only two of living players. Even by the start of the 1997 season, there were only 10 statues at MLB stadia and a handful more at Minor League parks (Stride & Thomas, 2011).

The Ty Cobb statue, sculpted by Felix de Weldon, depicts the great hustler sliding into base, spikes raised, his face stoic and determined as he beats the floundering baseman to the bag. The plaque text led with Cobb's Georgian heritage, reading as follows:

Plaque 1: TYRUS RAYMOND COBB. 1886—1961. KNOWN AS THE GEORGIA PEACH. CHARTER MEMBER OF BASEBALL HALL OF FAME. LEADING BATSMAN OF ALL MAJOR LEAGUE HISTORY. .367 AVERAGE, 4,191 HITS.
Plaque 2: FELIX de WELDON. SCULPTOR. 1977.

Cobb's statue was a gift from banker Mills B. Lane Jr., who, working alongside Mayor Allen, had been a pivotal figure in financing the Fulton County Stadium and thus bringing Major League sports to Atlanta a decade earlier (Fowler, 1989; Hatfield, 2014). Lane was intimately involved in city politics and was a booster of Atlanta. Unfortunately, the Braves were doing little to boost the city, managing eight losing seasons during the 1970s. Their stadium co-tenants, the NFL's Atlanta Falcons, were similarly hopeless. The Braves' nadir came in September 1975, when only 737 people showed up for their game against the Houston Astros (Caruso, 1995). In times of failure, tangible heritage objects such as a statue can provide a reminder of a glorious past and the possibility of a glorious future: Lane planned a series of sculptures of Georgian sporting heroes outside the Fulton County Stadium (Torpy, 2016).

There were few heroes on the Braves' roster at the time—aside from Hank

Aaron, who in 1974 broke Babe Ruth's long-standing record for career home runs. Born in Alabama and starting out in the Negro Leagues, Aaron had signed for the then Milwaukee Braves organization in 1952. He subsequently achieved both a stellar career at the plate and wider influence as a barrier-breaker (Aaron, 2007; Bryant, 2011). Having initially sworn never to return to the deep south where he was born, the Braves' move from Milwaukee to Atlanta placed Aaron at the center of integrating sport in a city where Jim Crow was still part of everyday life. Jimmy Carter, then a Georgian state senator and later United States president, commented that Aaron was "the first black man that white fans in the South cheered for" (Williams, 2014, p. 52).

So, why was Aaron not chosen by Lane as the first statue subject at Fulton County Stadium? The choice of Ty Cobb instead of Hank Aaron, a Black hero, makes this question particularly pointed. While undoubtedly among the greatest of all ballplayers, Cobb was widely regarded as cantankerous and feisty. Furthermore, since the publication of a scathing biography by Al Stump shortly after Cobb's death, Cobb's reputation had suffered serious damage, with several of his fights with African Americans cited as evidence of racism (Leerhsen, 2015). Recent and widely lauded research by Charles Leerhsen, exposing much of Stump's work as fraudulent, has countered this argument—Cobb was prone to fight anyone who rubbed up against him—and there is evidence that he both attended Negro League games and supported the racial integration of baseball (Leerhsen, 2015). Nevertheless, constructing a statue of Ty Cobb could be seen as racially provocative. Two years after the unveiling, Braves' owner Ted Turner publicly questioned the city's decision to erect a statue of Cobb at Fulton County Stadium, and suggested that, if he ran the city, the statue might be replaced with one of Aaron (Picking, 1979).

However, Lane's deep involvement in driving desegregationist policies make any accusation that his celebration of Cobb was motivated by racism appear to be misplaced (Teepen, 1989; Fowler, 1989). The explanation given by Bob Hope, a Braves' marketing executive of the time, was that Lane wished to commemorate Georgian-born greats, whereas Aaron was born in Alabama (Torpy, 2016). Another possible factor at play was that statues are dedicated to the deceased, or at least the long retired. When the statue was planned in 1976, not only was Aaron still alive but he was also an active player. It was not until the 2000s that baseball franchises began to routinely bronze recent ex-players (Stride & Thomas, 2011).

Whatever the truth behind Aaron being overlooked in 1977, four years

Figure 13.1. The original Hank Aaron statue, by Ed Dwight Jr. Photo by Beau White.

later a campaign was instigated by Hope to honor him with a statue (Caruso, 2001). The $85,000 cost was raised by public donations and fundraising events (Hinton, 1982; Atlanta Journal-Constitution, 1982). Hope's campaign group gifted the statue to Atlanta-Fulton County Recreation Authority (AF-CRA, henceforth referred to as the "stadium authority"), the public body who managed the stadium and its surroundings (Caruso, 2001).

Ed Dwight Jr., a Black sculptor whose father had played Negro League baseball, was chosen to sculpt the statue that was unveiled in September 1982 (McGrath, 1982). The pose chosen was Aaron following through in his record-home-run swing (Figure 13.1), eyes fixed on the ball as it soars into the sky and over the wall for a 715th time. The plaque references Aaron's crowning achievement and the site:

HENRY LOUIS "HANK" AARON. 715TH HOME RUN APRIL 6, 1974. ATLANTA-FULTON COUNTY STADIUM. DEDICATED SEPTEM-BER 7, 1982. SCULPTOR—ED DWIGHT, JR.

Phil Niekro's statue, also sculpted by Dwight, followed in 1986. Hall-of-famer Niekro, the winningest knuckleball pitcher, complemented his success with extreme longevity and loyalty, representing the Braves from 1964 to 1983. On moving to Turner Field, the Braves placed their statues of Cobb, Aaron, and Niekro together in Monument Grove, an area adjacent to the ticket windows and designed for pre-match gatherings, with trees and picnic benches arranged around the sculptures. There is no evidence of any dispute regarding the statues following the Braves from Fulton County Stadium to Turner Field. This is unsurprising given that the new stadium was only a few hundred yards from the location of the old venue, also on stadium authority land, and the statues forged tangible links with the Braves' past and with baseball at the new venue. On demolition of the Fulton County Stadium, further efforts were made to preserve and celebrate the scene and memory of Aaron's record. Though the Fulton County Stadium site became a parking lot for Turner Field, a bronze plaque marked the old home plate, and the stadium authority preserved—and placed a marker atop—the section of outfield wall cleared by Aaron's record-breaking home run (Pahigian, 2008). The Braves' three statues also gained a companion in 2003: a bronze of the Braves' most successful pitcher, "lefty" Warren Spahn. One of baseball's few fan-instigated ballpark statue projects, it is also atypical given that Spahn, while a Braves' great, had never appeared for the Atlanta incarnation of the franchise, having earned all of his 363 wins in either Boston or Milwaukee between 1940 and 1964. (DiLonardo, 2003; DeVault, 2003).

"Everybody wants The Hammer, nobody wants The Peach"

Spahn's statue was unveiled toward the end of an unprecedented run of success for the Braves, who, from 1991, reeled off 14 consecutive Divisional championships. Yet after the turn of the millennium, average attendances declined (Zygmont & Leadley, 2005; Baseball Reference, 2019). Supporters satiated by success were, no doubt, less willing to tolerate occasional losing seasons, but the Braves' organization was becoming increasingly unhappy with the location of Turner Field. The heavy traffic on adjacent freeways was a deterrent to fans, who were mostly drawn from Atlanta's northern, predominantly white suburbs (Catania, 2013). Though still a relatively new ballpark, Turner Field preceded the digital revolution and required substantial upgrading to maximize income and the fan experience. The Braves' management was also aware of how other franchises had successfully refurbished areas around their stadiums to supplement revenue streams: typically by buying and restoring real estate, leasing it to restaurants, bars, and associated entertainment, and so creating a gentrified "ballpark village" with an authentic urban feel (Diamond, 2016; Goldberger, 2019). As well as the game-day crowds, these areas offered year-round income by appealing to young, middle-class downtown residents. Turner Field, though, was a 1990s postmodern ballpark located in surroundings more akin to the 1960s concrete donut stadia: parking lots and freeways rather than precincts. It offered little suitable space for such ballpark-anchored redevelopment, nor a resident population considered wealthy enough to sustain it. The suburbs nearest to Turner Field, while benefiting from some improvements when the Olympic stadium was built, were still slightly down-at-heel residential areas, and were cut off from the ballpark by the freeways. Almost inevitably in Atlanta, race came into play, with these Black neighborhoods not re-garded as areas that white fans would be keen to visit, either before the ball game or at other times (Gustafson, 2013; French & Disher, 1997).

In 2013, the Braves announced that they would be moving 10 miles north to Cobb County for the start of the 2017 season (Tucker, 2013). The Cobb County site was closer to the majority of their supporter base and, cru-cially, offered space to develop around the ballpark. Atlanta's city leaders put on a brave face, with mayor Kasim Reed expressing excitement about redeveloping Turner Field for other uses. The reality was that neighbor-ing Cobb County, a separate municipal authority, had lured major league sport from Atlanta just as Atlanta had from Milwaukee 50 years earlier—by funding a new stadium that fit the franchise better than its existing home (Tucker, 2013). The Braves' management and players, on-message, trum-peted the economic benefits of the new development (O'Brien, 2013). Local media commentators were surprised but sanguine, focusing on the Braves' desire to move closer to their regular ticket-buyers, though quick to note that the new ballpark could suffer similar traffic congestion to Turner Field and that it lacked public transport access (Tomlinson, 2013; Burns, 2013). Some journalists and fans also noted echoes of "white flight" in the Braves' move away from a predominantly Black inner-city district, and linked this with Cobb County's refusal to fund a metro extension from the city center, thus "protecting" wealthier suburbs from poorer areas (Brown, 2013; Tom-linson, 2013; Henry, 2013). Despite the Braves' protestations that "We don't look at the exact makeup of the race, religion of that ticket buyer . . . what we're concerned about as a business that sells tickets is where do our ticket buyers come from?," issues of class, race, and wealth—as well as the ten-sion between public and privately owned space—are too deeply entangled in Atlanta for any economic decision to be uncoupled from these other factors (Henry, 2013; Glier, 2014).

The early discussions around the move to the new stadium largely ignored issues about stadium fixtures and fittings, but as the departure date drew closer, local media speculated on the fate of the Hank Aaron statue. In an April 2014 CNN interview, Aaron was keen for the old ACFS home plate and home-run wall markers to remain in situ: though not discussed with Aaron, the post-interview article assumed that the Braves would take Aaron's statue with them (Moore, 2014). However, a year later it was reported that fans were strongly against moving the statue, though the group of Atlanta-based fans in question were already "mad" at the move to Cobb County (Leslie, 2015a; Ove, 2015). The social media reaction to these reports was muted, with a handful of Twitter comments balanced across both sides of the argument (Arum, 2015; WSB-TV, 2015). Local politicians wanted the statue to remain in order to "memorialize the Braves and Aaron in Atlanta" (DeFeo, 2015a). Both the franchise, who felt it was their statue, and sculptor Dwight, who was concerned about the statue's upkeep, believed it should move with the Braves (Leslie, 2015a; Trubey, 2016a).

Nevertheless, the Braves were unable to provide legal documentation that they owned the statue (Saporta, 2015). An interview with the Aaron statue project organizer Bob Hope, now retired from the Braves' front office, cast doubt on the Braves' ownership claims. Hope, though personally happy to see the statue moved, believed it had been donated to the city in the guise of the stadium authority, but he considered Aaron the true owner (Leslie, 2015b; Saporta, 2015). Placed in an awkward position, Aaron was unsurprisingly even-handed: "On one hand, I think the statue should be wherever the baseball park is, wherever the Braves are playing . . . but on the other, the statue was paid for by fans . . . so if you had to think about it, it all belongs to Atlanta, to the people of Atlanta" (Leslie, 2015b). Parallel to the debate about the statue, the stadium authority negotiated the sale of Turner Field to Georgia State University (GSU), with the ballpark becoming the university's football stadium. In part to honor Aaron's and the site's memory, the deal included converting the parking lot on the old Fulton County Stadium site back to a small baseball stadium, with the 715th home-run wall preserved (Davis, 2015). Though physically movable, the wall is symbolically immovable heritage, as it is a tangible reminder of an important and historic moment in addition to its being located in the exact space where the moment happened. To move the wall would irrevocably change its meaning.

In February 2016, the dispute came to a head when the stadium authority claimed to have found documentation proving that they owned the statue, and stated that it would be remaining at the reconfigured Turner Field (Trubey, 2016b). The Braves briefly argued that Aaron should still decide the statue's fate, but when faced with Aaron's reluctance to get involved—and negative publicity in putting a franchise and city hero in an impossible position—the club backed down and instead announced the commissioning of a new Aaron statue for their new ballpark (Trubey, 2016c, 2016d).

The original statue stayed in situ. The statues of Niekro and Spahn were uncontested. Both were property of the Braves and were slated for transfer to the new stadium without controversy or dispute. On the other hand, the fate of Ty Cobb's statue also began to generate debate. Like the Aaron statue, there was a lack of documentation around the ownership of the Cobb artwork, which was by now almost 40 years old. However—ironically while claiming removal rights to the Aaron statue despite having no legal proof that it was theirs—the Braves used the same lack of evidence to waive their ownership claim over Ty Cobb's statue and to absolve themselves of deciding whether to take it with them (DeFeo, 2015b; Torpy, 2016). Braves fans appeared ambivalent, with just a handful of comments for or against Ty Cobb on internet forums, the negatives relating to his not having played for the Braves (Schafer, 2015; Mile High Chopper, 2017). Neither the stadium authority nor GSU publicly stated any wish to retain the statue. The Atlanta Journal-Constitution contrasted the Ty Cobb statue with Hank Aaron's, declaring, "Everybody wants The Hammer, nobody wants The Peach" (Torpy, 2016).

But there was one interested party. The Ty Cobb Museum, in Cobb's birthplace of Royston, Georgia, in addition to the Royston public authorities and Cobb's descendants successfully lobbied the stadium authority and GSU for permission to take the unwanted Cobb statue to Royston (Baruchman, 2017; Fricks, 2017). Royston, a small rural town of approximately 3,000 residents approximately 100 miles northeast of Atlanta had, since Cobb's death, increasingly branded itself as the "Home of Ty Cobb," complementing the museum with historical markers and Cobb-branded signage. Cobb's statue was removed from Turner Field in January 2017 and formally unveiled in the center of Royston (Figure 13.2) four months later (Hornick, 2017). The statues of Spahn and Niekro were movable, Hank Aaron's proved immovable, but Ty Cobb's was simply removable.

Figure 13.2. Ty Cobb statue, by Felix de Weldon, relocated to Royston. Photo by Gregory Ramshaw.

Changed Locations, Changed Meanings

Statues are markers of ownership—both physically (in terms of space and territory) and sociopolitically (in terms of culture and social narrative). Statues are rarely just benign monuments to celebrated figures: they often act as political symbols, both promoting the values that society wishes to preserve and celebrate, as well as, through absence or removal, those values they wish to forget or ignore (Dupré, 2007). The Braves' intentions for their statues upon their move from Turner Field to Truist Park likewise tell much about which parts of their past they wanted to celebrate at their new ballpark. Of those statues they had hoped could be movable heritage objects, Niekro's offered a nostalgic link to their Atlanta days, and Spahn's to a deeper franchise history and the associated authenticity and legitimacy that this provides. Aaron's statue at Turner Field was multivalent, depicting a heroic figure, a barrier breaker, and a specific moment of record-breaking glory: Aaron's 715th home run, an individual feat that could be cast as the Braves' achievement.

The new Aaron statue created for Truist Park (Figure 13.3) depicts this same scene, carrying this achievement to a new site. Baseball bats stacked to shape the number 755—Aaron's final MLB career home-run tally—and a screen showing images of Aaron's record-breaking home run serve as a backdrop. The plaque simply lists Aaron's name and sculptor Ross Rossin, neglecting both the site and city of Aaron's monumental homer, and his ongoing role in Civil Rights and racial integration. Hank Aaron's original statue may not have become movable heritage itself, but as a celebration of his crowning achievement, it has proved replaceable.

Ty Cobb's statue was removable, his legacy treated as best forgotten by the Braves' organization. It was somewhat disingenuous for the Braves to suggest that they were not taking Cobb to Cobb County purely because they didn't own the statue. They did not attempt to claim ownership, unlike with Aaron's statue: even without ownership, it is likely that they could have

Figure 13.3. The new Hank Aaron statue, by Ross Rossin, at Truist Park. Photo by Jeremy Dawson.

taken Cobb's statue with them, given that the stadium authority later gave it away to Royston. Neither did they replace Cobb's original statue with a new version at Truist Park.

Cobb's statue was inherited from a different past, in which his reputation was possibly less embedded or was ignored, and organizational sensitivity to racism was less acute. Today, even taking account of the contemporary arguments that dispute Cobb's racism, depicting a white, rural, southern hero from the segregationist era in a predominantly Black city is provocative. It is therefore unsurprising that the city of Atlanta, under the auspices of the stadium authority, didn't fight to retain the statue either. Furthermore, in the four decades since erecting Cobb's statue, the Braves have had numerous other franchise heroes of their own and no longer need Cobb to bolster their heritage credentials. For example, soon after arriving in Cobb County, the Braves unveiled a statue of Bobby Cox, their most successful manager (Schultz, 2017).

Meanwhile, Ty Cobb's statue found a home in Royston. Originally erected as a "home-state hero" tribute, his transmutation to "hometown hero" is in line with the typical distribution of non-franchise-funded baseball statues. These are often found in small towns, where a homegrown sports star is the biggest claim to fame, including such baseball stars as Christy Mathewson (Factoryville, Pennsylvania) and Lefty Grove (Lonaconing, Maryland). Sports statues are less common in big cities, where there will be a wider choice of potential heroes from politics, industry, and the performing arts—and where political considerations over who is honored may face scrutiny from a less partisan committee.

The arguments over the original Aaron statue at Turner Field reveal conflicts around competing notions of "ownership" of sports teams. Legal owners are beholden to advertisers and sponsors, to fans (both as ballpark spectators and via broadcast media), and to local political and civic figures who may invest in and maintain facilities that make operations easier or more profitable. The Braves, their fans, the Atlanta civic authorities, and the local community all had a stake in Hank Aaron's statue and, to a broader extent, the club's history, heritage, and culture. This in turn raises the following questions: to what extent are fans and the city one and the same, and to what extent were fans' interests represented by the city's stadium authority?

In the early days of organized baseball, fans lived near the ballpark, which in turn was a physical part of their daily lives. The flight from the cities into suburbs, as well as the global growth and availability of televised sport have combined to geographically separate the fan from the ballpark.

Districts adjacent to Turner Field were poorer areas, supplying correspondingly fewer regular ticket buyers than Atlanta's wealthier northern suburbs (Berg, 2013). Fans regularly visiting Turner Field, and therefore seeing Aaron's statue, were a largely distinct entity from residents living within walking distance of the ballpark (and, indeed, from out-of-town fans who interact purely through broadcast media). Aaron's statement that "the statue was paid for by fans . . . it all belongs to Atlanta, to the people of Atlanta," hence conflating these groups, probably made little sense when donations were collected in 1982, but even less so in 2017.

Ironically, neither the Braves nor the stadium authority sought the opinions of fans or local residents for or against the statue being removed—nor were fans or local residents particularly vocal in terms of organized protests, extensive discussions on social media, or comments reported in the media. Given Aaron's status as a Black hero and barrier breaker, and given the presence of the predominantly Black communities surrounding Turner Field, the lack of discussion might seem surprising. Yet with the stadium site marooned between freeways—and therefore attracting relatively sparse foot traffic—few local residents or visitors would encounter the statue unless attending a ball game. A monument invisible to a community rarely becomes symbolic. The lack of fan comment or protest could also be due to the absence of organized fan bodies to channel it, or fan deference to the Braves or Aaron himself. It also suggests that arguments concerning heritage installations are a relatively minor concern to fans. The presenters of Braves' fan podcast Talking Chop noted that the statue dispute had become "a bit embarrassing," and they wished for Spring Training to begin so that everyone had real baseball issues to discuss (Rowland & Collazo, 2016).

Civic figures were the most vocal in the Aaron statue dispute, notably the stadium authority's spokespeople. In terms of the balance sheet, their determination to retain Aaron's statue was mystifying. This was an artwork gifted to them rather than commissioned by them. With the Braves departing Turner Field and the arrival of GSU, it was now incongruously sited outside a college football stadium. The statue "saved for Atlanta" would be hidden from most Atlantans, yet it would still require maintenance. However, the stadium authority was still smarting from the loss of their Major League tenants, and was at the sharp end of negotiations with the Braves over disputed parking revenues (Meltzer, 2016). To acquiesce to the statue's removal would have added to the loss of face.

Further, issues of race can never be ignored in Atlanta. A million-dollar sports franchise owned by rich white men, with a predominantly white fan base, was leaving a majority-Black city for a prosperous suburb—and attempting to take the statue of a Black hero as well. This offered the city authority a way of being seen to defend the interests of the Black community. If the city authority were unable to keep baseball in Atlanta, they could at least retain baseball's Black heritage. In this way, despite not moving, the sculpture has taken on a new meaning. Further, along with the old Fulton County Stadium outfield wall—that Aaron's 715th home run flew over and that was retained as a monument in its original location just outside of Turner Field—Aaron's statue is a memorial to the loss of the Braves, as well as a celebration and claim of city ownership of Aaron's achievement.

Cobb's statue provides an interesting juxtaposition with Aaron's statue. In both cases, a civic body fought strongly for—and ultimately claimed—the artwork. The rehabilitation of Cobb's sculpture is a metaphor for Royston's campaign to rehabilitate Cobb's image. Cobb is Royston's main point of historical distinction and, as such, the town has much to gain from restoring his reputation. Coinciding with Charles Leerhsen's (2015) recent research that supports a more generous interpretation of Cobb's life, rescuing his statue from decrepitude or destruction provided a perfect opportunity for the community and its Ty Cobb museum. Furthermore, the statue serves as another attraction—alongside the museum—for baseball fans to visit in the community. In its new Royston home, Cobb's statue has become a symbol of a collective, community-wide ownership of Cobb's legacy that offers income through sports tourism and civic identity through reflected glory.

Moving Statues

It is interesting to speculate how the meanings of Aaron's and Cobb's statues would have changed if they had moved with the Braves to their new ballpark. In the future, other franchises will move venues—and even cities—and face the same issues. Is it better to leave such forms of tangible heritage in place, preserving a physical link to their origins, yet hidden away from fans who will most appreciate them? In one sense, Aaron's sculpture is site-specific—the record home run depicted happened at Fulton County Stadium. Or would Aaron's statue have been more appropriate at Truist Park, geographically separated from the moment sculpted but among those who would most appreciate both the significance of the moment and the player who achieved it? To what extent is the authenticity of the setting or the viewer most critical to tangible, movable heritage? This is an open question—one that museum curators grapple with when collecting and displaying artifacts, and one that sports teams, as they increasingly acknowledge the power of their heritage to engage fans, will have to address.

If Aaron's statue had moved with the Braves, it would have likewise symbolized Major League sports' move away from inner-city Atlanta to the wealthier suburbs, also for economic reasons. Profit margins ultimately drive corporate behavior within American sports: if these considerations coincide with wider social considerations, that is a bonus for teams and their ownership. Nonetheless, again from a symbolic viewpoint, the new, replacement Aaron statue is also appropriate for the Braves' new home. The Truist Park development enabled the Braves to create the ballpark village they so coveted. However, the ballpark is in a suburban location. The shops and precincts surrounding it, while built in a retro style, are new. While other MLB franchises have built retro ballparks—essentially faux-heritage stadiums—within actual downtown locations, the Braves built an entire faux-heritage neighborhood around their park (Goldberger, 2019). They control of all aspects of this ersatz locale, most crucially income streams, but also the suitably sanitized environment, which has none of the wear and tear of true urbanity (Goldberger, 2019).

The new Hank Aaron statue at Truist Park, similar in style to the one left in Atlanta but cleaner and shinier, on Braves' land and under their ownership is the perfect fit. Through the design and the backdrop, the statue is framed as a celebration of Aaron's baseball achievements for the franchise, specifically the home-run record. This is the primary meaning and message that the Braves want their fans and sports tourists to take from Aaron's monument. The statue plaque and surrounding materials offer little information regarding Aaron's achievements in bridging the racial divide of 1960s Atlanta. However, while the racial politics of the past are seemingly too delicate a subject to highlight at this ballpark, the very presence of a statue of a Black hero does serve an important purpose for the Braves in negotiating the racial politics of the present. The Braves franchise has often been criticized for the use of its moniker—and especially their fans' "Tomahawk Chop" celebration and chant—with respect to its caricature and stereotyping of Native American culture. Though the Braves have recently urged fans to refrain from doing "the chop," the franchise remains reluctant to change its name given its heritage and recognition (Kurtz, 2020). Aaron's statue offers an immediate visual riposte to any claims of racism.

Ty Cobb, on the other hand, was an imperfect fit for the Braves and their ballpark long before his statue was deemed removable. Even without accusations of racism, the success of Aaron and the later Braves teams of the

1990s—and the fact that Cobb's playing days are beyond living memory—diminished Cobb's status in Atlanta. This indicates how statue meanings can change—and how heritage can become devalued or even redundant. In Cobb's case, it was not only due to events changing the perception of his statue and heritage, but also through other, newer heroes becoming more notable or relevant, as well as the simple passage of time. For sporting heritage to maintain relevance beyond living memory, it needs to be about more than just statistics and must include a deeper local resonance or a wider social impact. Statues reflect perceived immortality of the subject at a point in time but do not grant immortality.

Hank Aaron and Ty Cobb were both celebrated ballplayers who held (or hold) significant records within baseball. With Aaron's home-run record now broken, his role in Atlanta's integration will most likely give his original statue a greater permanence in the city beyond his baseball career. However, even the brightness of such seismic social change may one day fade. Atlanta, a vast, dynamic, and global city of multiple traditions and identities, will face changing political considerations and produce other heroes to celebrate. Royston, on the other hand, may not produce a figure with a national profile as great as Ty Cobb for many generations, and so the community has invested in Cobb as a long-term identity for the town. Cobb's legacy to Royston has survived and even grown well beyond the living memory of his feats.

References

Aaron, H. (2007). *I had a hammer: The Hank Aaron story.* New York: Harper Collins.

Anderson, W. B. (2000). Sports page boosterism: Atlanta and its newspapers accomplish the unprecedented. *American Journalism, 17*(3), 89–107. doi:10.1080/08821127.2000.10739254

Arum, M. (2015, 13 February). 'Here is the Hank Aaron statue. Should the #Braves be allowed to take it to Cobb even though Atlanta owns it?' *Twitter.* https://twitter.com/MarkArum/status/566077690449788928 (accessed December 6, 2020).

Atlanta Journal-Constitution (Editorial) (1982, 5 September). Atlanta goes to bat for Hank Aaron. *Atlanta Journal-Constitution.* https://ajc.newspapers.com/image/399133043 (accessed December 6, 2020).

Bale, J. (1993). *Sport, space, and the city.* London: Routledge.

Barr, J. (2012, August 19). Life expectancy of arenas. *NHL to Seattle.* https://nhltoseattle.com/2012/08/19/life-expectancy-of-arenas/ (accessed December 6, 2020).

Baruchman, M. (2017, February 17). Ty Cobb statue is heading home to Royston. *Atlanta Journal-Constitution.* https://www.ajc.com/news/state—regional-govt—politics/cobb-statue-heading-home-royston/aCoxIMOX11j002Dy1KBuTM/# (accessed December 6, 2020).

Baseball Reference (2019). Atlanta braves attendance, stadiums and park factors. *Baseball Reference.* https://www.baseball-reference.com/teams/ATL/attend.shtml (accessed December 6, 2020).

Bayor, R. H. (2000). *Race and the shaping of twentieth-century Atlanta* (revised ed.). Chapel Hill: University of North Carolina Press.

Berg, T. (2013, November 13). Why the Braves want to move, in one ticket-sales map. *USA Today.* https://ftw.usatoday.com/2013/11/why-the-braves-want-to-move-in-one-ticket-sales-map (accessed December 6, 2020).

Bisher, F. (1966). *Miracle in Atlanta: The Atlanta Braves story.* Cleveland, OH: World Publishing.

Brown, E. (2013, November 14). The Atlanta Braves' move to Cobb County is about race, not transportation. *International Business Times.* https://www.ibtimes.com/atlanta-braves-move-cobb-county-about-race-not-transportation-1470814 (accessed December 6, 2020).

Bryant, H. (2011). *The last hero: A life of Henry Aaron.* New York: Anchor Books.

Burns, R. (2013, November 11). The Atlanta Braves are moving to Cobb County and everyone is kind of stunned. *Atlanta Magazine.* https://www.atlantamagazine.com/news-culture-articles/the-atlanta-braves-are-moving-to-cobb-county-and-every-one-is-kind-of-stunned/ (accessed December 6, 2020).

Caruso, G. (1995). *The Braves encyclopedia.* Philadelphia: Temple University Press.

Caruso, G. (2001). *Turner Field: Rarest of diamonds.* Marietta, GA: Taylor Trade Publishing.

Catania, J. (2013). Are the Braves making a big mistake deserting Turner Field? *Bleacher Report.* https://bleacherreport.com/articles/1846057-are-the-braves-making-a-big-mistake-deserting-the-turner-field (accessed December 6, 2020).

Davis, J. (2015, December 26). Turner Field holds future for Georgia State, neighborhoods. *Atlanta Journal-Constitution.* https://www.ajc.com/news/local-govt—politics/turner-field-holds-future-for-georgia-state-neighborhoods/flvzS1009IT9pqf-NgFwUgL/ (accessed December 6, 2020).

DeFeo, T. (2015a, March 18). What will happen to Hank Aaron statue at Turner Field? *The Travel Trolley.* http://thetraveltrolley.com/2015/03/what-will-happen-to-hank-aaron-statue-at-turner-field/ (accessed December 6, 2020).

DeFeo, T. (2015b, October 8). What should happen to the Ty Cobb statue at Turner Field? *Express Telegraph.* http://expresstelegraph.com/2015/10/08/what-should-happen-to-the-ty-cobb-statue-at-turner-field/ (accessed December 6, 2020).

DeVault, D. (2003). The Warren Spahn statue story. *New York Mets Hall of Records.* http://www.hagenspan.com/NYMHall/essays/statue.html (accessed December 6, 2020).

Diamond, J. (2016, September 27). Chicago Cubs and the last days of old, weird, Wrigleyville. *Rolling Stone.* https://www.rollingstone.com/culture/culture-sports/chicago-cubs-and-the-last-days-of-old-weird-wrigleyville-120220/ (accessed December 6, 2020).

DiLonardo, M. J. (2003, February). Hero worship: One fan's crusade honors the legendary lefty. *Atlanta Magazine,* 42 (11).

Donnellon, S. (2011, August 17). Harry Kalas statue is missing something. *Philadelphia Inquirer.* https://www.inquirer.com/philly/sports/phillies/20110817_Sam_Donnellon__Harry_Kalas_statue_is_missing_something.html (accessed December 6, 2020).

Dupre, J. (2007). *Monuments: America's history in art and memory.* New York: Random House.

Enders, E. (2018). *Ballparks: A journey through the fields of the past, present, and future.* New York: Chartwell Books.

Fowler, G. (1989, May 10). Mills B. Lane Jr., Atlanta banker, is dead at 77. *New York Times.* https://www.nytimes.com/1989/05/10/obituaries/mills-b-lane-jr-atlanta-banker-is-dead-at-77.html (accessed December 6, 2020).

Freedman, L. (2013). *Football stadiums: A guide to professional and top college stadiums.* Ontario: Firefly Books Ltd.

French, S. P., & Disher, M. E. (1997). Atlanta and the Olympics: A one-year retrospective. *Journal of the American Planning Association, 63*(3), 379–392. doi:10.1080/01944369708975930

Fricks, W. (2017, January 22). Forty-year-old statue comes home to Royston! *Ty Cobb Museum.* https://tycobb.org/blog/forty-year-old-ty-cobb-statue-comes-home-to-royston (accessed December 6, 2020).

Glier, R. (2014). If we win again, we'll be one again. *Bitter Southerner.* https://bitter-southerner.com/atlanta-hawks-if-we-win-again-well-be-one-again#.Xc2wky10ei5 (accessed December 6, 2020).

Goldberger, P. (2019). *Baseball in the American city: Baseball, ballparks, and the American city.* New York: Knopf.

Gustafson, S. (2013). Displacement and the racial state in Olympic Atlanta: 1990–1996. *Southeastern Geographer, 53*(2), 198–213. doi:10.1353/sg0.2013.0016

Hatfield, E. A. (2014, September 16). Mills B. Lane Jr. (1912–1989). *New Georgia Encyclopedia.* https://www.georgiaencyclopedia.org/articles/business-economy/mills-b-lane-jr-1912–1989 (accessed December 6, 2020).

Henry, R. (2013, December 14). Planned Braves stadium move highlights race, class. *San Diego Union-Tribune.* https://www.sandiegouniontribune.com/sdut-planned-braves-stadium-move-highlights-race-class-2013dec14-story.html (accessed December 6, 2020).

Hinton, E. (1982, 18 April). Crowd of 1000 attends fete to raise Aaron statue funds. *Atlanta Journal-Constitution.* https://ajc.newspapers.com/image/399319093/ (accessed December 6, 2020).

Holbrook, M. B., & Schindler, R. M. (2003). Nostalgic bonding: Exploring the role of nostalgia in the consumption experience. *Journal of Consumer Behaviour, 3,* 107–127. doi:10.1002/cb.127

Hornick, A. (2017, May 22). Ty Cobb statue officially makes new home in Royston. *92.1 WLHR Lake Hartwell Radio.* https://921wlhr.com/ty-cobb-statue-officially-makes-new-home-in-royston/ (accessed December 6, 2020).

Kurtz, J. (2020, July 13). Atlanta Braves will keep their name but review the 'Tomahawk Chop.' *CNN.* https://edition.cnn.com/2020/07/13/us/atlanta-braves-name-tomahawk -chop-trnd/index.html (accessed December 6, 2020).

Leerhsen, C. (2015). *Ty Cobb: A terrible beauty.* New York: Simon & Schuster Paperbacks.

Leslie, K. (2015a, February 11). Monument man: Is Hank Aaron's statue heading to the suburbs? *Atlanta Journal-Constitution.* https://www.ajc.com/news/mo nument-man-hank-aaron-statue-heading-the-suburbs/QAnRM3UjCPzPaB7wrLchvK/ (accessed December 6, 2020).

Leslie, K. (2015b, February 13). Future of Hank Aaron statue unclear as Braves move. *At-lanta Journal-Constitution.* https://eu.delawareonline.com/story/sports/mlb/2015/02 /12/future-hank-aaron-statue-unclear-braves-move/23327063/ (accessed December 6, 2020).

McGrath, J., (1982, 8 September). Aaron statue worthy of inspiration. *Atlanta Journal-Constitution.* https://ajc.newspapers.com/image/399194069 (accessed December 6, 2020).

Meltzer, M. (2016, September 23). Braves, Recreation Authority in $400,000 dispute. Atlanta Business Chronicle. https://www.bizjournals.com/atlanta/news/2016/09/23/ braves-recreation-authority-in-400–000-dispute.html (accessed December 6, 2020).

Mile High Chopper (2017, March 13). 'I'm glad the Cobb statue won't be at Sun Trust. Nothing against Ty Cobb' *Reddit.* [Comment on the online forum post *SunTrust Park won't have a museum, it will be a museum . . .*]. https://www.reddit.com/r/Braves/ comments/5z4w01/suntrust_park_wont_have_a_museum_it_will_be_a/ (accessed December 6, 2020).

Moore, T. (2014, April 8). Don't erase Hank Aaron's spot in history. *CNN.* https://edi-tion.cnn.com/2014/04/08/opinion/moore-hank-aaron-the-715-spot/index.html (ac-cessed December 6, 2020).

O'Brien, D. (2013, November 11). Quote: Reaction to Braves' new stadium plans. *At-lanta Journal-Constitution.* https://www.ajc.com/sports/baseball/quotes-reaction-braves-new-stadium-plans/JCvdKdLWM44jwPDUHbZH4M/ (accessed December 6, 2020).

Osmond, G., Phillips, M. G., & O'Neill, M. (2006). Putting up your Dukes: Statues social memory and Duke Paoa Kahanamoku. *International Journal of the History of Sport, 23*(1), 82–103. doi:10.1080/09523360500386484

Ove, J. (2015, February 12). Should Hank Aaron statue move with Braves? *patch.com.* https://patch.com/georgia/marietta/should-hank-aaron-statue-move-braves-0 (ac-cessed December 6, 2020).

Pahigian, J. (2008). *101 baseball places to see before you die.* Guilford, CT: Lyons Press.

Picking, K. (1979, 23 August). Turner says Braves' ship not sunk yet. *Atlanta Constitution.* https://ajc.newspapers.com/image/398628107 (accessed December 6, 2020).

Ramshaw, G. (2020). *Heritage and sport: An introduction.* Bristol: Channel View Publica-tions.

Ramshaw, G., Gammon, S., & Huang, W-J. (2013). Acquired pasts and the commodifica-tion of borrowed heritage: The case of the Bank of America Stadium tour. *Journal of Sport & Tourism, 18,* 17–31. doi:10.1080/14775085.2013.799334

Reichard, K. (2017, September 15). NFL stadiums, listed oldest to newest. *Football Stadium Digest.* https://footballstadiumdigest.com/2017/09/nfl-stadiums-listed-oldest-to-newest/ (accessed December 6, 2020).

Rowland, B., & Collazo, C. (Presenters). (2016, February 15). Episode 2: Prospects and Sabermetrics, with Ivan the Great [Audio podcast]. In B. Rowland (Producer), *Talking Chop.* https://radiopublic.com/talking-chop-for-atlanta-braves-f-WaYq2Q/s1!b6e70 (accessed December 6, 2020).

Saporta, M. (2015, February 16). Where does Hank Aaron statue belong? Only one solution exists. *Saporta Report.* https://saportareport.com/where-does-hank-aarons-statue-belong-only-one-solution-exists/ (accessed December 6, 2020).

Savage, K. (1994). The politics of memory: Black emancipation and the Civil War monument. In J. R. Gikllis (Ed.), *Commemorations: The politics of national identity* (pp. 127–149). Princeton, NJ: Princeton University Press.

Schafer, J. (2015, September 30). 'Atlanta Braves News: The Morning Chop, Box Score, Ty Cobb Statue.' *Tomahawk Take.* https://tomahawktake.com/2015/09/30/atlanta-braves-news-the-morning-chop-box-score-ty-cobb-statue (accessed December 6, 2020).

Schein, R. H. (2006). *Landscape and race in the United States.* New York: Routledge.

Schultz, J. (2017, April 13). Bobby Cox built Braves first time, was right man to honor with statue. *Atlanta Journal-Constitution.* https://www.ajc.com/sports/baseball/bobby-cox-built-braves-first-time-was-right-man-honor-with-statue/x30kwdFH00WhLvZp03e51H/ (accessed December 6, 2020).

Seifried, C., & Meyer, K. (2010). Nostalgia-related aspects of professional sports facilities: A facility audit of Major League Baseball and National Football League strategies to evoke the past. *International Journal of Sport Management Recreation and Tourism, 5,* 51–76. doi:10.5199/ijsmart-1791–874X-5c

Slotnik, D. E. (2013, March 27). Hjalmar Andersen, Norwegian speedskater, dies at 90. *New York Times.* https://www.nytimes.com/2013/03/28/sports/hjalmar-andersen-norwegian-speedskater-dies-at-90.html (accessed December 6, 2020).

Stanton, J. (2012). Monument to musial: The history of a statue. *NINE: A Journal of Baseball History and Culture, 20*(2), 27–42. doi:10.1353/nin.2012.0019

Stride, C., & Thomas, F. E. (2011). The Sporting Statues Project. http://www.sportingstatues.com (accessed December 6, 2020)

Stride, C., & Thomas, F. E. (2017). Tension in the union of art and sport: Competition for the ownership of the baseball statuary and its influence upon design. *NINE: A Journal of Baseball History and Culture, 24*(1), 1–28. doi:10.1353/nin.2015.0030

Teepen, T. (1989, May 14). Bonding of biracial Atlanta was Lane's biggest contribution to city. *Atlanta Sunday Journal-Constitution.* https://www.newspapers.com/newspage/400393059/ (accessed December 6, 2020).

Tomlinson, T. (2013, November 11). 13 ways of looking at the Atlanta Braves' move to the suburbs. *Forbes.* https://www.forbes.com/sites/tommytomlinson/2013/11/11/13-ways-of-looking-at-the-atlanta-braves-move/#34c2a85e49d3 (accessed December 6, 2020).

Torpy, B. (2016, February 17). Statue of Ty Cobb at Turner Field will be orphaned by the Braves. *Atlanta Journal-Constitution*. https://www.ajc.com/news/local/torpy-large-everybody-wants-the-hammer-nobody-wants-the-peach/7ChUqy4qLJjekXzx6 DdY9O/ (accessed December 6, 2020).

Trubey, J. S. (2016a, January 6). Turner Field plan raises questions about sports landmarks. *Atlanta Journal-Constitution*. https://www.ajc.com/news/local/turner-field-plan-raises-questions-about-sports-landmarks/VQ70QY4cX3zVe70YepKk70/ (accessed December 6, 2020).

Trubey, J. S. (2016b, February 10). Rec authority says Hank Aaron statue to stay, Braves say no deal yet. *Atlanta Journal-Constitution*. https://www.ajc.com/news/local-govt—politics/rec-authority-says-hank-aaron-statue-stay-braves-say-deal-yet /0BYDVyNcK2PMXdqNBzMo7O/ (accessed December 6, 2020).

Trubey, J. S. (2016c, February 12). Aarons wants authority, Atlanta Braves to make statue decision. *Atlanta Journal-Constitution*. https://www.ajc.com/news/local-govt—poli-tics/aarons-want-authority-atlanta-braves-make-statue decision/6pnikdvbjKSPHCh Gck9bBI/ (accessed December 6, 2020).

Trubey, J. S. (2016d, February 12). Braves: Hank Aaron statue to remain in Atlanta, new monument in Cobb. *Atlanta Journal-Constitution*. https://www.ajc.com/news/local/ braves-hank-aaron-statue-remain-atlanta-new-monumentcobb/3A2S4TVvrCxkpTl dCHxsEK/ (accessed December 6, 2020).

Tucker, T. (2013, November 12). Braves plan to build new stadium in Cobb. *Atlanta Journal-Constitution*. https://www.ajc.com/sports/baseball/braves-plan-build-new-stadium-cobb/g4N4VC7nuSPUX62DykwQ9K/ (accessed December 6, 2020).

Williams, D. (2014). *Hank Aaron: Groundbreaking baseball slugger*. Minnesota: ABDO Publishing Company.

WSB-TV (2015, 13 February). 'Will Hank get left behind? The fight to get Hank Aar-on's statue to the new Braves' stadium.' *Twitter*. https://twitter.com/wsbtv/status /565970231508893696 (accessed December 6, 2020).

Zygmont, Z. X., & Leadley, J. C. (2005). When is the honeymoon over? Major league baseball attendance 1970–2000. *Journal of Sport Management, 19*(3), 278–299. doi :10.1123/jsm.19.3.278

14

Chewing Gum, Cracker Jack, and Crab Cakes

Considering Baseball's Food Heritage

ALANA N. SEAMAN

Baseball's heritage is more intimately linked to food than any other sport. While golf has drinks such as the Arnold Palmer (half lemonade and half iced tea), football has the Green Bay Packers "Cheeseheads" fans and Super Bowl parties, and bowling is synonymous with cheap beer in plastic pitchers, baseball's relationship with food is central to both the sport itself and its spectator experience. Baseball's culinary heritage incorporates elements of the past meant to symbolize the game's commonality and links to its idealized pastoral and simple origins while simultaneously inviting the modern reinterpretation of its time-honored food traditions. In turn, within baseball, food is employed to create new heroes, provide connections between different generations, reinforce ties to place, cultivate team loyalty, and reinvigorate the links between health and the sport. It strengthens individual and collective identities, makes nostalgia both personal and social, and reflects long-standing, uniquely American traditions and national patriotism while at the same time conveniently glossing over or, in many cases, actively neglecting the controversy, corruption, and racism of baseball's earlier eras.

Indeed, baseball's food heritage has managed to strike a delicate and enduring balance between tradition—in part fueled by a collective enthusiasm for selective remembrance—and historic amnesia, likely unmatched by any other athletic endeavor. In this sense, baseball has seemingly managed to negotiate the tension between the past and the present—frequently an insurmountable friction inherent in many forms of heritage. The close relationship between the game itself and food is clearly integral to the sport, so much so that certain ingredients and dishes are instantly recognizable even to those outside of the sport. Thanks to a combination of serendipitous timing, Hollywood depictions, and the design of baseball stadia (which allows for control over how and where food is sold at games), the relationship of baseball and food has become inexorably entrenched in the traditions, experience, spaces, and culture of the sport. This chapter will therefore explore the relationship between food, heritage, and baseball by looking at the early development of the food-baseball relationship; the depictions of the food-baseball relationship in popular culture; the culture and heritage of the dining experience at ballparks; and the recent developments in the food-baseball relationship that both reinforce and challenge the role of food in the baseball heritage experience.

Early Baseball and the Emergence of the Modern Food Industry

Baseball "grew up with America" (Rossi, 2007). The story of its founding in 1839 in the picturesque lakeside hamlet of Cooperstown, New York, binds the sport with romanticized images of open spaces, in happy, quaint, and prosperous small towns existing harmoniously alongside beautiful wild and agricultural landscapes. While scholars argue that the sport really originated in the less aesthetically pleasing Hoboken, New Jersey (Thorn, 2011), or was perhaps even the derivative of an older sport possibly played as early as 1735 (Thorn, 2011), the Cooperstown version of the story prevails and cements the sports' links to idealized notions of pastoral, peaceful, small-town Americana (Fyfe, 2008; Springwood, 2019). Early versions of the game differed regionally, but by the 1850s baseball had become America's favorite sport. Given how the sport had evolved with the country, the game became heavily associated with the young nation. In turn, participation in baseball as a casual endeavor, serious player, or even as a fan has long been associated with patriotism, a way for Americans to connect with their home country (Rossi, 2007).

Food was a part of the game from the very beginning. As soon as crowds began to gather to watch baseball games, enterprising street vendors rolled their food carts up near the spectators, and the tradition of eating at a ball game was born. From that point forward, food and its consumption have been an integral part of the baseball fan experience. Hot dogs likely became game-time fan favorites because they were cheap, easy to transport and consume, and mild in flavor, consisting of simply salty meat and carbohydrates—truly the meal for the everyman (Kraig, 2005). Thus, engaging in the tradition of having a hot dog at a ball game was historically a way to "feel American," particularly as immigration soared in the late 19th and early 20th centuries. Baseball's intimate links to romanticized ideals of Americana positioned the gastronomic ritual as a patriotic endeavor. Playing, watching, and enjoying a hot dog at the ballpark was (and still is) a way of demonstrating that one had developed a taste for the country's sport (Rossi, 2007). Today, having a hot dog at a baseball game is the embodiment of Americana and the American sport-spectating experience. It therefore comes as no surprise that—despite the many changes and innovations to ballparks' fare over the decades—hot dogs remain the most popular concession item at Major League Baseball (MLB) parks across the United States (Clabough, 2019).

While the hot dog is often held up as a symbol of the sport's inclusiveness, this item marginalizes some of baseball's more challenging heritages and traditions. Derived from German culinary traditions (Kraig, 2005), the hot dog commemorates baseball's segregated past by inviting fans to "feel American" by consuming an item commemorating only Caucasian culinary influences. Other sports have had to address other much more subtle symbols of historic racial inequalities, yet baseball's iconic hot dog has seemingly escaped such scrutiny—perhaps because it appears to be an innocuous, if traditional, menu item. Yet, as Ashworth and Tunbridge (1996) noted, many heritages—even those which appear to be uncontroversial—are nevertheless contested and can reinforce narratives of marginalization.

Baseball's popularity continued to grow over the following decades. Simultaneously, the modern food industry was emerging. In the late 19th and early 20th centuries, new methods and technologies for food production, preservation, and distribution created new companies in a few short years, including global corporations such as Heinz, established in 1869; Hershey's, started in the 1880s; Kellogg's, founded in 1900; and Birds Eye Frozen Foods, created in 1927. As a result, healthier foods became more accessible and affordable than ever before (Burstein & Stone, 2019) and, in turn, people had more time, energy, and money to spend on leisure pursuits such as baseball. Conditions were ripe for the professionalization of the sport, and in 1871 the National League was founded, followed by the American League in 1901. In short, baseball and food became intricately intertwined because of how their histories parallel one another.

The professionalization of baseball brought with it an array of new opportunities that those in the food sector were quick to take advantage of. In fact, the Wrigley family's historic association with the sport traces its origins to this era. While the recently industrialized global food market afforded William Wrigley his wealth, it was his partnership with another food entrepreneur in 1916 that introduced him to baseball and initiated the family's legacy that endures today. With the help of area meatpacking baron J. Ogden Armour, the candy magnet Wrigley originally bought into the early Chicago Cubs' professional baseball organization before becoming the majority owner a few short years later in 1921. Wrigley's investment was vital to the historic Cubs franchise, with the beloved and historic Wrigley Field cementing the legacy of the food icon's importance to the team and the game. While the stadium remains one of the oldest in Major League Baseball (Cubs, n.d.), it was originally the merging of beef and confection money that set in motion the Wrigleys' long-standing baseball heritage (Fletcher & Castle, 2015).

Some twenty years later, with World War II looming and professional baseball on the verge of collapse, the popularity of gum in the global market again lent the Wrigleys the clout to put an indelible mark on baseball's history. Philip K. Wrigley, William's son, took it upon himself to search for solutions to the challenge of keeping a professional baseball league alive during the war, believing it to be an important part of keeping American spirits up. In 1943, he put money toward the development of a women's softball league, which would eventually become the All-American Girls Professional Baseball League (AAGPBL) (Lesko, 2014). With the men off to war, and the league keeping the country's game going on at home, the links between patriotism, food, and baseball were solidified—particularly as a reflection of patriotism and American identity. The enduringly popular Penny Marshall film *A League of Their Own* (1992) commemorates the chewing gum heir's patriotic endeavor. The film introduces new generations to baseball's historic and patriotic position in American culture with the fictional Mr. Harvey, played by Hollywood icon Gary Marshall, owner of the popular fictional Harvey Bars Company, paying homage to the younger Wrigley and the food industry's facilitation of baseball.

Popular Culture

A number of popular films also highlight, perpetuate, and reinforce the relationship between baseball and food. In *The Sandlot* (1993), for instance, several scenes feature the group of young boys drinking out of coke bottles in order to trade the bottles for money to buy a new baseball after having lost theirs to the neighborhood dog. In baseball films such as *Rookie of the*

Year (1993) and *Fever Pitch* (2005), scenes play out between main characters while eating at a ball game. In Robinson's (1989) *Field of Dreams*, a ballpark dining incident prompts one of the pivotal moments in the film, when protagonist Ray Kinsella's young daughter chokes on a hot dog after falling from a small set of bleachers (and then is saved by one of the ghostly players from the "Field of Dreams"—"Moonlight Graham"—who transforms from a young ballplayer to an elderly doctor upon leaving the mystical field in order to save the young girl). Even in non-baseball film genres, characters are often depicted eating in the stands when attending a ball game. Characters in films such as *Big* (1988), *Ferris Bueller's Day Off* (1986), and *Naked Gun* (1988) are shown consuming concession staples such as hot dogs while watching their favorite teams go head-to-head. In the romantic comedy *The Breakup* (2006), hot dogs at a ball game serve as a catalyst for the relationship between the main characters, while television characters such as Carrie Bradshaw in *Sex and the City* (1998–2004) and Homer Simpson in *The Simpsons* (1989–present) are depicted eating at baseball games during particular scenes in the series. Popular culture continues to symbolically immortalize food's role in baseball, perpetuating the notion that eating certain foods in the stands is something that you're *supposed* to do when attending a ball game; that part of the experience, tradition, and ritual of going to the game is the food. Though other sports are often depicted on-screen, and sport movies in particular represent one of the most popular genres of film, few depict food traditions to a similar degree or manner as those associated with baseball.

Baseball Foods and the Ballpark Dining Experience

As baseball's popularity exploded into the first half of the 20th century, so, too, did competition in the quickly expanding food industry. New competition demanded new promotional approaches and methods for marketing food—and baseball offered a viable channel for new promotional tactics. These tactics were so effective that baseball still serves a popular food marketing platform today. In fact, many food corporations have or still sponsor contemporary MLB stadiums. Tropicana Field, named for the well-known orange juice manufacturer, is home of the Tampa Bay Rays. Minute Maid Field in Houston has been home of the Astros since it was named for the lemonade brand in 2002, while beer companies such as Miller (Milwaukee), Coors (Denver), and Busch (St. Louis) have or continue to sponsor MLB stadia. While other sport venues feature food sponsors and arena walls plastered with advertisements, baseball stadiums are well suited for sideline marketing, given the slower pace of the game and the wide, steady camera angles used to catch play. Moreover, baseball stadiums have historically boasted longer life spans than many venues hosting other sports, thus allowing their food-linked names to become synonymous with not only the teams they are home to but also the area where they reside (such as the Wrigleyville neighborhood surrounding Wrigley Field in Chicago).

Historically, one of the oldest baseball food traditions—cracking and eating dry-roasted peanuts at the ball game—can be traced back to the marketing of food. In 1895, a peanut farmer couldn't pay the local ballclub's fee for advertising his product on the back of the scorecards provided to fans and instead settled up with loads of the thick-shelled legume (National Peanut Board, 2019). To earn back some of the lost funds, the team owner decided to sell the peanuts to fans as a concession item. Cracking the shells, as it turned out, gave nervous fans something to do with their hands, and peanuts quickly became standard fare in stadiums across the country (National Peanut Board, 2019). Fans' love of dry-roasted peanuts, however, echoes a similar pattern of remembrance and collective amnesia, as the legume itself is an iconic product of the same south that practiced slavery, segregation, and perpetuated Jim Crow laws much longer than the rest of the country. This, of course, is rarely addressed, or likely even considered by players, fans, or concessionaires hawking the salty snack between batters. Still widely available at most ballparks, the simple snack is instead practically positioned as the antithesis of modernity—low-tech, hands-on (thus phone-free), and, given that peanuts are a relatively unprocessed agricultural product, reminiscent of baseball's idealized pastoral past (see Fyfe, 2008; Springwood, 2019).

Cracker Jack is similarly synonymous with baseball, its legacy also largely based in historic marketing tactics. While singing "Take Me Out to the Ball Game" remains a popular ritual during baseball's seventh-inning stretch, sales of the often referenced salty-sweet Cracker Jack snack have declined at many MLB stadiums in recent years (Branch, 2009). However, attempts to remove or replace Cracker Jack from several MLB ballparks upon slowing sales was met with hordes of upset fans (Branch, 2009), highlighting the role that food nostalgia plays in the baseball fan experience. One would be hard-pressed to find another example of sports fans who are so passionate about a single food item. Perhaps even sadder, in 2016 Frito-Lay, the company that currently owns and makes the treat, announced that the product would no longer offer tangible prizes in its packages. Instead, the trinkets would be replaced with "virtual prizes" redeemable only online (Dawn, 2016). This is particularly notable for baseball, as Cracker Jack was one of the first large-scale producers and distributors of baseball cards that were included as prizes early in the company's history (McKay, n.d.). Baseball cards are, for many, a valued, hero-making childhood currency that was traded, cherished, and poured over for decades by multiple generations. Thus, while Cracker Jack is still marketed to kids, it also likely reminds adult fans of their own childhood experiences; with the fun of eating the snack and finding the prize while taking in a ball game. While this move toward the future has caused some tension in the way of disappointed fans, the snack's longtime existence in the ballpark still provides multiple generations with a common experience to bond over (Branch, 2009; see also Timothy, 2018). Given its declining sales, Cracker Jack has, in this sense, become fetishized by fans who evidently value the *idea* of the snack and the nostalgia it represents over the product itself or the experience of consuming it. Nonetheless, baseball still pays musical homage to Cracker Jack to celebrate their unique historic ties to the treat, in turn justifying their distinctive heritage and claims to the culinary icon.

Nostalgic components of the ballparks themselves also contribute positively to the overall fan experience (Slavich et al., 2019). Ballpark sights, sounds, tactile feelings, and smells inspire a sense of nostalgia by invoking happy memories, often about childhood (Lee et al., 2012). Along with taste, which is widely recognized as bringing about strong emotionally charged memories (Hirsch, 1992), food incorporates many of these other sensory elements as well. Food is both tangible and intangible (see Ramshaw & Gammon, 2005), encompassing both personal experience and collective traditions. Fans, for instance, can both top their own hot dogs to suit their personal tastes or reflect their regional identity, and join other, even opposing, fans in the traditional singing of "Take Me Out to the Ball Game" during the same game experience. Above all else, food is immersive and affects all the senses, thereby contributing to the overall atmospherics of the ball game (Ramshaw, 2020). Baseball's relatively slow pace and outdoor setting, for example, allows for the tradition of shelling sunflower seeds or roasted peanuts by fans in the stands. The warm weather and tightly packed seating increase the demand for salty snacks and cold beers. Coupled with the gentle rise of the stadium stands, the game is also particularly well suited for the hawking of foods and beverages by concessionaires. Given that sound is important in creating unique place experiences (TaunTuan, 1974), particularly within sport venues (Gaffney & Bale, 2004), concessionaires' calls for "hot dogs" and "iced cold beer" have become synonymous with the ballpark (Ramshaw, 2020). Whether directly tuned in or as a sort of ambient background, the calls of concessionaries, the sounds of the crowd and the crack of the bat, the smell of hot dogs, the taste of salty snacks, and the heat of the season are all central to what makes attending a baseball game a distinctive experience.

Baseball's unique conditions were even the catalyst for one of sport spectators' favorite junk foods, stadium nachos. The dish of salty corn chips covered in (unmistakable and clearly unnatural) orange cheese-product—pumped from large countertop canisters—and jalapeño slices was actually created specifically to address the unique conditions associated with eating at a baseball game. Created for the Texas Rangers in 1986, they were cheap, easy to carry and eat, relatively mild in flavor, and quick to prepare and distribute, meaning that fans could spend more time watching the game (Smith, 2013). Fulfilling the needs of hungry baseball fans everywhere, stadium nachos quickly caught on and can be found at ballparks everywhere from recreational facilities to modern MLB stadiums today. They've even become commonplace at other sporting events, though baseball is truly the sport to be credited with producing its own, widely recognizable culinary dish—a claim to primacy that few, if any, other sports can boast.

Experiences involving food and dining are particularly impactful because they are social, immersive, and laden with nostalgia (Getz & Robinson, 2014b; Getz et al., 2014). This is likely why, until recently, the experience of eating and drinking at the ballpark, unique as it is, had changed little in over 150 years, despite the fact that stadiums, uniforms, and even the rules of the game have changed somewhat drastically over the same time frame. For decades, the concessions associated with baseball remained unchanged at community ballparks and modern professional stadiums alike. They all served the same processed, frozen, and often overly salty concession-stand staples of roasted peanuts, hot dogs, nachos, Cracker Jack, and beer. Today, however, baseball's relationship with food is changing.

Local Foods: Culture, Place, and Health

In the current experience economy, in which almost every organization in every industry is creating unique and immersive experiences (see Pine & Gilmore, 1998), ballparks are utilizing local culinary heritages to set stadium experiences apart from one another, particularly as demand for distinctive and authentic products increase. Neo-localism, a cultural and social response to the rise of homogenous and placeless chain stores and restaurants that have dotted the American landscape (Eberts, 2014; Flack, 1997; Schnell & Reese, 2003; Watson, 2016), has also helped shaped the food culture at ballparks. The neo-localist movement has shaped food culture in the United States in particular (Adams & Adams, 2011; Adams & Salois, 2010; Boyce, 2013; Casselman, 2010; Delind, 2006; Feagan et al., 2004; Giovannucci et al., 2010; Richards, 2012; Sims, 2009; Timmons, 2006), and, as a result, many MLB and Minor League Baseball stadiums have moved beyond traditional ballpark fare and now focus on local delicacies curated by iconic local restaurants and establishments. The concessions cultivate a sense of being "local" and reinforce loyalty and allegiance to an area, given that food is widely seen as a way to connect with place (UNWTO, 2017; Richards, 2012). Fans can now find lobster rolls at the Washington Nationals Park in DC (Figure 14.1), crab cakes in Baltimore's Camden Yards, Seaside Market's "Cardiff crack" at San Diego's Petco Park (Figure 14.2), or fried cheese curds and Smoke Shack BBQ over macaroni and cheese at Milwaukee Brewers Miller Park (Figure 14.3) among a host of other options in other cities.

Figure 14.1. Lobster roll stand at Washington Nationals Park. Photo by Alana Seaman.

Figure 14.2. Seaside Market at San Diego's Petco Park, where fans can order tri-tip marinated in a secret recipe and served over a choice of carbs affectionately known locally as "Cardiff crack." Photo by Alana Seaman.

EAT

BBQ SANDWICH

CHOPPED BRISKET	13.25
SERVED WITH KETTLE CHIPS	
SMOKED PULLED PORK	11.75
SERVED WITH KETTLE CHIPS	
SHREDDED CHICKEN	8.25
SERVED WITH KETTLE CHIPS	

BBQ NACHOS	10.00
MAC & CHEESE	7.50
BACON MAC & CHEESE	10.00
PULLED PORK MAC & CHEESE	11.00
KOSHER BEEF HOT DOG	6.00
BRATWURST	6.25

DRINK

REGULAR SODA	5.00
LARGE SODA	7.00
SOUVENIR SODA CUP	9.00
BOTTLED WATER	5.00
LARGE DRAFT BEER	8.75
REGULAR DRAFT BEER	7.00

SNACK

BBQ FRIED CORN	7.50
LICORICE	5.00
PEANUTS	4.75
BAVARIAN PRETZEL	5.75
CHEESE CUP	2.25

Figure 14.3. Smoke Shack menu items featuring pulled pork mac and cheese at Milwaukee Brewers Miller Park. Photo by Alana Seaman.

Figure 14.4. Local beers featured at San Diego's Petco Park. Photo by Alana Seaman.

Recent renovations at Chicago's Wrigley Field even included the creation of a dedicated concession space, Sheffield's Kitchen, meant to host a rotation of regionally recognized chefs and their own baseball inspired creations, which was marketed as the Chef Series presented by Maker's Mark.

Local beers are similarly curated and marketed to fans, further reinforcing a sense of place. Small-scale breweries are often intimately connected to their local communities (Fletchall, 2016; Schnell & Reese, 2003), given how many host locally focused fundraisers, artists, and chefs; brew seasonal ales reminiscent of area traditions; and recall and memorialize local histories, icons, and geographic features in their company branding, décor, and beer names (Argent, 2017; Eberts, 2014; Seaman & Schroeder, 2018) (Figure 14.5). Thus, selling these beers at the ballparks conveys particular place values and reminds fans of the unique heritage of the team and its home city. Further, these local products elicit emotional connections between brews, brands, and place (Hede & Watne, 2013). Not only are regional beers now offered at many concession stands (Figure 14.4), but stadiums are also now incorporating taprooms into their stadiums, and some teams are even collaborating with local breweries to create limited-release beers themed around specific players, events, and historic moments (Figure 14.5). Given that visiting local pubs around baseball stadia is often part of the game-day experience, ballparks are working to incorporate that pre-game excitement into the stadium experience. In-stadium taprooms often open before games start, and they symbolically encourage fans to socialize in order to develop camaraderie and energy with fellow fans. Specially brewed beers commemorate the role of the team in local culture, remind fans of historic accomplishments of the franchise and why they should be proud to show their allegiance to the

Figure 14.5. Cans of Summer Shandy for sale at Milwaukee Brewers Miller Park stadium. Summer Shandy is a traditional brew commonly associated with the upper Great Lakes region of the United States. This one is made by Wisconsin's own Leinenkugel's beer company and depicts the state's lush green rolling countryside. Photo by Alana Seaman.

team, and reinforce the relationship between baseball and American culture. Other locally created or inspired alcoholic beverages are increasingly available at MLB ballparks. Regionally influenced cocktails are now served in team-branded plastic Mason-jar style containers, thematically juxtaposing contemporary culture's affinity for artisan ingredients with nostalgia for the rural notions of baseball's past. Given that an energetic crowd is a central form of intangible cultural heritage at sporting events, providing an array of local beverages, many of which are branded on local heritage, in stadiums seems to both invite and encourage the crowd's loud, rambunctious, and lively involvement in the game—perhaps reminiscent of the ball games of yesteryear before the perpetual distraction of smartphones.

While these new food and drink options create unique and enticing ballpark experiences ideally attractive to both fans and tourists, they are also powerful reminders of the local area's culinary and agricultural heritages. Anecdotal evidence suggests that the wider array of concession options available at many stadiums represent a greater range of local culinary and cultural diversity honoring, celebrating, and including more of the population in America's game than ever before. However, the selective showcasing of particular foods, food brands, and restaurants inherently places value upon certain establishments, food-related industries, and local culinary heritages. Often showcasing only one or two (sometimes modified) versions of original dishes, selected for both recognition and ease of procuring and eating in the stands, these selective offerings have important placemaking and place-based implications, given how food reflects local culture and reinforces a sense of place (Sims, 2009; Richards, 2012).

Culinary heritages and traditions are examples of the central intangible components that make spaces meaningful places (Lefebvre, 1974; Tuan, 1974). Thus, food and place are inexorably linked, and boasting local foods within the fan experience likely increases fan loyalty, given how place is also emotionally tied to identity (Hernandez et al., 2007). The foods together work to reinforce a team's unique links to place by providing fans with unique experiences, in turn eliciting new facets of team allegiance. Much like the Milwaukee Brewers or historic teams such as the Rockford Peaches or the Kansas City Packers pay homage to the beer, fruit, stockyards, and meatpacking sectors of the food industry that once dominated their respective cities' economies, these local concessions tell fans which food traditions are worthy of being honored and engaged with, while also showing how both the team and the food they memorialize are integral to the local culture.

Local foods also have connotations of health credited to lower food miles traveled, which is thought to make them fresher than traditionally sourced foods (Berlin et al., 2009; Winter, 2003). Thus, while featuring local foods in stadiums honors local culinary heritages, the approach also works to reinvigorate the links between health, food, and sports. Moreover, healthy foods are trendy and culturally resonant. In fact, functional foods or foods that are *perceived* to be healthy and are eaten for their health benefits have comprised the fastest growing sector of the food market for several years running (Verbeke, 2005). More stadiums are now offering "healthier" concession alternatives. Items such as gluten-free lobster rolls, acai bowls, plant-based-meat burgers, and avocado toast, for example, are available at numerous baseball parks around the country and could be classified as "functional foods." While the more diverse food options make the baseball fan experience more relevant in a competitive market, as people are increasingly concerned about health and wellness and its relationship with food (Siro et al., 2008), the increased menu options also subtly highlight the link between sports and health in new ways.

The public's interest in the health and locality of food is being fueled in part by growing concerns over the ethics, nutrition, and social practices of the current corporate-dominated food system (Delind, 2006) that is also widely known to be unsustainable (Delind, 2006; Feagan, 2007). Thus, people are more interested not only in the taste, quality, and sourcing of food but also in the environmental impacts associated with the production and consumption. Anecdotal evidence suggests little effort on behalf of the MLB to "green" either professional baseball or the fan experience, as evidenced by the travel patterns and exceptional amount of resources used to sustain the sport—such as water for fields and concrete for parking lots—and the sheer quantity of single-use plastics used at virtually every MLB ballpark nationwide. But some teams are addressing environmental issues and celebrating their hometown heritage in new and innovative ways at the same time. The San Francisco Giants, for example, planted an on-site garden in the stadium, sacrificing increased prime seating in favor of garden beds (Schulman, 2019). The gardens not only add aesthetic appeal to fan common areas but also grow fresh fruits and vegetables for use in several in-stadium restaurants (Bamco, n.d., SFGiants, n.d.). Reminiscent of the concept of "terroir," wherein the place-specific growing conditions of an agricultural product are thought to contribute to the item's taste (Trubek, 2008), the new tradition of eating foods produced in the same soil as the historic ball-game moments cherished by the team ensures that fans can literally "taste" the past. Additionally, the garden at the San Francisco Giants' stadium serves as a living and applied learning classroom for local children (Bamco, n.d.). Classes visit on field trips to learn about agriculture, nutrition, and sustainability (SFGiants, n.d.), presumably as related to sport. Education aside, it is perhaps fitting that such a memorialization of nature in an urban setting harkening back to baseball's pastoral past would be placed in California, a place widely recognized as one of the country's leading agricultural producers. While the garden may be a fun and healthy reminder of the state's agricultural heritage, the placement of fresh edible plants within the stadium emphasizes holistic notions of sport, food, and health.

While many sports organizations design facilities that capitalize on local culinary traditions and popular gastronomic trends, baseball is uniquely positioned to employ and celebrate its own local and trend-inspired culinary creations, as games are played in stadiums seldomly shared by other teams or sports. This gives baseball organizations far more influence over their food heritage, particularly when compared with other multisport venues. This effectively gives each club freedom to choose how they might connect their food and beverage offerings with local culinary traditions, implement aspects of larger culinary trends to cater to visitor expectations, and to utilize emergent heritage, nostalgia, and traditions at the concession stands. Add to this the number of games played in each baseball season—normally 81 home dates for each MLB team each year—and the role of connecting local culinary traditions and ballpark concession spaces all the more important. If going to a number of games per season, fans will probably want to try a variety of different foods, not the same old fare that is sold at every stand in the stadium.

Team Chefs: Creating Heroes and Cultivating Rivalries

Thanks in large part to baseball's dedicated stadia, a number of MLB teams now employ executive chefs. Given free rein to create new and exciting dishes featured both at their home stadiums and at league and community events, these individuals act as team representatives—much like an updated version of the team mascot—and their creations are utilized to create new heroes and fuel rivalries. In their home stadiums, team chefs are helping to create new heroes by creating concession items inspired by specific players. Featured dishes are based on individual players' favorite meals and cultural heritage, as well as their professional and personal histories. The Miami Marlins' Change Up food stand, the Los Angeles Angels' similarly named Change Up Kitchen, and other teams' dedicated varying-food venues feature different players and related food items on a rotating schedule. Accompanying the menu descriptions are often little facts, quotes, stats, or personal vignettes about the player and the meal curated to represent them (Figure 14.6).

Rotating culinary options offer loyal fans variety and frame players as heroes, often memorializing their contribution to the team. Historic icons are often similarly commemorated with various snack items named in their honor, though these food items appear to pay homage to the heroes in name only, rather than reflecting the person's actual food preferences or team affiliation. Nonetheless, the unique culinary offerings provide fans with new ways to bond with the team and to develop personal connections and memories associated with individual players.

Introduced in 2018, the annual MLB Food Fest celebrates the league's food traditions every September, rotating between American cities. At the event, fans can taste an array of culinary creations presented by every participating team's head chef. The event honors baseball's food heritage by inviting MLB chefs to unofficially compete for recognition for their best ballpark recipes from new versions of ballpark classics (e.g., hot dogs with unique toppings or cooked in a particular way) to contemporarily inspired fusion desserts. While no official awards are involved, menus representing teams are listed much like playoff brackets, with teams' social media accounts taunting rival clubs about their chefs' creations. The event has proven wildly popular, offering fans a new way to engage with the sport and highlighting the unique culinary experiences available at each ballpark. The event and featured creations are in part a nostalgic nod to childhood, particularly the fun of going to the game and the fact that chefs are literally

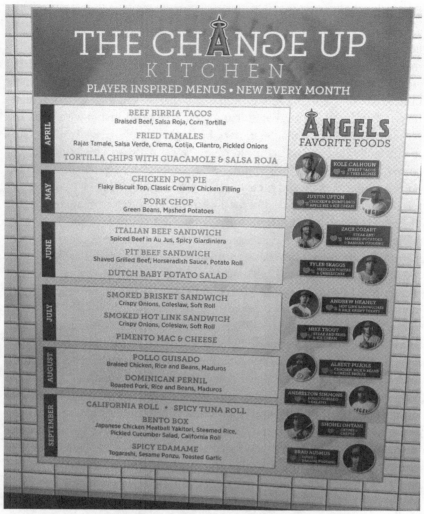

Figure 14.6. The Change Up Kitchen's menu, at Angel Stadium in Los Angeles, includes dishes honoring specific players. Photo by Alana Seaman.

playing with food. Furthering the carnivalization of ballpark food, dishes served at the event are usually bright, bold, and aesthetically over-the-top. In the current sharing economy, in which people, particularly members of the younger generations, are enamored by Instagram, "likes," and other attention on social media (see Hamari et al., 2015), the festival also includes unique food-inspired experiences—such as ball pits made to look like containers of popcorn where fans can dive in and "swim" around the kernels;

a giant teeter-totter shaped like a hot dog where fans can sit on each end of the sausage that hangs over its bun; and an equally oversized but empty hot dog bun with a slide built down the middle where attendees can enjoy their favorite treat from a new perspective. The wild aesthetics are aimed at enticing those often preoccupied with social media to engage with the sport in new ways, essentially reinterpreting baseball's food past for contemporary audiences. However, recognizing its special relationship with food, the self-celebration of baseball's culinary heritage also effectively works to further reinforce the sport's claims to uniquity, primacy, and tradition when it comes to food. In turn, the memorialized elements of its gastro past are thus bound to the sport by and for a whole new generation of fans. In this sense, the festivalization of baseball's food customs essentially ritualizes specific dishes and practices, in turn fetishizing the central facets of the fan dining experience and making them, in some cases, as important as the sport itself. Certainly, no other sport is as identifiable through food as baseball, much the less so deserving as to celebrate their own culinary customs. This self-recognition nonetheless once again highlights how the game's food heritage has become and remains so special.

Further challenging baseball's long-standing and simple culinary traditions are the dining lounges or clubs that are now featured in almost every new or upgraded MLB stadium. Stadium clubs such as the Lexus Diamond Club in the Los Angeles Angels' Angel Stadium, the Porsche Grille in the New York Mets' Citi Field, or the Delta Sky360 Club in Washington Nationals Park boast of high-end brands and corporate partnerships, swanky décor, and signature kitchens—which frequently double as home kitchens for team chefs. Foods in these spaces are not the typical, casual ballpark fare but rather unique culinary parings, new preparation techniques, high-quality and locally sourced ingredients, and gourmet-style foods. Served in pay-for-access high-end restaurant facilities integrated into stadiums—often with climate control, premium views, televisions for instant replays, and fully stocked bars—these venues hardly reflect baseball's pastoral or egalitarian heritage. While premium stadium seat prices have long been determined by a free market, these club-like lounges are clearly places for those fans with the means and taste to consume and enjoy—both literally and figuratively—the unique, exotic, and gourmet dishes being featured. Perhaps the exclusive food venues are simply an attempt to capitalize on the opportunities presented by the increasing number of people classifying themselves as "foodies," or individuals whose identity is linked in part to food, particularly as these people are thought to be willing to pay more for unique dining experiences (Ambrozas, 2003; Getz & Robinson, 2014a). However, the popularity of these places raises questions about class and the spectator experience, particularly within a sport that has been traditionally and romantically seen as a game for *all* Americans. Nonetheless, while simple staples like hot dogs, beer, Cracker Jack, and peanuts evoke nostalgia, fans also flock to new food vendors, craft breweries, and high-end in-stadium dining venues, exemplifying how baseball has managed to incorporate innovation alongside tradition when it comes to food. In this sense, baseball has set the standard for successfully merging the nostalgic and the postmodern in sport food heritage by both encouraging the perpetuation of long-standing legacies and embracing change like no other sport has.

Baseball and Food: Special and Sport-Wide

Regardless of how food is utilized, reinvented, and memorialized, baseball's special relationship with food is evident sport-wide. Shucked shells littering recreational ballparks suggest that Little Leaguers chew sunflower seeds from the first time they put on a glove. Parents and boosters often volunteer in community ballpark concession stands to help fund high school and select baseball teams for teens. Minor League organizations have long used food and beverage promotions as a way to attract fans. Concession classics are refashioned into attention-grabbing dishes such as hot dogs coated in funnel cake batter, Philly cheesesteak nachos, and even beer milkshakes (Zellers, 2013). Venues host specials such as "Thirsty Thursdays," "Seniors Eat Free," "Dollar Dogs and Beers," "Date-Night Two-fers," "Wiener Wednesday," "Bands and Brews," "Tacos and Tallboys," and the like. And recently, teams have even begun to temporarily change their names, logos, and uniforms to both honor iconic local-food traditions and to entice fans with related limited-time food choices, branded memorabilia and apparel, as well as special in-game contests and giveaways (Jackson, 2017). And Major League Baseball's history has been intimately intertwined with food since the sport began.

Not only has food in many ways shaped baseball's history, but eating at the game has also become a time-honored tradition. The ritual consumption of certain foods has transcended time and place and has permeated almost every facet of the sport from sponsorship to spectatorship. Concession classics are memorialized in popular culture and are cherished across generations, yet these options now exist alongside contemporary choices. The juxtaposition of these menu items seems to symbolize baseball itself; a game seeped in nostalgia and surrounded by romantic ideals of Americana aiming to maintain its place in an increasingly modernized world. Food is what ties the sport together, yet in many ways it is what sets teams and fans apart. Food is perhaps the ultimate example of heritage in baseball. It is used to recall and commemorate historic moments, memorialize heroes, and immerse fans in nostalgic experience, yet it is also constantly reinvented to maintain the sport's relevancy in an ever-changing world. No other sport boasts the rich, varied, and intimate links to food. Food is central to baseball's game-day traditions, venues, and franchises. It is also connected to people's notion of the game itself, thanks to historic parallels, popular culture, and team-specific stadiums; for other sports, food is often only a small part of the spectator experience or is merely a means of satisfying a hungry crowd.

References

Adams, D. C., & Adams, A. E. (2011). De-Placing local at the farmers' market: Consumer conceptions of local foods. *Journal of Rural Social Sciences, 26*(2), 74.

Adams, D. C., & Salois, M. J. (2010). Local versus organic: A turn in consumer preferences and willingness-to-pay. *Renewable Agriculture and Food Systems, 25*(4), 331–341. doi:10.1017/S1742170510000219

All American Girls Professional Baseball League (AAGPBL), (2017). League History. AAGPBL.org (accessed December 6, 2020).

Ambrozas, D. (2003). *Serious feast: Vancouver foodies in globalized consumer society* [Doctoral dissertation, School of Communication-Simon Fraser University].

Argent, N. (2017). Heading down to the local? Australian rural development and the evolving spatiality of the craft beer sector. *Journal of Rural Studies, 61,* 84–99.

Ashworth, G. J., & Tunbridge, J. E.(1996). *Dissonant heritage: The management of the past as a resource in conflict.* London: Wiley & Sons.

BAMCO (n.d.). The Garden at Oracle Park. *Bon Appetit Management Company.* http://www.bamco.com/giants-garden/ (accessed December 6, 2020).

Berlin, L., Lockereta, W., & Bell, R. (2009). Purchasing foods produced on organic, small and local farms: A mixed method analysis of New England consumers. *Renewable Agriculture and Food Systems, 24*(4), 267–275. doi:10.1017/S1742170509990111

Boyce, B. (2013). Trends in farm-to-table from a sociological perspective. *Journal of the Academy of Nutrition and Dietetics, 113*(7), 895.

Branch, J. (2009). Cracker Jack: The seventh-inning snack. *New York Times.* https://www.nytimes.com/2009/10/14/sports/baseball/14cracker.html (accessed December 6, 2020).

Burstein, B., & Stone, Y. (writers), & White, N. (director). (2019). *The Food that Built America* [television series].

Casselman, A. L. (2010). *Local foods movement in the Iowa catering industry* [Master's thesis, Iowa State University].

Clabaugh, J. (2019). Hot dogs still reign supreme at MLB ballparks. *WTOP Washington.* https://wtop.com/business-finance/2019/03/hot-dogs-still-reign-supreme-at-mlb-ballparks/ (accessed December 6, 2020).

Dawn, R. (2016). Cracker Jack is replacing toy prizes inside with digital codes. *Today.* https://www.today.com/food/cracker-jack-replacing-toy-prizes-inside-digital-codes-t87811 (accessed December 6, 2020).

Delind, L. B. (2006). Of bodies, place, and culture: Re-situating local food. *Journal of Agricultural and Environmental Ethics, 19*(2), 121–146. doi:10.1007/s10806-005-1803-z

Eberts, D. (2014). Neolocalism and the branding and marketing of place by Canadian microbreweries. In M. Patterson & N. Hoalst-Pullen (Eds.), *The geography of beer: Regions, environment, and societies.* New York: Springer.

Feagan, R., Morris, D., & Krug, K. (2004). Niagara region farmers' markets: Local food systems and sustainability considerations. *Local Environment, 9*(3), 235–254. doi:10.1080/1354983042000219351

Feagan, R. (2007). The place of food: Mapping out the 'local' in local food systems. *Progress in Human Geography, 31*(1), 23–42. doi:10.1177%2F0309132507073527

Flack, W. (1997). American microbreweries and neolocalism: "Ale-ing" for a sense of place. *Journal of Cultural Geography, 16*(2), 37–53.

Fletchall, A. M. (2016). Place-making through beer-drinking: A case study of Montana's craft breweries. *Geographical Review, 106*(4), 539–566.

Fletcher, D., & Castle, G. (2015). William Wrigley Jr. In G. H. Wolf (Ed.), *Winning on the north side: The 1929 Chicago Cubs.* Retrieved from sabr.org.

Fyfe, D. A. (2008). Birthplace of baseball or village of museums? The packaging of heritage tourism in Cooperstown, New York. *Journal of Sport & Tourism, 13*(2), 135–153.

Gaffney, C., & Bale, J. (2004). Sensing the stadium. In J. Bale & P. Vertinsky (Eds.), *Sites of sport: Space, place and experience.* London: Routledge.

Getz, D., & Robinson, R. N. (2014a). "Foodies" and their travel preferences. *Tourism Analysis, 19*(6), 659–672. doi:10.3727/108354214X14116690097693

Getz, D., & Robinson, R. N. (2014b). Foodies and food events. *Scandinavian Journal of Hospitality and Tourism, 14*(3), 315–330. doi:10.1080/15022250.2014.946227

Getz, D., Robinson, R., Andersson, T. & Vujicic, S. (2014). *Foodies and food tourism.* Oxford: Goodfellow Publishers.

Giovannucci, D., Barham, E., & Pirog, R. (2010). Defining and marketing "local" foods: Geographical indications for US products. *Journal of World Intellectual Property, 13*(2), 94–120. doi:10.1111/j.1747–1796.2009.00370.x

Hamari, J., Sjoklint, M., & Ukkonen, A. (2015). The sharing economy: Why people participate in collaborative consumption. *The Association for Information Science and Technology.*

Hede, A. M., & Watne, T. (2013). Leveraging the human side of the brand using a sense of place: Case studies of craft breweries. *Journal of Marketing Management, 29*(1–2), 207–224.

Hernández, B., Hidalgo, M. C., Salazar-Laplace, M. E., & Hess, S. (2007). Place attachment and place identity in natives and non-natives. *Journal of Environmental Psychology, 27*(4), 310–319.

Hirsch, A. R. (1992). Nostalgia: A neuropsychiatric understanding. *Advances in Consumer Research,* 19, 390–395.

Jackson, J. (2017). Fare game: Teams turn up heat on food theme. *Minor League Baseball.* https://www.milb.com/milb/news/brooklyn-slices-rochester-plates-continue-regional-food-trend-245642422 (accessed December 6, 2020).

Kraig, B. (2005). Man eats dogs: The hot dog stands of Chicago. *Gastronomica,* 5(1), 56–64.

Lee, S., Lee, H. J., Seo, W. J., & Green, C. (2012). A new approach to stadium experience: The dynamics of the sensoryscape, social interaction, and sense of home. *Journal of Sport Management, 26*(6), 490–505.

Lefebvre, H. (1974). *The production of space.* Hoboken, NJ: Wiley-Blackwell.

Lesko, J. (2014). AAGPBL League History. *All-American Girls Professional Baseball League Players Association.* https://www.aagpbl.org/history/league-history (accessed December 6, 2020).

MacKay, S. (n.d.). The cards your mother threw away—and other tales. *National Baseball Hall of Fame.* https://baseballhall.org/discover/baseball-card-preservation (accessed December 6, 2020).

National Peanut Board (2019). The story behind peanuts and baseball. https://www.nationalpeanutboard.org/news/whats-story-behind-peanuts-and-baseball.htm (accessed December 6, 2020).

Pine, B. J., & Gilmore, J. H. (1998). *Welcome to the experience economy.* Harvard Business Review.

Ramshaw, G. (2005, April). Nostalgia, heritage, and imaginative sports geographies: Sport and cultural landscapes. In *Forum UNESCO University and Heritage 10th International Seminar "Cultural Landscapes in the 21st Century,"* Newcastle upon Tyne, UK. https://www.researchgate.net/profile/Gregory_Ramshaw/publication/281624806_Nostalgia_Heritage_and_Imaginative_Sports_Geographies_Sport_and_Cultural_Landscapes/links/55f048f008ae199d47c1fb74.pdf (accessed December 6, 2020).

Ramshaw, G. (2018). Food, heritage, nationalism. In D. Timothy (Ed.), *Heritage cuisines: Traditions, identities, and tourism.* London: Routledge.

Ramshaw, G. (2020). *Heritage and sport: An introduction.* Bristol: Channel View.

Ramshaw, G., & Gammon, S. (2005). More than just nostalgia? Exploring the heritage/sport tourism nexus. *Journal of Sport Tourism, 10*(4), 229–241.

Richards, G. (2012). An overview of food and tourism trends and policies. In *Food and the tourism experience: The OECD-Korea Workshop.* Paris: OECD Publishing (pp. 13–46).

Rossi, J. P. (2007). Baseball and American history. *Pennsylvania Legacies, 7*(1), 36–37.

Seaman, A., & Schroeder, L. (2018). Crafting the Carolina Coast: Brewing a new sense of place. *Mid-Atlantic Popular and American Culture Conference.* Baltimore, Maryland.

Schnell, S. M., & Reese, J. F. (2003). Microbreweries as tools of local identity. *Journal of Cultural Geography, 21*(1), 45–69.

Schulman, H. (2019). Giants begin construction on new bullpens: How Oracle Park is changing. *San Francisco Chronicle*. https://www.sfchronicle.com/giants/article/Giants-begin-construction-of-new-bullpens-How-14821599.php (accessed December 6, 2020).

SFGiants (n.d.). Ballpark attractions: The Garden. *MLB: San Francisco Giants*. https://www.mlb.com/giants/ballpark/garden (accessed December 6, 2020).

Sims, R. (2009). Food, place and authenticity: Local food and the sustainable tourism experience. *Journal of Sustainable Tourism, 17*(3), 321–336.

Siro, I., Kápolna, E., Kápolna, B., & Lugasi, A. (2008). Functional food. Product development, marketing and consumer acceptance—A review. *Appetite, 51*(3), 456–467.

Slavich, M. A., Dwyer, B., & Hungerberg, E. (2019). Taken back at the ballgame: The impact of nostalgia within the Minor League Baseball spectator experience. *Journal of Sport Behavior, 42*(2), 200.

Smith, K. A. (2013). The history of baseball stadium nachos. *Smithsonian Magazine*. https://www.smithsonianmag.com/arts-culture/the-history-of-baseball-stadium-nachos-53046650/ (accessed January 28, 2022).

Springwood, C. F. (2019). *Cooperstown to Dyersville: A geography of baseball nostalgia*. New York: Routledge.

Thorn, J. (2011). The 'secret history' of baseball's earliest days. *NPR Fresh Air*. https://www.npr.org/2011/03/16/134570236/the-secret-history-of-baseballs-earliest-days (accessed December 6, 2020).

Timmons, D. S. (2006). *Measuring and understanding local foods: The case of Vermont* [Doctoral dissertation, University of Vermont].

Timothy, D. J. (2018). Personal heritage, intergenerational food and nostalgia. In D. Timothy (Ed.), *Heritage cuisines: Traditions, identities, and tourism*. London: Routledge.

Trubek, A. B. (2008). *The taste of place: A cultural journey into terroir* (Vol 20). Oakland: University of California Press.

Tuan, Y. F. (1974). *Topophilia: A study of environmental perception, attitudes, and values*. Englewood Cliffs, NJ: Prentice-Hall.

Verbeke, W. (2005). Consumer acceptance of functional foods: Socio-demographic, cognitive and attitudinal determinants. *Food Quality and Preference, 16*(1), 45–57.

Watson, A. A. (2016). Neolocalism and activating the urban landscape: Economics, social networks, and creation of place [Doctoral dissertation, Florida Atlantic University].

Winter, M. (2003). Embeddedness, the new food economy and defensive localism. *Journal of Rural Studies, 19*(1), 23–32.

Zellers, Z. (2013). 12 outrageous foods at minor league ballparks. *USA Today*. https://www.usatoday.com/story/travel/destinations/2013/06/01/12-outrageous-foods-at-minor-league-ballparks/2376915/ (accessed December 6, 2020).

15

Extra Innings: A Conclusion

Baseball and Heritage in Times of Change

SEAN GAMMON AND GREGORY RAMSHAW

Baseball undoubtedly shares a strong relationship with its past. This relationship has inspired any number of academic and popular outputs, from books and journal articles to documentaries to Hollywood films. And yet, despite the strong bond between baseball and history, the connection between baseball and heritage—all those things we inherit from the past and are used in the present (Timothy, 2011)—has largely been overlooked. Of course, heritages are inherited because either contemporary society has deemed them of importance and value, or previous generations decided them worthy of protection, education, and (in some cases) conservation. Baseball is no different in this regard. Many people, places, records, artifacts, memories, and traditions of baseball's past are regularly used in baseball today. Indeed, much of baseball's heritage exists because of its cultural value. Baseball has many treasured heirlooms of both the tangible (e.g., ballparks and historic artifacts) and intangible (e.g., traditions like the seventh-inning stretch) variety. However, reflecting Graham et al.'s (2000) duality of heritage, baseball's heritage is also a commodity. It is packaged, marketed, sold, and consumed as a "taste of baseball's past" (see Kulczycki et al., Chapter 2). And increasingly, as baseball competes for attention with other sports and entertainment options across the globe, its heritage (which includes a gradually more antiquated relationship with time, pace, seasons, and endurance) may be both an albatross and an asset. Ramshaw's (2014) article about cricket—a sport with a similar relationship to heritage as baseball—suggests that being "old-fashioned" perhaps benefits sports that were created in a different era but that are played and watched today. Couple this with a near-infinite treasure-trove of magnificent heroes, memorable teams, lavish uniforms, and time-honored traditions, and perhaps the baseball/heritage relationship will not only endure but flourish. Undoubtedly, baseball—like any number of social institutions—will keep the heritage that is valuable today and toss aside or ignore that which no longer serves a cultural or economic purpose (see Stride, Chapter 13). If baseball falls behind—or, perhaps, continues to fall behind—other pastimes, will the baseball/heritage relationship remain as central to the sport as it is now?

Indeed, the fact that baseball generates deeply meaningful experiences is of course predictable—yet there is a risk that these significant personal and collective attachments are predominantly associated with an older demographic. There have been concerns over the last four decades about the slow demise of a game that once defined a nation (Elias, 2010)—and while its heritage has much to offer, it must not define it. Over much of the 20th century, baseball and America were the closest of companions; the oft-quoted speech from the character Terence Mann in film *Field of Dreams* describes this relationship, remarking that while "America has rolled by like an army of steamrollers . . . baseball has marked the time." These two concepts stood by and supported each other through times of change and upheaval; offering a much-needed constant when each were at their most vulnerable. In the latter part of the century, however, they grew apart and didn't communicate anywhere near as often. There is no doubt that throughout the proceeding years of the 21st century, the gap has widened, primarily because America has found new distractions and new passions. And while it is obvious what America can do for baseball, it is less clear what baseball can offer America. Perhaps its heritage is perceived as an irrelevant anachronism—a point raised by Koppett (2001), who observed, "Tradition and history, so integral a part of baseball interest, are in themselves less powerful in society than they once were" (p. 221). But as we move into the third decade of the 21st century, the past continues to be used as a political tool, keen on reminding a nation of its past glories—however romantic they may be. Moreover, a stronger case must be made that the heritage of baseball is also the heritage of America, and that it still has relevance today.

The fact that the game has changed little over the last centuries is unquestionably a double-edged sword: on the one hand, it represents much needed stability and cultural familiarity in a world of change (Prentice & Andersen, 2007); on the other, it characterizes a past that is largely incompatible with modern life and leisure. The great players are not as eulogized as they once were, perhaps because "our taste for heroes has changed, as more effort is devoted to tearing down the mighty than to admiring them" (Koppett, 2001,

p. 221). Yet this is common across all sports, not just baseball. Perhaps the answer is to consider ways to make the game more relatable to a younger demographic, much like cricket in the United Kingdom. In this case, different forms of the game were introduced that were shorter (Twenty20 format) and more action-filled than regular matches. The outcome not only increased attendance by younger people but also created an upsurge of interest in the traditional format of the game. One of Major League Baseball's marketing initiatives in recent years is to highlight the personalities of the game's young batch of star players, many of whom are willing to violate the unwritten rules of the game (such as showboating when hitting a home-run). Clearly it is vital that any changes made to the game do not affect the loyalty and appetite that current fans still share. In many ways, appealing to a younger, less heritage-centric audience now may lead to more heritage-focused fans of the future. To this end, it is worth reflecting on the words of the late Bill Rigney (former Los Angeles Angels manager); when asked why he still bothered watching baseball, Rigney replied, "The piano's a little different but the tune plays the same" (Ryan, 2001). Baseball's task is now to ensure that the tune is still worth listening to.

As this collection has demonstrated, the baseball relationship remains vital, despite recent travails. In the United States, at first glance, it is tempting to suggest that the heritage well has run dry. Indeed, how many more "retro ballparks" (see Ramshaw & Gammon, Chapter 6), "throwback jerseys," or any number of heritage-themed promotions (see Seaman, Chapter 14) and traditions does one sport need? And yet, there are still pasts to discover, pasts from which to learn, and, indeed, pasts to commodify. One need only look at how the heritage of the Negro Leagues has evolved, from an obscure and overlooked part of American baseball history in the late 1980s to a widely recognized and celebrated past (see Hogan, 2006), which includes popular museums (most notably, the Negro League Baseball Museum in Kansas City—see Gordon, Chapter 7) and several lines of Negro Leagues–themed clothing and souvenirs (including from Ebbets Field Flannels and Team Brown Apparel, among others). But as this collection demonstrates, there are many baseball histories—and, by extension, baseball heritages in the United States—that remain in the shadows (see Downs & Pfleegor, Chapter 5). Heritages of women's baseball (see Heaphy, Chapter 4), for example, have not been fully realized, while others—such as from the many Mill Leagues in the industrial towns and cities across the United States—are still largely unexplored. In this, baseball heritage mirrors other heritage constructions—it ignores and marginalizes as often as it represents and celebrates (see McGregor, Chapter 3).

While baseball heritage remains an important part of the American heritage landscape, this collection demonstrates that baseball heritage is increasingly global. Explorations of baseball heritage in places like Japan (see Ito et al., Chapter 8), South Korea (see Choi, Chapter 9), Brazil (see Tobar, Chapter 10), the Caribbean (see Van Hyning, Chapter 11), and Britain (see Lashua, Chapter 12) reflect the "present use of the past" in these contexts and societies. Like their American counterparts, these heritages reflect cultural identities, marginalized and contested pasts, and economic development, while also demonstrating heritages that may be unfamiliar to followers of American baseball. Understanding, for example, the culture of Japanese high school baseball, the fan traditions of South Korean baseball, the rivalries of Brazilian baseball, the meanings of baseball events in the Caribbean, and the Anglo-American identity of baseball in Britain shows that understanding the baseball-heritage relationship involves more than the United States. Indeed, while global influences may be placing baseball heritage under threat in the United States, these same influences are helping baseball—and its heritage—thrive in many different parts of the globe.

The Future of Baseball's Past

This collection positioned the baseball/heritage relationship under three broad themes: people, place, and promotion. Unsurprisingly, most of the chapters in this collection fit into more than one category; a promotion can reveal something about place, for example, while place is constructed in part through the people who played there. Naturally, there are many facets of the baseball/heritage relationship that were not explored in this collection and that would also reveal the baseball/heritage relationship.

People

Baseball's past is filled with remarkable performances, great athletes, creative managers, and inspired executives. Figures from baseball's past have become heritage icons in their own right, having been enshrined in museums and halls of fame, memorialized in sculpture, and commodified in souvenirs—from jerseys to bobbleheads. However, essential representational questions—in particular, which heritage gets represented, by whom, and for what purpose (Smith, 2006)—are key in understanding baseball's heritage.

Several of the chapters in this collection examined the representation (and marginalization) of players in heritage settings, and this vital work needs to continue. In addition, people who have been involved outside of the field of play—ballpark architects, labor negotiators, and technology developers—are also part of the heritage of baseball and will likely garner future heritage recognition. A broader understanding of heritage "people" in baseball would also impact material culture. For example, one of the National Baseball Hall of Fame and Museum's artifact acquisitions was the Washington Nationals–themed face mask of Dr. Anthony Fauci, lead member of the White House coronavirus task force, when he threw out the first pitch at Nationals Park in July 2020. The fact that an artifact from an infectious-disease specialist is part of the collection in Cooperstown helps demonstrate that the people representing baseball heritage are beyond the game itself.

As has been revealed in this collection, many of baseball's pioneers plied their trade outside of the United States. Baseball museums and halls of fame exist in many other countries, including Canada, Australia, Mexico, Japan, and Venezuela. How baseball heritage—including the enshrinement of members as well as the politics of heritage representation—is characterized at these museums, in addition to how they compare with well-established museums and halls of fame in the United States is another avenue for exploration. Similarly, there must be a consideration of how the broader forms of heritage commemoration and the commodification of baseball players, such as statues, sculptures, and souvenirs, are understood and used outside of the United States. Finally, many baseball players competed in different countries during different times of the year. Negro Leagues players regularly competed in Cuba, for example, while current players play Winter League baseball in places like Mexico. How this transnational labor migration played out, and how it fits into contemporary heritage identities today, represents a more intangible heritage approach to baseball heritage.

Much like the great athletes from other sports, the revered players from the past in baseball are denoted the status of national icon. Their names—Babe Ruth, Joe DiMaggio, and Jackie Robinson, for example—are as familiar to non-baseball fans as they are to the serious baseball connoisseur. They not only represent a specific period in the sport but are also emblematic of a specific time in American history. Today, there remains a collective learned nostalgia (especially concerning the earlier players) that gazes back to a simpler, less cynical devotion to the national pastime. These instantly recognizable heroes irrefutably comprise baseball heritage—not only through the tangible artifacts found in sport museums and halls of fame but also by way of their extraordinary achievements during their careers. Yet there are numerous great players whose achievements took place in the more recent past who can be considered tangible living heritage (Gammon, 2014; Ramshaw, 2010). Players like Willie Mays and Ken Griffey Jr. exemplify this form of heritage, representing a living conduit to important eras of the game that fans and followers will pay premium prices to access (Gammon, 2014). Further research is required to explore the motives that drive these fans to see their heroes—as well as the resulting experiences when they do. Moreover, it would be interesting to note how perceptions may differ between those who saw the players perform in their heyday and those who have learned of their greatness in more recent times.

Place

Heritage is an important factor in place creation and construction. Ballparks in particular help create a sense of place, and while there are several historic ballparks that have received historic designation and protection—such as Fenway Park in Boston, Wrigley Field in Chicago, and Rickwood Field in Birmingham—there are new conservation matters on the horizon. Historic Minor League ballparks are likely to be important repositories for local and regional sport heritage, while venues that hosted Negro Leagues teams or All-American Girls Professional Baseball League teams may be part of a wider network of hidden sport heritage (Ramshaw, 2020); researchers can help uncover and interpret forgotten or marginalized pasts. Several communities have also turned the sites of beloved ballparks into heritage-themed recreational spaces. The sites where Tiger Stadium in Detroit and Yankee Stadium in New York once stood are now public baseball fields, not only providing a sporting space for local people but also helping to create (or continue) the symbolic meanings and identities of these spaces. Perhaps one of the more challenging ballpark conservation issues on the horizon is that of multipurpose domed stadiums, which were staples of baseball in the 1960s, 1970s, and 1980s but are increasingly being abandoned and demolished. Few of these venues are mentioned in the same breath as a Fenway Park or Wrigley Field, and yet they are important monuments of architectural history. A case for their preservation should be made, and examining the potential for the adaptive reuse of these stadiums—as is happening in Houston with the Astrodome (Trumpbur & Womack, 2016)—should be part of a baseball heritage/conservation agenda. Finally, the role of heritage in placemaking at ballparks outside of the United States should be examined—in particular, understanding how (and what kinds) of heritage are represented at these ballparks and how these heritages create a sense of place.

Museums and halls of fame also share significant connections to place and heritage (see Gordon, Chapter 7) not only through the exhibits and heritage interpretation residing within them, but also in the significance of the sites in which they are situated. Moreover, the cultural significance of the edifices that house the collections have become heritage structures in their own right—not through any inherent architectural value but through their authoritative status and reputation. The National Baseball Hall of Fame and Museum (NBHF) in Cooperstown is a case in point, where part of the desire of the 260,000 annual visitors is to experience the place as much as to view the exhibits. The NBHF has become, for baseball fans, what Cohen (1992, p. 35) described "as the center out there"; a sacred, remote place in which the spirit of the game is retained and protected. The heritage components of both Cooperstown and the NBHF are used symbiotically to support and influence the authenticity and integrity of the organization and the location. The extent to which each impact the heritage of the other requires further understanding and investigation.

Promotion

Heritage will undoubtedly remain part of baseball marketing and consumption. One of the more significant areas of this is the baseball card and memorabilia industry, which includes ties to personal and collective heritages and nostalgias. How and why fans collect baseball cards and memorabilia into adulthood, and how this links with areas such serious leisure (Stebbins, 1982), necessitates consideration. Similarly, the role of baseball fantasy camps, where participants play with or against their childhood sporting heroes (Gammon, 2002), has strong links with both nostalgia and the commodification of baseball heritage. Indeed, while baseball may not capture the imagination of the youth as readily as it once did, there is seemingly a market for those in middle-age and older to "grow" into the game and its heritage. The reasons for this are certainly worth exploring.

Heritage is still a major part of the ballpark experience. Traditional aspects—such as particular foods (beer and hotdogs), rituals (seventh-inning stretch), mascots, and promotional giveaways—are anticipated elements of any game, particularly in the United States. How these rituals and traditions influence consumer behavior—particularly in Minor League Baseball, where the promotions are often more important than the game itself—necessitates further consideration. The uses of non-baseball heritage in baseball settings, such as popular culture—for example, from films, television, books, and music (Ramshaw, 2019)—in baseball marketing and promotions is another baseball/heritage relationship that could be an avenue for exploration. For example, baseball teams host promotions such as "*Star Wars* Night" or "Grateful Dead Night," which often have little to do with baseball's heritage. These types of popular culture–themed heritage/nostalgia promotions may attract new and different audiences, many of whom have a strong personal connection to a particular film or type of music rather than an abiding interest in baseball. Finally, a greater understanding of baseball rituals, traditions, and promotions outside of the United States should be explored. The cheering culture of South Korean baseball, for example, is very different than the more sedate fan cultures in the United States, and it may help illuminate understandings of cultural performance and identity through baseball fandom and spectatorship.

Finally, many baseball heritage attractions—such as museums and halls of fame—have to balance both cultural outcomes (such as providing an authentic and accurate representation of baseball's past) and economic outcomes (such as creating fun and memorable experiences for visitors) (Ramshaw et al., 2019). How baseball heritage sites balance these duties, particularly when faced with both representing challenging pasts (Ramshaw & Gammon, 2020) and increasing visitor attendance and spend (particularly if visitors want a more nostalgic experience), needs more exploration. This will be particularly important as baseball heritage sites look to broader topical concerns, including labor issues, performance-enhancing drugs, gambling, social justice movements, and public health (such as the long-term impact of the coronavirus pandemic on baseball's heritage).

Conclusion

Baseball has always had a strong relationship with its past. While this relationship has primarily been explored through history, the way baseball uses its past in heritage contexts requires further consideration. Though baseball has remained essentially the same game for more than a century, the margins of baseball—how it is understood, promoted, and consumed—have changed immensely. Baseball heritage has changed as well. At times, teams, leagues, and communities have embraced baseball heritage, using it to illuminate any number of contemporary cultural and economic concerns. At other times, baseball's heritage has been sidelined or ignored, particularly when it was viewed as an impediment to present concerns and future development. While baseball's heritage "in times of change" suggests threat—and, as this collection undoubtedly demonstrates, aspects of baseball heritage that are at risk—the sport has emerged as a global game in which new and different heritages can thrive. Exploring and understanding these heritages—as well as their uses, controversies, and developments—should be part of baseball scholarship for decades to come.

References

Cohen, E. (1992). Pilgrimage centers: Concentric and excentric. *Annals of Tourism Research, 19,* 33–50.

Elias, R. (2010) (ed.). *Baseball and the American dream: Race, class, gender and the national pastime.* London: Routledge.

Gammon, S. (2002). Fantasy, nostalgia and the pursuit of what never was. In S. Gammon & J. Kurtzman (Eds.), *Sport tourism: Principles and practice* (pp. 61–72), Eastbourne: Leisure Studies Association.

Gammon, S. (2014). Heroes as heritage: The commoditization of sporting achievement. *Journal of Heritage Tourism, 9*(3), 246–256.

Graham, B., Ashworth, G. J., & Tunbridge, J. E. (2000). *A geography of heritage: Power, culture & economy.* London: Arnold.

Hogan, L. D. (2006). *Shades of glory: The Negro Leagues and the story of African-American baseball.* New York: National Geographic Books.

Koppett, L. (2016). A new golden age? An evolving baseball dream. In R. Elias (Ed.), *Baseball and the American dream: Race, class, gender, and the national pastime* (pp. 214–225). London: Routledge.

Prentice, R., & Andersen, V. (2007). Interpreting heritage essentialisms: Familiarity and felt history. *Tourism Management, 28*(3), 661–676.

Ramshaw, G. (2010). Living heritage and the sports museum: Athletes, legacy and the Olympic hall of fame and museum, Canada Olympic park. *Journal of Sport and Tourism, 15*(1), 45–70.

Ramshaw, G. (2014). A Canterbury tale: Imaginative genealogies and existential heritage tourism at the St. Lawrence ground. *Journal of Heritage Tourism, 9*(3), 257–269.

Ramshaw, G. (2019). Long strange trips: Tourism, events, and the Grateful Dead. *Event Management, 23*(6), 945–952.

Ramshaw, G. (2020). *Heritage and sport: An introduction.* Bristol: Channel View.

Ramshaw, G., & Gammon, S. (2020). Difference, dissonance, and redemption in sport heritage: Interpreting the tangled legacy of Pete Rose at two museums. *Journal of Heritage Tourism, 15*(2), 217–227.

Ramshaw, G., Gammon, S., & Tobar, F. (2019). Negotiating the cultural and economic outcomes of sport heritage attractions: The case of the National Baseball Hall of Fame. *Journal of Sport & Tourism, 23*(2–3), 79–95.

Ryan, J. (2001). The tune plays the same. In R. Elias (Ed.), *Baseball and the American dream: Race, class, gender and the national pastime* (pp. 262–264). London: Routledge.

Smith, L. (2006). *Uses of heritage*. London: Routledge.

Stebbins, R. A. (1982). Serious leisure: A conceptual statement. *Pacific Sociological Review, 25*(2), 251–272.

Timothy, D. J. (2011). *Cultural heritage and tourism: An introduction*. Bristol: Channel View Publications.

Trumpbour, R. C., & Womack, K. (2016). *The eighth Wonder of the World: The life of Houston's iconic Astrodome*. Lincoln: University of Nebraska Press.

Contributors

Makoto Chogahara is professor in the Faculty of Global Human Sciences at Kobe University, Japan. Chogahara's research interests include the support methods for active and healthy aging through investigating health and sport promotion.

Jungah Choi is a PhD candidate in the Department of Parks, Recreation, and Tourism Management at Clemson University. Her research focuses on sport tourism and sport heritage, especially in relation to mega-sporting events. She is also interested in sport tourist behavior.

Benjamin J. Downs is assistant professor of Sport Administration at Ball State University. Dr. Downs is a sport management/management history hybrid scholar who focuses his research on the evolution of urban multipurpose facilities. He utilizes history within sport management to better understand the construction and renovation trends related to multipurpose arenas.

Jonathon Edwards is assistant dean of Graduate Studies and Research, and associate professor in the Faculty of Kinesiology at the University of New Brunswick (UNB) in Fredericton, New Brunswick. He teaches courses in Sport Marketing and Sponsorship, and Sport Delivery Systems for the undergraduate and MBA in Sport and Recreation Management programs at UNB. His research interests include nonprofit sport organizations and the government, hockey organizations and structures, coaching, institutional work, and sport development systems in a sport and recreation organization and management context. Dr. Edwards has published in the *Journal of Sport Management*, *Sport Management Review*, *Managing Sport and Leisure*, and the *International Journal of Sport Coaching*.

Sean Gammon is a reader based in the Lancashire School of Business and Enterprise at the University of Central Lancashire. His main areas of research involve sport-related heritage and nostalgia as an instigator of tourism. He also has published in the fields of leisure, human geography, and identity.

Kiernan O. Gordon is assistant professor of Sport and Recreation Management at the University of New England in the United States. His research examines the role of built and natural environments in both creating and solidifying ritual behavior in sport and recreational contexts. Dr. Gordon's recent publications involve analyses of humans' engagement with place and space in sport tourism, sport venue design, and sport safety and security.

Leslie Heaphy is associate professor of history at Kent State University at Stark. Heaphy's research focuses on the Negro Leagues and women's baseball. She is coeditor of *Encyclopedia of Women and Baseball*.

Kei Hikoji is associate professor in the Faculty of Education at Wakayama University, Japan. He is engaged in sports promotion from the perspective of gerontology of sports, in particular the Sports for Life and Masters Sports Movement.

Eiji Ito is associate professor in the School of Health and Sport Sciences at Chukyo University, Japan. His areas of research are sport tourism, leisure studies, and cultural psychology. He serves as an associate editor of the *Journal of Leisure Research*.

Cory Kulczycki is assistant professor in the Faculty of Kinesiology and Health Studies at the University of Regina, Saskatchewan, Canada. His research examines leisure, recreation, and sport tourism with an interest in individual and group place experiences (e.g., event spectators and participants) as well as the media framing of sport events.

Brett Lashua teaches sociology of media at University College London (UCL). His scholarship spans questions of youth leisure, popular music, cultural heritage, and cities. His most recent book is *Popular Music, Popular Myth and Cultural Heritage in Cleveland: The Moondog, the Buzzard and the Battle for the Rock and Roll Hall of Fame*.

Andrew McGregor is professor of history at Dallas College. He is also the founder and coeditor of the "Sport in American History" group blog and has been featured as a guest on radio and televisions programs, including ESPN2's "Outside the Lines," and written an op-ed for the *Washington Post's* Made by

History section. His research focuses on American culture, politics, race, and the history of sports.

Adam G. Pfleegor is associate professor of Sport Administration at Belmont University in Nashville, Tennessee, United States. His research employs ethical theory to examine contemporary and historical issues in sport and recreation.

Luke Potwarka is associate professor in the Department of Recreation and Leisure Studies at the University of Waterloo. His research examines the behaviors and experiences of sport spectators, with a specific focus on the roles that elite sport events play in inspiring grassroots participation.

Gregory Ramshaw is professor in the Department of Parks, Recreation and Tourism Management at Clemson University, and is the author of *Heritage and Sport: An Introduction*. His research explores the social construction and cultural production of heritage, with a particular interest in sport-based heritage.

Alana N. Seaman is associate professor of tourism, recreation, and sport at the University of North Carolina Wilmington. Her research focuses on the links between tourism, popular culture, and heritage, particularly as related to neolocalism, placemaking, and food.

Chris Stride is senior lecturer and applied statistician at the University of Sheffield. He is also the founder of "From Pitch to Plinth: The Sporting Statues Project," a website and database that records and researches statues of sportsmen and sportswomen around the world.

Felipe Bertazzo Tobar is a PhD candidate in the Department of Parks, Recreation, and Tourism Management at Clemson University. His research focuses on football (soccer), heritage, and tourism—in particular, how difficult heritages are presented, interpreted, or marginalized on public stadium tours and in club museums.

Thomas E. Van Hyning is tourism economist/researcher at the Mississippi Development Authority and charter member of the Society for American Baseball Research's (SABR) Mississippi Cool Papa Bell Chapter. He contributes blogs about Caribbean baseball to www.béisb01101.com and SABR bios. His research articles have appeared in SABR's *The National Pastime and Baseball Research Journal*. He authored two books: *Puerto Rico's Winter League* and *The Santurce*

Crabbers; and coauthored Puerto Rico baseball chapters in two other books: *Baseball without Borders: The International Pastime* and *Baseball beyond Our Borders: An International Pastime*. Van Hyning presented at SABR National Conferences and regional meetings in Arkansas and Mississippi. He covered the February 1–7, 2020, Caribbean Series in San Juan, Puerto Rico—where he lived for 25 years—and wrote a two-part essay on Roberto Clemente's Puerto Rico Winter League career for a 2022 SABR book titled *"Arriba!": The Heroic Life of Roberto Clemente.*

Index

CULTURAL HERITAGE STUDIES
Edited by Paul A. Shackel, University of Maryland

Heritage of Value, Archaeology of Renown: Reshaping Archaeological Assessment and Significance, edited by Clay Mathers, Timothy Darvill, and Barbara J. Little (2005)

Archaeology, Cultural Heritage, and the Antiquities Trade, edited by Neil Brodie, Morag M. Kersel, Christina Luke, and Kathryn Walker Tubb (2006)

Archaeological Site Museums in Latin America, edited by Helaine Silverman (2006)

Crossroads and Cosmologies: Diasporas and Ethnogenesis in the New World, by Christopher C. Fennell (2007)

Ethnographies and Archaeologies: Iterations of the Past, edited by Lena Mortensen and Julie Hollowell (2009)

Cultural Heritage Management: A Global Perspective, edited by Phyllis Mauch Messenger and George S. Smith (2010; first paperback edition, 2014)

God's Fields: Landscape, Religion, and Race in Moravian Wachovia, by Leland Ferguson (2011; first paperback edition, 2013)

Ancestors of Worthy Life: Plantation Slavery and Black Heritage at Mount Clare, by Teresa S. Moyer (2015)

Slavery behind the Wall: An Archaeology of a Cuban Coffee Plantation, by Theresa A. Singleton (2015; first paperback edition, 2016)

Excavating Memory: Sites of Remembering and Forgetting, edited by Maria Theresia Starzmann and John R. Roby (2016)

Mythic Frontiers: Remembering, Forgetting, and Profiting with Cultural Heritage Tourism, by Daniel R. Maher (2016; first paperback edition, 2019)

Critical Theory and the Anthropology of Heritage Landscapes, by Melissa F. Baird (2017)

Heritage at the Interface: Interpretation and Identity, edited by Glenn Hooper (2018)

Cuban Cultural Heritage: A Rebel Past for a Revolutionary Nation, by Pablo Alonso González (2018)

The Rosewood Massacre: An Archaeology and History of Intersectional Violence, by Edward González-Tennant (2018; first paperback edition, 2019)

Race, Place, and Memory: Deep Currents in Wilmington, North Carolina, by Margaret M. Mulrooney (2018; first paperback edition, 2022)

An Archaeology of Structural Violence: Life in a Twentieth-Century Coal Town, by Michael P. Roller (2018)

Colonialism, Community, and Heritage in Native New England, by Siobhan M. Hart (2019)

Pedagogy and Practice in Heritage Studies, edited by Susan J. Bender and Phyllis Mauch Messenger (2019)

History and Approaches to Heritage Studies, edited by Phyllis Mauch Messenger and Susan J. Bender (2019)

A Struggle for Heritage: Archaeology and Civil Rights in a Long Island Community, by Christopher N. Matthews (2020; first paperback edition, 2022)

Earth Politics and Intangible Heritage: Three Case Studies in the Americas, by Jessica Joyce Christie (2021)

Negotiating Heritage through Education and Archaeology: Colonialism, National Identity, and Resistance in Belize, by Alicia Ebbitt McGill (2021)

Baseball and Cultural Heritage, edited by Gregory Ramshaw and Sean Gammon (2022)